Canaan,
Dim and Far

Canaan, Dim and Far

BLACK REFORMERS AND
THE PURSUIT OF CITIZENSHIP
IN PITTSBURGH, 1915–1945

Adam Lee Cilli

THE UNIVERSITY OF
GEORGIA PRESS
ATHENS

© 2021 by the University of Georgia Press
Athens, Georgia 30602
www.ugapress.org
All rights reserved
Designed by Kaelin Chappell Broaddus
Set in 10/13.5 LTC Italian Old Style by Kaelin Chappell Broaddus

Most University of Georgia Press titles are
available from popular e-book vendors.

Printed digitally

Library of Congress Cataloging-in-Publication Data

Names: Cilli, Adam Lee, author.
Title: Canaan, dim and far : black reformers and the pursuit of
 citizenship in Pittsburgh, 1915–1945 / Adam Lee Cilli.
Description: Athens : The University of Georgia Press, [2021] |
 Includes bibliographical references and index.
Identifiers: LCCN 2020035737 (print) | LCCN 2020035738 (ebook)
 | ISBN 9780820358871 (hardcover) | ISBN 9780820358888
 (paperback) | ISBN 9780820358895 (epub)
Subjects: LCSH: African Americans—Civil rights—
 Pennsylvania—Pittsburgh—History—20th century. | African
 Americans—Pennsylvania—Pittsburgh—Social conditions—
 20th century. | Civil rights movements—Pennsylvania—
 Pittsburgh—History—20th century. | Pittsburgh (Pa.)—Race
 relations—History—20th century. | Pittsburgh (Pa.)—Social
 conditions—20th century.
Classification: LCC F159.P69 N435 2021 (print) | LCC F159.P69
 (ebook) |
DDC 323.1196/0730748860904—dc23
LC record available at https://lccn.loc.gov/2020035737
LC ebook record available at https://lccn.loc.gov/2020035738

FOR MY GREAT-GRANDPARENTS,
Nicola Cilli
AND
Antonia Vittoria Fiocca,
AND ALL MIGRATING PEOPLE WHO
VENTURE INTO UNFAMILIAR LANDS
IN SEARCH OF A BETTER LIFE

IN MEMORY OF MY GRANDMOTHER,
Marie Rose (Plunkett) Cilli,
1926–2020

CONTENTS

LIST OF ILLUSTRATIONS   xi

ACKNOWLEDGMENTS   xiii

INTRODUCTION
The Meaning of Progress
1

CHAPTER 1
"The Ugliest, Deadest Town"
MIGRANTS AND REFORMERS IN
THE STEEL CITY, 1915–1929
18

CHAPTER 2
"A Healthy and Prosperous Race"
THE URBAN LEAGUE OF PITTSBURGH AND
THE STRUGGLE FOR JOBS, HOUSING,
AND HEALTH, 1915–1929
54

CHAPTER 3
"The Weapons of Legal Defense"
THE PITTSBURGH NAACP AND THE
CRIMINAL JUSTICE SYSTEM, 1924–1934
83

CHAPTER 4
"The Ranks of This New Army"
THE *PITTSBURGH COURIER* AND THE
FIGHT FOR POLITICAL POWER AND
NATIONAL RECOGNITION, 1929–1933
108

CHAPTER 5
"The Taken-for-Granted Rights
of American Citizenship"
REFORMERS AND THE QUEST FOR CIVIL EQUALITY
AND EDUCATIONAL JUSTICE, 1934–1937
147

CHAPTER 6
"This Great Crusade"
REFORMERS AND THE INDUSTRIAL
LABOR MOVEMENT, 1933–1939
168

CHAPTER 7
"The Freedoms We Cherish"
REFORMERS AND THE STATE, 1933–1945
205

CONCLUSION
The Legacy of the Black Reform Era
237

INDEX 247

ILLUSTRATIONS

Migrants arriving in Pittsburgh	24
Monticello Street, ca. 1930	26
African American boardinghouse overlooking Pittsburgh, ca. 1925	27
African American tenement in Pittsburgh, ca. 1925	27
Shoeshine parlor in the Hill District	28
Hill District street scene, July 29, 1935	28
Wylie Avenue	29
African American communities in interwar Pittsburgh	29
Concentration of African Americans in Pittsburgh by 1930	30
Major black communities in western Pennsylvania	30
The Pittsburgh Crawfords, 1926	33
Black reformers in Pittsburgh	66
Grace Lowndes at a neighborhood unit meeting	69
Better Baby Show, ca. 1930	73
The grim reaper in Pittsburgh	73
Homer Brown	92
Daisy Lampkin	92
The Highland Park pool, ca. 1952–1955	95
Robert L. Vann, ca. 1935	116
Newspaper boys standing outside the *Courier* office	117
Courier staff at work in the editorial department, ca. 1945	117

Typesetters, one of several kinds of African American technicians employed by the *Courier*	118
The *Courier*'s printing press, which required several operators and maintenance men	118
The political cartoons of Wilbert Holloway	134
Georgine Pearce, ca. 1932	150
William E. Hill	182
R. Maurice Moss, ca. 1932	182
Pittsburgh Urban League Office, ca. 1930	183
Ben Careathers, August or September 1960	191
Phillip Murray	194
Black and white steelworkers	196
Ernest Moses at the Carnegie Steel Plant	197
Frank Bolden, war correspondent, ca. 1940s	209
Robert L. Vann, Percival Prattis, and an unknown government official, ca. 1936	213
Eleanor Roosevelt greets black reformers in Pittsburgh	213
African American dignitaries at the Vann dedication ceremony	220
Homer Brown and Ira Lewis in Portland, Maine	220
The *Courier*'s Double V emblem	226
The Ink Spots	228
A banquet honoring Daisy Lampkin	243
Interracial protest demonstration	243

ACKNOWLEDGMENTS
🐦 🐦 🐦

This book illuminates the social justice efforts of African American reformers in the Urban League of Pittsburgh and other key racial advancement centers. These activists provided crucial advocacy and support in the working-class black neighborhoods of Pittsburgh—services that improved healthcare, expanded employment opportunities, promoted interracial labor unions, and advanced civil rights. Yet behind a book's arguments and supporting evidence, there is a story about how the book was written in the first place. That story for *Canaan, Dim and Far* includes a large cast of generous institutions and people who provided funding, expert advice, encouragement, and friendship.

The University of Maine funded numerous archival trips to Pittsburgh and Washington DC during the early stages of this project; later, Texas A&M University-San Antonio and the University of Pittsburgh at Bradford provided research support as well. The staff at the University of Pittsburgh Archives Service Center made me feel like a welcomed friend. They called my attention to important sources, cheerfully assisted me with locating hard-to-find information, and even invited me to join them at their annual Christmas lunch. I could say similar things about the friendly staff at the circulation desk of UMaine's Fogler Library.

Many scholars read portions of my work and offered suggestions that made this book incalculably better. These include Priscilla Dowden-White, William S. Bush, Dennis C. Dickerson, Larry Glasco, and Michael J. Socolow. I owe a special thanks to Richard W. Judd, Liam Riordan, and Joe W. Trotter. They have supported me since 2013 when I first developed my ideas for this book. Over the ensuing years, they repeatedly took time out of their busy schedules to review my manuscript chapters as well as my articles in the *Journal of Women's History, Journal of Urban History,* and the *Pennsylvania Magazine of History and Biography.* I am also grateful to those journals for allowing me to reproduce some of my findings in this book.

Several anonymous reviewers read part or all of the book manuscript on behalf of the University of Georgia Press, and they provided key suggestions for broadening its scope and strengthening some of its core arguments. Walter Biggins, executive editor at the press, saw worth in this project from the outset, and he patiently worked with me through its early iterations. When he accepted a position at another university press, Rebecca Norton stepped in and capably shepherded this book through the final stages of publication.

I also owe a debt to the scholars who came before me in chronicling the history of the black community in Pittsburgh from its early formation through the New Deal period, especially Peter Gottlieb, Dennis C. Dickerson, Larry Glasco, Rob Ruck, John Bodnar, Roger Simon, and Michael P. Weber. Additionally, Joe W. Trotter and Jared N. Day produced a valuable book on African Americans in the Steel City since World War II. Although I interpreted a few things differently from some of these historians, their detailed studies of the black working class provided critical background information for my work that enabled me to concentrate on actors that had not gotten as much scholarly attention.

Writing a book involves countless hours of solitary labor, and any author will attest to the importance of having friends and family to spend time with after a day of effort and to lean on when times get tough. In this regard, I have been extremely fortunate. Greg Rogers provided unwavering friendship as we pursued our history PhDs at UMaine, and he helped ensure that my weeks included board-game nights, watching *Survivor,* and playing flag football. Sarah Ann Drahovzal took me hiking in Maine, Arizona, and Texas whenever I reached a new cairn in my career; she listened with enthusiasm as I spoke about my ideas for this book, even while rambling through rugged terrain, and she provided moral support and encouragement throughout the process of writing it.

No matter what was going on in my life, I could always count on my grandma, Marie Rose Cilli, as a source of comfort and continuity. She poured her love and prayers into all eighteen of her grandchildren until the day she died, at the age of 94, in late August 2020. Her son, my uncle Ralph, who introduced me to wine-making and Christmas sing-a-longs, has taught me about courage and grace through his battle with lung cancer.

Among grandma's many great-grandchildren are my rowdy pack of nephews—Jackson, Nicolas, and Bennett—who bring chaos and joy into my world every time my sister-in-law Laura brings them over. For that matter, so does Puddles the Cat, beloved by humans and feared by local chipmunks.

Whenever I need logistical support, I never have to look far. My dad (Nick) and my brothers (Garrett and Michael) have helped me with multiple moves across the country, from Maine to Pennsylvania, Pennsylvania to Texas, and Texas to Pennsylvania. Through it all, they loved me unconditionally, cheerfully tolerated me as I blabbed endlessly about this book, and laughed at my stupid jokes. The importance of that kind of support defies quantification.

Most especially, I owe thanks to my mom, Leslie Cilli. She has enthusiastically stood in my corner through every round of my career and championed my work in all its aspects. In addition to reading each chapter draft multiple times, Mom attended one of my history lectures in San Antonio, joined me at a conference in Cincinnati, helped me do archival research in Washington DC, visited a historic gravesite with me in Pittsburgh, and patiently probed census records for me through Ancestry.com. I feel immensely grateful to have a mother who is so interested and engaged in my professional life, and I will always cherish these memories.

Canaan, Dim and Far

INTRODUCTION

The Meaning of Progress

> Lo! We are diseased and dying, cried the dark hosts; we cannot write, our voting is vain; what need of education, since we must always cook and serve? And the Nation echoed ... Be content to be servants, and nothing more; what need of higher culture for half-men? Away with the black man's ballot, by force or fraud,— and behold the suicide of a race! Nevertheless, out of the evil came something good,—the more careful adjustment of education to real life, the clearer perception of the Negroes' social responsibilities, and the sobering realization of the meaning of progress.
>
> —W. E. B. Du Bois, *The Souls of Black Folk*

The Souls of Black Folk sent a jolt through the racial advancement community when it appeared in 1903. In it, the scholar, activist, and poet W. E. B. Du Bois called for a new direction in the freedom struggle and repudiated the methods of America's leading black spokesperson, Booker T. Washington. Washington had long advocated for African Americans to temporarily accept segregation and disfranchisement in exchange for a quality vocational education and access to skilled jobs with decent wages. While others had criticized this accommodationist philosophy before, no one matched the force and eloquence of Du Bois in *Souls*. Beyond a full dinner plate and a good job, he argued that a complete life necessarily included self-respect, which could not come if African Americans acquiesced to second-class citizenship.

Du Bois characterized the postemancipation pursuit of racial equality as a long and ongoing journey best led by the "talented tenth"—college-educated black professionals familiar with the needs of ordinary African Americans and conversant with the mores of white society. Drawing from the Exodus story that gave hope to generations of slaves, he explained how the "advance guard" guided the black masses from bondage toward an elusive promised land. Yet for all their striving, "the horizon was ever dark, the mists were often cold, the Canaan was always dim and far away."[1]

This short passage foreshadowed crucial features of black reform work during the Great Migration. Drawn by the promise of good jobs and greater freedom, from 1915 to 1940 over 1.6 million African Americans moved from rural communities in the South to urban industrial centers in the North.[2] For many of them, the Ohio River symbolized the biblical River Jordan in their exodus from the South. But the prospect of full citizenship disappeared from view as whites in cities across the North raised racial barriers that inhibited black economic and social mobility. As one migrant complained, "Everyplace I had gone, including Pittsburgh, I found that Mr. Jim Crow dominated the scene."[3]

In these urban communities, reform-minded black professionals joined organizations that fought to democratize access to economic opportunity and secure equal rights for all African Americans. They saw themselves as Du Bois's "advance guard," tasked with negotiating the fraught racial landscape of interwar northern cities while acclimating southern black migrants to urban life. Thus, among other projects, they developed "adjustment" programs to impress on migrants the importance of workplace reliability, temperance, good home economics, proper hygiene, and restrained public conduct. This effort to address structural inequality through moral reform, which contemporaries termed "racial uplift," sometimes clashed with the designs of migrants who had their own means of asserting their agency. Yet racial uplift represented only one star in a constellation of strategies that black leaders hoped would guide them all to Canaan.

This book spotlights neglected elements of middle-class black activism in the decades preceding the civil rights movement. It features a revolving cast of social workers, medical professionals, journalists, scholars, and lawyers who experimented with a variety of tactics as they moved fluidly across ideologies and political alliances to find practical solutions to profound inequities. In the period under study, these black reformers developed crucial social safety supports in African American communities that buffered southern migrants against the physical, civil, and legal impositions of northern Jim Crow; they waged comprehensive campaigns to combat antiblack stereotypes, shape racial discourse, and enhance black political power; and they facilitated black inclusion in the industrial labor movement.[4]

Pittsburgh represents a crucial site for illuminating how reformers maneuvered within a political culture driven by industrial capitalism and informed by white supremacist rhetorics. The city was a national hub of steel production, ethnic diversity, and labor activity. Along with that, it was a major site of black migration, hosted a leading black newspaper, the *Courier*, and had very active branches of the Urban League and NAACP. These features permit a detailed examination of the dynamic relationships that reformers developed with migrants, steel executives, labor leaders, communists, progressives, and politicians in order to advance their goals.

In some ways, the subjects of this book reflected the larger reform impulse that characterized the Progressive Era. They came from the middle class (defined in the black community by occupation and education), formed leagues and associations committed to specific issues, and relied on muckraking journalism and social science to expose "social ills" and offer concrete steps for remediation. Yet while most white progressives ignored racial injustice, black reformers made it their central concern.

As members of the talented tenth, they felt they had a moral obligation to lead the black masses, but they did not fit neatly on the Washington–Du Bois spectrum, or on any political spectrum. For while black reformers insisted on political equality as Du Bois understood it, they also embraced some of Washington's initiatives, such as Negro Health Week. And if at the national level the Urban League was more conservative than the NAACP, as one study has maintained, the local Pittsburgh chapter does not fit that mold.[5] Membership between the Urban League of Pittsburgh (ULP) and the Pittsburgh NAACP (PNAACP) often overlapped, and staff in both organizations frequently collaborated. Moreover, at various times in the twenties and thirties, black reformers worked with both laissez-faire capitalists and committed socialists. As many of them saw it, the reality on the ground presented too many challenges and the available allies seemed too scarce to permit an exclusive commitment to any one ideology or tactical formula.

In this study, I consider reformers' outlook and options in the context of their time and place. Migrants constituted two-thirds of all African Americans in Pittsburgh by 1930, and the city hosted the nation's fifth largest black community.[6] In response to the sudden and extensive influx of southern blacks, white Pittsburghers from all social ranks adopted measures to exploit, exclude, and marginalize them. Employers in area mills confined them to the lowest-paying and most dangerous jobs while targeting them for layoffs during economic downturns. Polish workers, whose numerical dominance of certain departments in local plants enabled them to reserve positions for their kin and friends, militated against outside intrusion by black migrants. Native white workers barred African Americans from joining local unions, and they occasionally threatened to go on strike to prevent their having to work alongside them.

Black women confronted an even more restrictive employment situation in the Steel City. For most of the interwar period, they found themselves shut out of a host of occupations considered appropriate for white women only. White women, but not black women, could work as telephone operators, typists, secretaries, saleswomen, nurses, and teachers. With few options available to them, about 90 percent of employed black women in Pittsburgh worked as domestic laborers for whites who could subject them to long hours, low wages, sudden wage reductions, and arbitrary terminations.

Black migrants in Pittsburgh also faced a bleak housing situation. Racially restrictive neighborhood covenants combined with economic poverty to trap them in the lower Hill District and other poor black enclaves in the inner city, where they crowded into dilapidated and unsanitary boardinghouses and tenements. These difficult economic and physical conditions created a health crisis in the black community. Over the first decade of the Great Migration, black adults in Pittsburgh suffered disproportionately from tuberculosis and pneumonia, and their infants died twice as often as white infants.

Along with these dire physical challenges, African Americans in western Pennsylvania endured daily insults from whites of all ethnic backgrounds. Italians at the Highland Park public pool repeatedly attacked and harassed would-be black swimmers to prevent them from using "their pool." By 1924, about 125,000 native whites had joined local Ku Klux Klan chapters in western Pennsylvania. They held regular parades through the main streets of towns like Aliquippa, attacked black migrants in Imperial, and burned crosses in Johnstown. In both Johnstown and Industry, white officials worked to deport black migrants back to the South; in Industry, they achieved partial success when police arrested over forty migrants on fraudulent charges and shipped them to the West Virginia border. Moreover, African Americans could find only one restaurant in downtown Pittsburgh that would serve food to them (a café in the basement of a department store), and white ushers led them to segregated seating on the B&O Railroad, in the balconies of local theaters, and at Forbes Field—home of the Pittsburgh Pirates. Most hotels denied services to African Americans as well, and a local amusement park would only allow them to use its pavilions on designated "Negro days."

Under these trying circumstances, middle-class black activists in Pittsburgh took a pragmatic, "race-first" approach to reform work. Lacking funds and dealing with grave challenges, they recognized the imperative to make compromises and accept tradeoffs for modest gains. The records reformers left behind attest to their commitment to face honestly their limited range of options, to direct their paltry resources toward achievable goals, and to shift positions to capitalize on changes in mainstream American political culture. Time and again, they demonstrated willingness to make and break alliances with whites across the political spectrum when it suited their racial goals, from Republicans, philanthropists, and business executives in the twenties to Democrats, labor leaders, and communists in the thirties. Observing this practical orientation in 1944, Swedish economist Gunnar Myrdal commented that they "*seem to be held in a state of eternal preparedness for a great number of contradictory opinions—ready to accept one type or another depending on how they are driven by pressures or where they see an opportunity.*"[7] The chapters in this book demonstrate the ideological mutability of the members of the black reform community in Pittsburgh and illustrate how they developed nuanced positions toward corporate elites, the state, existing political parties, and organized labor.[8]

In the 1920s, social workers in the Urban League rhetorically affixed racial justice to Victorian notions of respectability in order to gain white allies and obtain financial support from area businesses and philanthropists. With this funding, league staff developed programs to mitigate the most urgent practical problems in the black community. They launched health campaigns that helped save black lives, developed community initiatives to improve sanitation in poor neighborhoods, deployed welfare workers to area mills to improve living conditions for black industrial workers, advocated for black juveniles and prostitutes at the city morals court, lobbied local unions to open their doors to African Americans, and sponsored social scientific studies that raised public awareness of racial problems in Pittsburgh.

The league did not produce revolutionary changes for black Pittsburghers, as historians have often observed, but in the 1920s no organization did more to improve their day-to-day lives. Facing discriminatory unions and employers and a lack of basic government services in black neighborhoods, the ULP stitched together a meager but crucial social safety net that reduced mortality rates and improved working and housing conditions for some of the poorest and most economically vulnerable members of the community.

Activists in the PNAACP contributed to the league's social safety net by providing effective legal advocacy that buffered poor African Americans against the worst excesses of a racially biased criminal justice system. The deportation of migrants in Industry offers just one example of how police in western Pennsylvania targeted African Americans. When black swimmers protested their exclusion from the Highland Park pool, local officials locked them up while letting off the Italians with a warning. On other occasions, police assaulted African Americans for demanding explanations from them. When George Lewis protested the arrest of his housemate, the officers present proceeded to handcuff and beat him until he lay nearly unconscious in a pool of blood; the next day, while recovering in a hospital, they arrested him for obstruction of justice. African American arrest rates in Pittsburgh spiked during the Great Migration, and the city's criminal justice system swept hundreds of southern black men into its penitentiary. Connecting with a growing body of literature on the carceral state, this study examines how reformers in the PNAACP secured the release of the Highland Park protestors, prosecuted police officers who assaulted unarmed black men, and pursued justice for the forty migrants deported to West Virginia.[9]

Moving on the perilous racial terrain of interwar Pittsburgh, reformers prioritized achievable steps over sweeping strides likely to end in a painful fall. But while they traversed slowly and cautiously toward modest short-range goals, they had faith that their path eventually would lead to something greater. They pursued a vision of citizenship, somewhere on the horizon, that included more than civil rights. For them, full citizens should have access to gainful employment as well as the opportunity to bargain collectively for better wages and working conditions; they were entitled to live in decent, affordable, sanitary homes where they could raise healthy children; and they had a right to basic government services in their neighborhoods—including accessible medical facilities, adequate street cleanup and waste removal, a public bathhouse, good schools, and wholesome community outlets such as playgrounds, parks, pools, and recreation centers. Reformers rarely articulated this vision in its entirety. Yet their actions—the programs they sponsored, initiatives they pursued, and campaigns they launched—attested to an understanding of citizenship that encompassed economic opportunity, physical security, political empowerment, and civil equality.

My argument speaks to a broader literature in urban black history that tends to evaluate activism through a post–civil-rights lens. In the midst of a larger initiative to rewrite history "from the bottom up" and highlight the agency of everyday people, scholars from the sixties through the eighties generally showed little interest in middle-class black reformers except to stress how their efforts adversely affected ordinary African Americans. Their studies often cast reformers as bourgeois accommodationists who abhorred the folk culture of the black masses, promoted middle-class advancement to the exclusion of the working poor, and worried incessantly about their social status.[10]

Depictions of major racial-advancement organizations in Pittsburgh reflect this trend. In his study of black migrants in the Steel City, Peter Gottlieb gives the impression that the Urban League, NAACP, and *Courier* almost exclusively catered to the interests of black elites. His introductory chapter asserts that the league's "campaign to reform southern blacks served to protect and maintain the status of Pittsburgh's leading blacks," and his index listing for the *Courier* refers to "its ambivalence toward migrants." Similarly, John Bodnar, Richard Simon, and Michael Weber dismiss the *Courier* as a middle-class outlet that "had little to say about the concerns . . . of working people." Consequently, the nation's largest black weekly newspaper appears nowhere in the index, and neither does the NAACP, while the league features on just two pages. In the hands of New Left historians, even the *Courier*'s famous Double V campaign turned out to be a bourgeois scheme meant to preserve the capitalist order. As Lee Finkle maintains, it served conservative ends by subverting labor radicalism among black workers.[11]

Scholarly treatment of the Urban League in other communities further illustrates this pattern. Kimberly Phillips argues that Cleveland's Urban Leaguers focused narrowly on protecting their elite status in the black community while imposing middle-class values on migrants and stifling working-class activism.[12] Keona Ervin follows this model by arguing that domestic workers in St. Louis had to push, manipulate, and transform the local league to make it sponsor programs that actually benefited them.[13] Extending her analysis beyond local chapters, Nancy Weiss stresses the National Urban League's conservative orientation toward conciliation and moral uplift. Likewise, Touré Reed focuses on the league's "behavioral models of uplift" and devotes considerable space to showing how these approaches hurt working-class African Americans.[14]

To be sure, there have been noteworthy exceptions to this canon. Evelyn Brooks Higginbotham, Darlene Clark Hine, Stephanie Shaw, and others have skillfully reconceptualized the reform ethos of black social workers, club women, and professionals while demonstrating how they challenged the prevailing racial hierarchy.[15] Nevertheless, contemporary studies still tend to situate reformers in convenient but misleading class frameworks that obscure their complexity and miss important nuances.[16] What we are left with is an incomplete picture of racial activism in the decades preceding the civil rights movement. "Except for in the pages of social science," historian Thomas Sugrue reminds us, "political actors and ordinary citizens seldom hold consistent views. Their motivations vary; their ideologies shift; their sense of what is possible and impossible, pragmatic and impracticable changes with the times."[17]

Perhaps unconsciously, scholars often place ahistorical expectations on reformers that fail to account for the extraordinarily difficult environment in which they operated. Throughout the early twentieth century, African Americans of all classes faced overwhelming hostility from whites across the social and economic spectrum. Physicians and psychologists respectively conducted cranial studies and developed IQ tests that alleged to prove the mental superiority of Anglo-Saxons, while the writings of social Darwinists and eugenicists made their way into high school and college textbooks. Outside academia, ordinary Americans attended world's fairs that featured exhibits of primitive African and Asian villages alongside Western exhibits showcasing great scientific advancements. Meanwhile, a newly emerging mass culture disseminated crude antiblack stereotypes nationwide through films, radio programs, books, songs, magazines, and newspapers. The early twentieth century witnessed a surge of racist ideology, and mass culture served as the medium through which it gained expression. For millions of white Protestants who did not personally know any African Americans, it provided a racial education that justified upholding white supremacy. D. W. Griffith's 1915 silent film, *Birth of a Nation*, so inspired them that they established Ku Klux Klan chapters in cities and towns from California to Maine.[18]

Moreover, during the first phase of the Great Migration, from about 1915 to 1930, black reformers in Pittsburgh could not depend on support from local, state, or federal authorities. The state refused to address the discriminatory hiring and promotional policies of Pittsburgh's major employers. It would not force white landlords to provide basic upkeep to the housing units in the lower Hill District or make them charge reasonable rents. It did not make local hospitals admit and treat black patients in a timely manner or compel them to hire black nurses. It willfully ignored the exclusion of black teachers from Pittsburgh's public school system; no law prevented African Americans from becoming teachers in Pittsburgh, but in practice the school board never hired black applicants. By 1937, Pittsburgh was the only major northern city to have an all-white teaching staff.

Civil rights activists in the fifties and sixties risked extreme physical danger when they engaged in protest marches, freedom rides, and sit-in demonstrations, but in some ways they operated from a more advantageous position than reformers of the interwar years. As historian Mary Dudziak shows, after the Second World War racial activists could tether civil rights in America to the larger ideological struggle against Soviet totalitarianism. "As presidents and secretaries of state from 1946 to the mid-1960s worried about the impact of race discrimination on U.S. prestige abroad," Dudziak explains, "civil rights reform came to be seen as crucial to U.S. foreign relations."[19]

Both then and during the interwar years, activists formulated plans in dialogue with the world they observed around them. Larger political, economic, and international developments could at any time restrict or expand their range of options. Government inaction and the hostility of the white working class in the 1920s encouraged black leaders to cultivate ties with business executives and pursue a modest reform agenda based on actionable research.[20] In the 1930s, the increasing activism of the state created an opening for Pittsburgh's reformers to develop bolder strategies and forge alliances with the Democratic Party and the industrial labor movement. While racial activists in other cities adopted similar approaches, black Pittsburghers stood in the vanguard of this development.

During the New Deal period, the Steel City emerged as the epicenter of the black middle-class movement for full citizenship. The *Pittsburgh Courier* surpassed all other racial-advancement institutions in the effort to bring black voters into the New Deal coalition. Since emancipation African Americans had overwhelmingly supported the "party of Lincoln," but in 1932 *Courier* editor Robert L. Vann and his staff of columnists, journalists, feature writers, and cartoonists launched a national campaign to persuade them to abandon the GOP and cast their ballots for Franklin Roosevelt. Vann was among the first national black leaders to support Roosevelt, and in exchange he extracted major concessions from Pennsylvania Democrats. After FDR's election, black Pittsburghers gained a considerable number of patronage appointments as well as proportional employment in New Deal work-relief projects.[21]

The black reform community in Pittsburgh also stood in the forefront of the national effort to integrate the labor movement in the late thirties. The Congress of Industrial Organizations (CIO) made Pittsburgh the headquarters of its campaign to organize steelworkers. Members of its Steel Workers Organizing Committee (SWOC), led by Philip Murray, infiltrated mills, traveled the streets, and visited homes to persuade workers from all backgrounds to sign union cards. They rarely required much convincing. As Lizabeth Cohen's classic study of interwar Chicago shows, the pressures of the Great Depression often overwhelmed the mutual-aid societies developed in ethnic neighborhoods and consequently strengthened class consciousness among diverse groups of working people.[22] But in Pittsburgh, SWOC struggled to overcome black workers' mistrust of organized labor. Local unions had excluded them for years, and white workers (both native and foreign born) had often obstructed their movement to better-paying jobs.

The present study picks up where Cohen's analysis leaves off by demonstrating how African American reformers helped bridge these divisions. Convinced that unions could elevate the economic position of black workers, they crossed racial and class lines to coordinate with SWOC and bring them into the movement. They developed workers' councils, organized labor rallies, and pioneered legislation to integrate unions. At the insistence of state representative and Pittsburgh NAACP head Homer Brown, the Pennsylvania legislature added to its labor relations bill a clause that excluded discriminatory unions from its protections. The National Labor Relations Act, better known as the Wagner Act, included no such stipulation. Pennsylvania became the first state to enact a law like this.

The industrial labor movement in Pittsburgh highlights the intersections between reformers and radicals, those moments in which they found a common cause. Social workers in the ULP worked alongside black socialists and communists to organize labor rallies, and they coordinated with black labor organizers who secretly infiltrated area mills to persuade steelworkers to sign union cards. For his part, Ernest Rice McKinney, Pittsburgh's leading black socialist, served at a major settlement house, urged black Pittsburghers to donate to the local Urban League, joined reformers in the effort to open teaching jobs to black applicants, and worked alongside them in the labor movement. Their collective efforts yielded tangible results. By 1940, thousands of

African Americans across western Pennsylvania had joined CIO unions and consequently saw improvements in their wages, working conditions, and job security.

During World War II, black reformers in Pittsburgh again led the way by using wartime urgency to pressure the federal government to support racial justice. Appealing to patriotism and democracy, *Pittsburgh Courier* staff initiated a national Double V campaign that linked fascism abroad with racism at home. Through hundreds of articles, photographs, and drawings, in 1942 the paper led a frontal attack on Jim Crowism in America that reached black homes and street corners from Philadelphia to Los Angeles. Across the country, *Courier* subscribers held Double V parades, created Double V gardens, sponsored Double V baseball games, and joined Double V clubs that lobbied local and federal officials to combat segregation. The campaign infused new meaning into the war for thousands of African Americans, and it helped to push antiracist discourse closer to the mainstream of northern political culture.

By 1944, House Speaker John McCormack, CIO leader Phillip Murray, and AFL head William Green all wore Double V badges; the United Auto Workers passed a resolution endorsing the Double V campaign; and politicians on both sides of the aisle, including GOP presidential nominee Wendell Willkie, warned that fascism "within our own borders is as serious a threat to freedom as is the attack without."[23]

Ultimately, the Double V campaign likely hastened federal-level decisions to open the marines, air corps, and coast guard to African Americans, expand their role in the army and navy, and include black women in the women's corps. Like the March on Washington Movement in 1941 that pressured Roosevelt to issue an executive order barring discriminatory hiring practices in defense plants, the *Courier* demonstrated for future activists how the federal government could serve as a powerful weapon against racial injustice when it was forced to do so.

Still, division and failure mixed with these moments of unity and achievement. Reformers sometimes argued over the best course of action, struggled to balance their personal ambitions with the greater good of the community, and engaged in petty disputes both within and among their respective institutions. And although reformers made noteworthy contributions to the struggle for citizenship, sometimes their measures worked against the interests of ordinary African Americans. ULP head John T. Clark lobbied local unions to include black workers and pressed employers to open skilled positions to nonwhites, but occasionally he encouraged companies to fire migrants whose behavior did not conform to bourgeois standards of reliability, industriousness, and restrained personal conduct. And while state legislator and Pittsburgh NAACP president Homer Brown sponsored legislation that made it easier for black workers to join unions, later in his career he supported "urban renewal" projects in Pittsburgh's lower Hill District that displaced many working-class African Americans.

Moreover, male reformers sometimes perpetuated patterns of gender discrimination. Men almost always held key leadership posts in Pittsburgh's major racial-advancement organizations while confining women to positions that dealt with "women's issues" in the community.[24] Yet in these gendered roles, women reformers performed most of the gritty grassroots work for their respective organizations. Jeannette Washington, Pittsburgh's first black public health nurse, provided free health screenings for hundreds of black infants, registered babies with local medical facilities, and educated parents about preventative care. Grace Lowndes represented the ULP at the city morals court, where she advocated for black juveniles and prostitutes. Georgine Pearce, the league's home and school visitor, monitored the education of local youth at their schools and homes. These tasks placed professional women in intimate contact with poor and working-class African Americans. And while some migrants resented their intrusions, others welcomed them as friends. Through these personal connections, black women reformers played a major role in social reforms centered around children and families in the migrant community, a role whose dismissal by historians replicates the gendering of their labor.

The lives of reformers and migrants intersected in numerous ways as they pursued full citizenship in Pittsburgh. Members of both groups entered the city as outsiders hoping to find economic opportunity and greater personal freedom. They came from different regional, educational, and social backgrounds, but their shared identity as African Americans in a racially hostile society drew them together at critical moments, from their arrival at Union Station in downtown Pittsburgh at the beginning of the Great Migration to their deployment in the jungles of Southeast Asia during WWII. And while reformers initiated the major social justice campaigns of the era, migrants gave them shape and force. Harrison Gant, a Georgia migrant whose life I follow throughout the book, made his views clear when he joined other black Pittsburghers in rejecting the Republican Party in 1932; later, in the late thirties, he risked his livelihood to persuade his fellow black workers to join CIO unions. Reformers and migrants never reached Canaan, but their collective striving led to tangible improvements in the black community and pointed the way forward for the next generation of activists.

NOTES

1. Du Bois's 1903 publications collectively illustrate how he conceived of education and activism at that moment in his life. He maintained that racial progress depended on providing a good classical education for the most talented African Americans, who then would go on to lead black America toward first-class citizenship (*The Souls of Black Folk* [Greenwich, CT: Fawcett, 1961], 19–20). For his discussion of the talented tenth, see "The Talented Tenth," in *The Negro Problem* (New York: James Pott, 1903), 33–75.
2. The pace of migration slowed during the Great Depression as industrial jobs disappeared. However, with the onset of World War II and the revitalization of industry, the Great Migration entered its second phase. From about 1940 until 1970, another five million African Americans left the South. Rural-to-urban migration occurred *within* the South as well. See Earl Lewis, "Expectations, Economic Opportunities, and Life in the Industrial Age: Black Migration to Norfolk, Virginia, 1910–1945," in *The Great Migration in Historical Perspective: New Dimensions of Race, Class, and Gender*, ed. Joe W. Trotter (Bloomington: Indiana University Press, 1991), 22–45, and Luther Adams, "'Headed for Louisville': Rethinking Rural to Urban Migration in the South, 1930–1950," *Journal of Social History* 40, no. 2 (2006): 407–30.
3. Committee to Defend the Pittsburgh Five, "The Frame-Up of Benjamin Lowell Careathers," Communist Party pamphlet, May 1953, box 1, folder 7, Leon Swimmer Collection, University of Pittsburgh Archives Service Center.
4. Black reformers had high aspirations, but they tailored their tactics and short-term goals to the bleak racial reality they confronted. However, through their actions and exhortations, we can begin to discern a broader picture of citizenship. As *Courier* editor Robert L. Vann once explained in an editorial, black reformers had a duty to "see to it that Negroes get a square deal in employment; that they get a square deal from the labor unions; that they get a square deal from the relief agencies; that they get their proper share of education funds; that their legislative representatives work energetically in their interests to remove all disabilities imposed because of race and color." See "Does the Negro Need Defense?" *Pittsburgh Courier*, August 4, 1934.
5. Nancy J. Weiss, *The National Urban League, 1910–1940* (New York: Oxford University Press, 1974), 55–57.
6. Rob Ruck, *Sandlot Seasons: Sport in Black Pittsburgh* (Urbana: University of Illinois Press, 1993), 10; Dennis Dickerson, *Out of the Crucible: Black Steelworkers in Western Pennsylvania, 1875–1980* (Albany: State University of New York Press, 1986), 38–39.
7. Gunnar Myrdal, *An American Dilemma: The Negro Problem and Modern Democracy* (New York: Harper and Brothers, 1944), 782, emphasis in original.
8. Historian James Grossman has also noted this pragmatic, "race-first" orientation. In his case study of African Americans and organized labor in Chicago from 1916 to 1923, he explains that local Urban Leaguers' modest endorsement of unions "must be understood in terms of a world view dominated by the category of race. Like Abbott at the

Defender, black Urban Leaguers looked first to the interests of race, and middle-class values interacted with but did not determine the substance of their race-consciousness." The *Chicago Defender* displayed even greater ambivalence toward unions in the 1910s and early 1920s: "Because the principle of unionization was secondary to the question of what stockyards unions could do for the black community," writes Grossman, "the editors could change their minds easily, depending on the power equation in the stockyards and the level of interest in the black community" ("The White Man's Union: The Great Migration and the Resonance of Race and Class in Chicago, 1916–1922," in *The Great Migration in Historical Perspective*, 83–99).

9. For examples of recent studies examining the carceral state, see Rebecca M. McLennan, *The Crisis of Imprisonment: Protest, Politics, and the Making of the American Penal State, 1776–1941* (Cambridge: Cambridge University Press, 2008), Kali N. Gross, *Colored Amazons: Crime, Violence, and Black Women in the City of Brotherly Love, 1880–1910* (Durham, NC: Duke University Press, 2006), Cheryl D. Hicks, *Talk with You like a Woman: African American Women, Justice, and Reform in New York, 1890–1935* (Chapel Hill: University of North Carolina Press, 2010), David M. Oshinsky, *Capital Punishment on Trial: Furman v. Georgia and the Death Penalty in Modern America* (Lawrence: University Press of Kansas, 2010), Robert Perkinson, *Texas Tough: The Rise of America's Prison Empire* (New York: Metropolitan Books, 2010), Khalil Gibran Muhammad, *The Condemnation of Blackness: Race, Crime, and the Making of Modern Urban America* (Cambridge, MA: Harvard University Press, 2010), Heather Ann Thompson, "Why Mass Incarceration Matters: Rethinking Crisis, Decline, and Transformation in Postwar American History," *Journal of American History* 97, no. 3 (2010): 703–34, Talitha L. LeFlouria, *Chained in Silence: Black Women and Convict Labor in the New South* (Chapel Hill: University of North Carolina Press, 2015), and Jeffrey S. Adler, "Less Crime, More Punishment: Violence, Race, and Criminal Justice in Early Twentieth-Century America," *Journal of American History* 102, no. 1 (2015): 34–46. Also see Douglas A. Blackmon, *Slavery by Another Name: The Reenslavement of Black People in America from the Civil War to World War II* (New York: Doubleday, 2008), Michelle Alexander, *The New Jim Crow: Mass Incarceration in the Age of Colorblindness* (New York: New Press, 2010), and Bryan Stevenson, *Just Mercy: A Story of Justice and Redemption* (New York: Spiegel and Grau, 2014).

10. E. Franklin Frazier articulated this concept in *Black Bourgeoisie* (Glencoe, IL: Free Press), published in 1957: "When the opportunity has been present, the black bourgeoisie has exploited the Negro masses as ruthlessly as have whites. As the intellectual leaders in the Negro community, they have never dared think beyond a ... philosophy that provided a rationalization for their own advantages" (236). Historians from the 1960s through the 1980s offered similarly dismissive interpretations. See August Meier and Elliot Rudwick, *From Plantation to Ghetto* (New York: Hill and Wang, 1966), 242, Lee Finkle, "The Conservative Aims of Militant Rhetoric: Black Protest during World War II," *Journal of American History* 60, no. 3 (1973), 692–713, Nancy Weiss, *The National Urban League, 1910–1940* (New York: Oxford University Press, 1974), Andrew Buni, *Robert L. Vann of the Pittsburgh Courier: Politics and Black Journalism* (Pittsburgh: University of Pittsburgh Press, 1974), John Bodnar, Richard Simon, and Michael P. Weber, *Lives of Their Own: Blacks, Italians, and Poles in Pittsburgh, 1900–1960* (Urbana: University of Illinois Press, 1982), 9, and Peter Gottlieb, *Making*

Their Own Way: Southern Blacks' Migration to Pittsburgh, 1916–30 (Urbana: University of Illinois Press, 1987), 7.
11. Gottlieb, *Making Their Own Way*, 7, 248; Bodnar, Simon, and Weber, *Lives of Their Own*, 9; Finkle, "The Conservative Aims of Militant Rhetoric," 692–713. Buni offers a similarly dismissive take on black reform work in his biography of Vann (*Robert L. Vann of the* Pittsburgh Courier, xiii, 61).
12. Cleveland Urban League head William Conners and social welfare worker Jane Edna Hunter bear the brunt of Phillips's critique of black professionals in the city. For instance, without citing anything that Conners himself wrote, Phillips maintains that he "aggressively impeded black workers' efforts to organize unions" (*Alabama North: African-American Migrants, Community, and Working-Class Activism in Cleveland, 1915–1945* [Urbana: University of Illinois Press, 1999], 157).
13. Keona K. Ervin, "Breaking the 'Harness of Household Slavery': Domestic Workers, the Women's Division of the St. Louis Urban League, and the Politics of Labor Reform during the Great Depression," *International Labor and Working-Class History* 88 (Fall 2015), 49–66. In making her argument that domestic workers "transformed their local UL into a worker organization," Ervin tacitly implies that the league staff who developed programs tailored to their interests did not have agency. A closer reading of St. Louis Urban League head John T. Clark's career in New York City, Pittsburgh, and St. Louis, for example, suggests a long-standing commitment to promoting working-class issues. See my "The Pursuit of Happiness: Racial Utilitarianism and Black Reform Efforts in John T. Clark's Urban League," *Journal of Urban History* 45, no. 1 (2019): 6–22.
14. Weiss, *The National Urban League*; Touré F. Reed, *Not Alms but Opportunity: The Urban League and the Politics of Racial Uplift, 1910–1950* (Chapel Hill: University of North Carolina Press, 2008), 196. Although Reed seeks to position his work outside debates over the league's conservative or militant tendencies, *Not Alms But Opportunity* makes plain that Urban Leaguers pursued essentially conservative tactics that served a narrow subset of the black community.
15. Evelyn Brooks Higginbotham, *Righteous Discontent: The Women's Movement in the Black Baptist Church, 1880–1920* (Cambridge, MA: Harvard University Press, 1993); Charles Pete T. Banner-Haley, *To Do Good and to Do Well: Middle-Class Blacks and the Depression, Philadelphia, 1929–1941* (New York: Garland, 1993); Darlene Clark Hine, *Speak Truth to Power: Black Professional Class in United States History* (Brooklyn, NY: Carlson, 1996); Stephanie Shaw, *What a Woman Ought to Be and to Do: Black Professional Women Workers During the Jim Crow Era* (Chicago: University of Chicago Press, 1996); Glenda Elizabeth Gilmore, *Gender and Jim Crow: Women and the Politics of White Supremacy in North Carolina, 1896–1920* (Chapel Hill: University of North Carolina Press, 1996); Charles E. Coulter, *Take Up the Black Man's Burden: Kansas City's African American Communities, 1865–1939* (Columbia: University of Missouri Press, 2006); Danielle McGuire, *At the Dark End of the Street: Black Women, Rape, and Resistance—A New History of the Civil Rights Movement from Rosa Parks to the Rise of Black Power* (New York: Knopf, 2010); Priscilla A. Dowden-White, *Groping toward Democracy: African American Social Welfare Reform in St. Louis, 1910–1949* (Columbia: University of Missouri Press, 2011).
16. Notwithstanding the revisionist trends discussed above, concerning black reformers and mainstream racial advancement organizations, studies in the 1990s and 2000s usu-

ally hewed to E. Franklin Frazier's interpretive model. For instance, Kevin Gaines remarked that "black elites sought status, moral authority, and recognition of their humanity by distinguishing themselves...from the presumably underdeveloped black majority." See Gaines, *Uplifting the Race: Black Leadership, Politics, and Culture in the Twentieth Century* (Chapel Hill, NC: University of North Carolina Press, 1996), 2; Phillips, *Alabama North*, 157; Karen Ferguson, *Black Politics in New Deal Atlanta* (Chapel Hill: University of North Carolina Press, 2002), 5–11; Michele Mitchell, *Righteous Propagation: African Americans and the Politics of Racial Destiny after Reconstruction* (Chapel Hill: The University of North Carolina Press, 2004); Brian Kelly, "Industrial Sentinels Confront the 'Rabid Faction': Black Elites, Black Workers, and the Labor Question in the Jim Crow South," in *The Black Worker: A Reader*, ed. Eric Arnesen (Urbana: The University of Illinois Press, 2007): 98 and 110; Touré Reed, *Not Alms But Opportunity* (2008); Michelle Alexander, *The New Jim Crow* (2010), 210–214; Preston H. Smith, *Racial Democracy and the Black Metropolis: Housing Policy in Postwar Chicago* (Minneapolis, MN: University of Minnesota Press, 2012), xvi; Ervin, "Breaking the 'Harness of Household Slavery'", 49–66.

Numerous other studies enhance this narrative by marginalizing the contributions of black reformers while emphasizing the important roles of black leftists and the Communist Party in the freedom struggle. For instance, Glenda Elizabeth Gilmore confines the Urban League to one page in *Defying Dixie* and places communists at the center of the southern freedom struggle, stating that they "alone argued for complete equality between the races." See Mark Naison, *Communists in Harlem during the Depression* (New York: Grove Press, Inc., 1983); Robin D.G. Kelley, *Hammer and Hoe: Alabama Communists during the Great Depression* (Chapel Hill: University of North Carolina Press, 1990); ———, *Race Rebels: Culture, Politics, and the Black Working Class* (New York: The Free Press, 1996); Mark Solomon, *The Cry Was Unity: Communists and African Americans, 1917–1936* (Jackson, Mississippi: University Press of Mississippi, 1998); Martha Biondi, *To Stand and Fight: The Struggle for Civil Rights in Postwar New York City* (Cambridge, Massachusetts: Harvard University Press, 2003); Manning Marable, *Race, Reform, and Rebellion: The Second Reconstruction in Black America, 1945–2006* (Jackson: University Press of Mississippi, 2007; Third Edition), 27; Glenda Elizabeth Gilmore, *Defying Dixie: The Radical Roots of Civil Rights* (New York: W.W. Norton and Company, 2008), 4.

Moreover, while overlooking interwar-era reformers, scholars have generally praised the Black Panthers in Oakland, Chicago, and other major cities for developing community programs that performed similar functions as the ones Urban Leaguers sponsored in the 1920s. See Marable, *Race, Reform, and Rebellion*, 107; Andrew Witt, *The Black Panthers in the Midwest: The Community Programs and Services of the Black Panther Party in Milwaukee, 1966–1977* (New York: Routledge, 2007); *The Black Panther Party Service to the People Programs*, edited by David Hilliard (Albuquerque: University of New Mexico Press, 2008).

17. Thomas Sugrue, *Sweet Land of Liberty: The Forgotten Struggle for Civil Rights in the North* (New York: Random House, 2008), xxiv–xxv.
18. For an effective overview of racism during the Progressive Era, see David W. Southern, *The Progressive Era and Race: Reaction and Reform, 1900–1917* (Wheeling, IL: Harlan Davidson, 2005), 47–71.

19. Mary L. Dudziak, *Cold War Civil Rights: Race and the Image of American Democracy* (Princeton, NJ: Princeton University Press, 2000), 6.
20. The Urban League of Pittsburgh sponsored a fellowship program that encouraged black intellectuals to pursue graduate degrees in sociology, social work, and economics at the University of Pittsburgh. Concurrently, the *Pittsburgh Courier* published essays by leading black thinkers from Walter White and W. E. B. Du Bois to Marcus Garvey. As in Harlem and Chicago, the black reform community in Pittsburgh created a vital space for New Negro intellectual discourse on modernity, labor politics, urbanization, and other questions of social importance.
21. Vann's political defections reflected the pragmatic impulse of many black reformers to make and break alliances across the political spectrum whenever it suited their racial goals. As the *Courier*'s managing editor explained it, "The Negro vote should at all times remain organized and liquid; liquid that it might move from party to party where the political and economic interests of the Negro were factors." For Vann and other reformers at the *Courier*, citizenship both required and featured political empowerment—for without it African Americans could not compel the major parties to take their concerns seriously. See Ira F. Lewis, speech, October 10, 1943, box 31, Robert L. Vann Papers, Percival Prattis Collection, Mooreland-Spingarn Research Center, Howard University.
22. Lizabeth Cohen, *Making a New Deal: Industrial Workers in Chicago, 1919-1939* (New York: Cambridge University Press, 1990).
23. See the following *Pittsburgh Courier* articles: James Edmund Boyack, "Dewey Endorses Courier's 'Double V' Campaign: The True American Spirit . . . 'Double V' for Victory Campaign Gets White Support!" February 28, 1942, James Edmund Boyack, "Willkie Blasts 'Hate'," July 31, 1943, John R. Williams, "Epochal Radio Speeches Reflect Courier's 'Double V' Theme," July 31, 1943, and Horace Cayton, "UAW-CIO Adopts Courier 'Double-V' Program," August 15, 1942.
24. Daisy Lampkin and Jesse Vann are exceptions to this pattern. Lampkin rose to vice president of the Pittsburgh NAACP before accepting a position as a staff member for the association's national office in New York. Eventually, she became the NAACP's first female board member. For her part, Jesse Vann took over the *Pittsburgh Courier* publishing company after her husband died in 1940.

CHAPTER ONE

"The Ugliest, Deadest Town"
MIGRANTS AND REFORMERS IN
THE STEEL CITY, 1915–1929

The flat, verdant fields of Ohio gave way to hills and ravines as Harrison Gant's train crossed into western Pennsylvania in the summer of 1916. His journey had begun two years earlier, when at age fourteen he left his family's farm near Americus, Georgia, to find work in urban communities farther north. Like thousands of southern black peasants, young Gant faced increasingly poor economic prospects in his hometown as the price of cotton declined, and this factored into his decision to relocate. He moved first to Louisville and then Cincinnati before making his way to Pittsburgh.

Had he left home a year earlier he might have crossed paths with John T. Clark in Louisville. Clark was a native of the city. After earning a bachelor's degree at Ohio State and working at a naval yard in Portsmouth, Virginia, he returned to Louisville and taught math at a black school from 1908 to 1913.[1] Clark joined the Urban League movement in New York just as Gant arrived in Louisville. In Harlem, Clark directed a systematic study of black living conditions that convinced league officials to establish the Housing Bureau of New York.[2] He spent four years with the National Urban League (NUL) and eventually became its field secretary. This role led to his deployment to Pittsburgh in early 1918, where NUL director Eugene K. Jones charged him with the task of developing an Urban League affiliate.[3]

Gant had arrived in Pittsburgh almost two years earlier. As his train screeched to a stop at Union Station in the heart of the city, he felt a mixture of excitement and shock. Although Gant had grown accustomed to cities during his earlier travels, he never encountered industrial pollution on Pittsburgh's scale. "This was the ugliest, deadest town I ever seen in my life!" he declared. "Man, you couldn't see no sun around here! I'll tell you the truth, the first year I was here I betcha I didn't see the sun a half a dozen times." Gant eventually found a place to stay in the lower Hill District and got a job as a common laborer in a steel plant. When Clark arrived, he moved into a house in the upper Hill and directed the local Urban League that he helped establish. Both Gant and Clark were newcomers, outsiders in an unfamiliar landscape. One was a peasant farmer from the Deep South, the other a college-educated social worker from the upper South. Like other migrants and reformers settling in Pittsburgh, their racial, regional, and class identities shaped their experiences in the city: where they lived, worshipped, played, and worked. During the interwar period these newcomers permanently altered the demographic and political landscape of the city and laid the foundations for an effective social justice movement.

The Emergence of the Black Community in Pittsburgh

Migrants and reformers arrived in a city with an established black community. Over a thousand African Americans lived in Pittsburgh in 1865. Concentrated in a lower Hill District community dubbed Little Hayti, they gradually developed black-owned institutions and businesses as well as forms of social stratification. Particularly during the late nineteenth century, when in-migration and natural growth increased Pittsburgh's black population to twenty thousand, occupation, region of birth, and adherence to genteel customs became marks of distinction. Native Pittsburghers readily distinguished themselves from southern migrants through their commitment to "respectability," membership in prestigious social clubs like Loendi and the Aurora Reading Club, and attendance at elite churches such as Ebenezer Baptist, Grace Memorial Presbyterian, and Bethel AME. They also created an impressive array of businesses (around eighty-five by 1909), including barber shops, poolrooms, taverns, pharmacies, catering operations, and wig-making enterprises.[4]

When the Great Migration began, reformers and southern migrants settling in the Hill District thus encountered a black community with an institutional framework in place and a tradition of class distinction based on origins, comportment, place of worship, and occupation. Native black Pittsburghers usually held domestic or service jobs that provided greater financial security than the unskilled factory work migrants performed. Elite black natives, who called themselves Old Pittsburghers, or OPs, prided themselves on their heritage in the community. They worshipped apart from migrants at the prestigious churches their fathers and grandfathers helped establish, and they created new social clubs to augment the ones that already existed—the Frogs, for example, surpassed the older Loendi Club in its exclusivity. Increasingly, OPs lived apart from migrants as well. As conditions deteriorated in the lower Hill, many moved to the upper Hill (called Sugartop), East Liberty, and Homewood-Brushton.[5]

Reformers served as intermediaries between natives and migrants. Like their contemporaries elsewhere, Pittsburgh's black reformers lived and worked in multiple cities during their careers. Most arrived in the Steel City from other parts of the country and eventually left for appointments elsewhere. Clark spent time in Louisville, Portsmouth, and New York before arriving in Pittsburgh, and after eight years in the Steel City he left for St. Louis.[6] Daisy Lampkin grew up in eastern Pennsylvania, moved to Pittsburgh, and worked for the *Pittsburgh Courier* and the local chapter of the National Association for the Advancement of Colored People (NAACP) before becoming an officer in the NAACP's national branch in New York.[7] Abram Harris came from Virginia to pursue a master's degree at the University of Pittsburgh, and after completing his thesis he went on to teach at Howard University in Washington, DC. Although they were outsiders, reformers' education and comportment gained them entry into the elite churches, clubs, and neighborhoods of the OPs. *Courier* editor Robert L. Vann, who migrated from North Carolina, lived in Homewood.[8] Urban Leaguers Grace Lowndes and R. Maurice Moss, respectively from South Carolina and New York, lived in the upper Hill.[9] Reformers mixed and mingled with OPs, but their opposing perceptions of the migrant community strained the relationship at times. Many native Pittsburghers believed that migrants depleted the black community's limited financial resources and housing options, damaged their carefully cultivated image of respectability, and provoked white racial animosity.[10] As one minister recalled, local African Americans feared that migrants "were going to make it much worse for the resident population of blacks. Some of the so-called 'Old Ps' actually resented the presence of these people."[11]

Although they generally held better-paying jobs than migrants, most native black Pittsburghers could not afford to donate money to organizations like the Urban League of Pittsburgh (ULP). But even members of the black middle class—from clergymen to morticians, druggists, grocers, and barbers—often refused to support the league. Preferring instead that migrants leave the city, some OPs saw reformers like Clark and Lowndes as interlopers whose migrant "adjustment" programs undermined their interests. A ULP survey in 1923 revealed that most black churches did not offer any special services or programs to help the migrants adjust to urban life, and several preachers grumbled that the migrant influx in their churches was "not conducive to a high place of morality and decent standards."[12]

Reformers, in turn, often complained about the lack of support from native blacks.[13] Responding to the poor turnout at a ULP fundraising event, one of them reminded readers that "the Urban League works in the interest of us all, and it is the least that we can do to support it by buying a dollar ticket. Our disinterestedness along this line is alarming."[14] Contributing to this tension were the goals of the migrants themselves, which not infrequently conflicted with the designs of both OPs and reformers.

The Great Migration and the Journey to Pittsburgh

The First World War created industrial employment opportunities that catalyzed a mass migration of southern blacks eager to escape deteriorating economic and social conditions in their home states. In the early twentieth century a boll weevil infestation devastated fields throughout the cotton belt, deepening the poverty of black tenant farmers, and across the South white vigilantes terrorized African American communities. Lynch mobs hanged an average of more than two black men a week from 1880 to 1930, and local Democrats implemented poll taxes and literacy tests to disfranchise black voters. Under Jim Crow, southern blacks lived apart from whites, studied in black schools, traveled in segregated railroad and trolley cars, and buried their dead in segregated cemeteries. Hoping to escape these conditions and improve their employment prospects, southern migrants undertook a long and uncertain journey north, across the Ohio River and Mason-Dixon Line, to Chicago, Detroit, Cleveland, Pittsburgh, Philadelphia, and New York.[15]

The Great War cut off the supply of cheap labor from southern and eastern Europe just as American industries had begun accelerating production to furnish war materials. Consequently, northern industries sought to meet their labor needs domestically by recruiting poor whites and blacks from the South. Their labor agents scoured the South for new recruits, and they often offered to pay the transportation fare for any able-bodied men willing to work for them. Prospective migrants also learned about northern jobs from black newspapers, letters from friends and relatives who already migrated, word of mouth, and correspondences with city branches of the Urban League. They collected information, weighed their options, and made calculated decisions about whether, when, and where to migrate.[16]

The Reverend James Simmons recalled moving to Pittsburgh in 1924 when his wife's parents "sent for him." His father was a tenant farmer on a sprawling fifty-acre plantation in Albany, Georgia, where he grew watermelon, potatoes, rice, cotton, corn, and sugarcane. Simmons was one of fourteen children, only six of whom survived infancy. Simmons and his siblings worked on their father's farm, but during slack seasons he supplemented his family's income through a job building and maintaining railroad tracks.[17]

At age fourteen, Ben Irving, who grew up in Bullet County, Alabama, began working at a nearby lumberyard when he was not needed on his family's sixty-acre farm. A few years earlier a boll weevil infestation had destroyed his father's cotton crop, so he switched to beans, peas, and corn. Irving's parents encountered serious financial difficulties thereafter, which may have damaged their relationship. They divorced around 1914, and his father moved to the Pittsburgh area to work at a coal mine. Irving's mother died shortly afterward, and he remained on the farm with his grandparents. Like Simmons, he migrated to Pittsburgh in 1924 upon receiving a letter from his father suggesting that he do so because "he figured it would better my condition."[18]

Bartow Tipper remembered seeing labor agents on the streets of Americus, Georgia, representing the Jones and Laughlin Steel Company of western Pennsylvania. One of the agents, with pockets full of company money to pay migrants' transportation fares, shouted "I want a hundred people to go to Woodlawn" (later renamed Aliquippa). Once there, the agent promised that "we'll furnish you a place to stay until you're able to make enough money to get a place that you want."[19]

Simmons, Irving, and Tipper joined a multitude of African Americans moving north during the interwar period. Between 1916 and 1930 as many as 1.5 million southern blacks participated in the exodus to what they hoped would be their Canaan. While New York, Philadelphia, and Chicago attracted the largest share of migrants, the black populations of smaller cities also grew dramatically. From 1910 to 1920 Detroit's increased from 5,741 to 40,838; Cincinnati went from 19,337 to 30,079; and Cleveland's spiked from 8,448 to 34,451.[20]

As one of the nation's major centers of steel production, Pittsburgh and its surrounding communities attracted thousands of migrants. Between 1910 and 1920 the city's black population grew from 24,623 to 37,725, and by 1930 it approached 55,000—making it the fifth largest black population in the country.[21] Although some of this can be attributed to natural growth, historian Peter Gottlieb calculates that over 21,000 black migrants settled in Pittsburgh between 1910 and 1930.[22]

Migrants from the Deep South initially comprised the majority of newcomers to Pittsburgh. In a 1918 survey of 567 migrants, social researcher Abraham Epstein discovered that 47 percent of them came from either Alabama or Georgia. African Americans departing from the Birmingham area, the South's steel-producing capital, encountered resistance from white steel managers desiring to safeguard their supply of cheap labor. Local police confiscated migrants' train tickets, and they were known to arrest blacks for "conspiring to go north," using fabricated charges to detain them. To avoid detection, Birmingham migrants often left in secret and boarded trains several miles from their homes. Even then, they sometimes faced additional discouragement while awaiting departure. In June 1917 a white railroad employee approached several black passengers and pointed to the adjacent car containing coffins: "Yo Niggahs goin' to Pittsburgh, eh? We all are jes shippin' five of yo back from thah. They froze to death in Pittsburgh."[23] Once under way, northbound trains traveled to Cincinnati, from where most migrants headed to Midwest cities like Chicago and Milwaukee. Those traveling east to Pittsburgh boarded either the Pennsylvania Railroad or B & O lines.[24]

No matter which train they took to the Steel City, migrants arrived downtown at Union Station, where the landscape presented a stark contrast to the hometowns they left behind. Gottlieb notes that black peasants in the South often supplemented their earnings by working seasonally in small-scale factories nearby. Still, transitioning from these semi-industrial communities to Pittsburgh was not easy. Many migrants likely shared Harrison Gant's first impressions of the Steel City in 1916. Industrial smoke spewing from the region's factories darkened both the sky above and the moods of incoming rural migrants who "couldn't see no sun around here!"[25] H. L. Mencken, the nationally renowned journalist and satirist, corroborated Gant's assessment ten

Migrants arriving in Pittsburgh.
Jacob Lawrence, Migration Series, Panel 45, 1940–1941,
Phillips Collection, Washington, DC.

years later, writing that the greater Pittsburgh area was "so intolerably bleak and forlorn that it reduced the whole aspiration of man to a macabre and depressing joke."[26]

Housing and Residential Patterns in Black Pittsburgh

Migrants exiting Union Station made their way to one of several black enclaves in Pittsburgh. The Hill District hosted the largest concentration of African Americans, about 50 percent by 1930, but housing shortages forced many migrants to settle elsewhere. Smaller black neighborhoods emerged west and east of the Hill, respectively in Northside and East Liberty, as well as below it in the Strip District and Lawrenceville, which lay along the bank of the Allegheny.[27] The city's hills and ravines served as geographic barriers between these neighborhoods and prevented the black community from fully consolidating its political and financial strength.[28]

The Hill District comprised Pittsburgh's third and fifth wards and resembled the shape of a rectangle. Its short side to the southwest abutted the central business district at the junction of the Allegheny, Monongahela, and

Ohio rivers. From there it climbed steeply to the northeast, roughly parallel to the Allegheny, before ending in the upper Hill, which overlooked the entire district. Migrants typically settled along Wylie, Centre, and Bedford Avenues in the lower Hill, near downtown Pittsburgh.[29]

Jews and Italians made up the majority of Hill District residents during the early twentieth century, and the small black population lived alongside them in ethnically diverse neighborhoods and apartment complexes. "The housing situation, before the great exodus of blacks from the South took place, was not too bad," the Reverend Harold Tolliver remembered. "People could live in mixed neighborhoods. They were able to buy or to rent. There was no rigid real estate constriction at that time."[30] As of 1910 African Americans comprised less than a quarter of the Hill District's population, but their numbers steadily increased with the influx of southern migrants. Meanwhile, Europeans and their children gradually left the inner city as their economic conditions improved, settling in peripheral communities such as East Liberty, Homewood-Brushton, and Beltzhoover. By 1930 about twenty-six thousand African Americans resided in the Hill and represented 53 percent of its total population.[31]

Like local whites and OPs, black reformers gradually left the lower Hill District as conditions deteriorated there. R. Maurice Moss, Grace Lowndes, Daisy Lampkin, and Homer Brown settled in the upper Hill, but others, like Vann and Ernest Rice McKinney, a social worker and political activist, moved to the Homewood-Brushton area east of the Hill.[32] When Vann first moved to Homewood's Monticello Street, few of his white neighbors expressed any reservations, and he lived there for the next six years without incident. Whites tolerated Vann's presence until 1917, when he bought the house next to him and rented it to a black family. Thereafter they waged what Vann later called "the battle for Monticello Street." Fearing a trend, they passed out handbills calling for the removal of African Americans in the neighborhood, and they held meetings to discuss how they might reclaim the street. After a few months, when it became clear that Vann would not leave, his neighbors gradually moved out. By 1927 Monticello Street was predominantly black, and Vann counted McKinney among his neighbors.[33]

In the inner city, incoming migrants confronted a more serious lodging situation. Many of the lower Hill's housing units had fallen into disrepair years before they arrived, and few developers invested in building new homes there. The stagnant housing market and deteriorating infrastructure placed severe limits on migrants' choice of lodging, and the situation was lit-

Monticello Street, ca. 1930.
Urban League Collection, box 10, folder 513,
University of Pittsburgh Archives Service Center.

tle better elsewhere. In Pittsburgh and its satellite communities like Homestead and Braddock, migrants crowded into dilapidated tenements, boardinghouses, and company bunkhouses.[34] "When I first moved to Pittsburgh," Gant recalled, "you couldn't find a colored family from downtown all the way out to East Liberty [that] lived all by themselves. Everybody [was] living with everybody else."[35] Another migrant, Bartow Tipper, remembered sharing his bed in shifts with another steelworker and living in a house with twelve men.[36]

Social researchers expressed deep concern over the state of migrant boardinghouses. To supplement their meager earnings and offset the cost of rent, local African Americans lodged migrants in their spare rooms, basements, attics, and even kitchens.[37] "The conditions in these rooming houses often beggar description," Epstein wrote in 1918. They often had drooping plaster, low ceilings, poor lighting, and inadequate ventilation. Like Tipper, almost two-thirds of the lodgers Epstein observed shared their beds with at least one other person. Workers on the night shift slept during the day, and their counterparts on the day shift used the bed at night. In most cases, boardinghouses did not have indoor toilets or sinks, compelling migrants to use privies to relieve themselves and an outdoor pump for washing and drinking.[38]

Conditions improved little over the ensuing decade. Eighty percent of the black homes surveyed in the region in 1925 lacked bathtubs, and half relied on outhouses and water closets.[39] A 1929 study of housing in the Hill described decrepit boardinghouses with holes in the flooring, broken door panels, faulty

African American boardinghouse overlooking Pittsburgh, ca. 1925.
Historic Pittsburgh Image Collection, 8III50606.UL,
University of Pittsburgh Archives Service Center.

African American tenement in Pittsburgh, ca. 1925.
Historic Pittsburgh Image Collections, 8III50606.UL,
University of Pittsburgh Archives Service Center.

A shoeshine parlor and a west-facing view of the Hill from 1213 Wylie Avenue, April 29, 1920.
Pittsburgh City Photographer Collection, 1901–2002, AIS.1971.05,
University of Pittsburgh Archives Service Center.

Wylie Avenue and Pittsburgh's hilly terrain, July 29, 1935.
Pittsburgh City Photographer Collection, 1901–2002, AIS.1971.05,
University of Pittsburgh Archives Service Center.

A west-facing view of the Hill from 1232 Wylie Avenue, October 20, 1936.
Pittsburgh City Photographer Collection, 1901–2002, AIS.1971.05, University of Pittsburgh Archives Service Center.

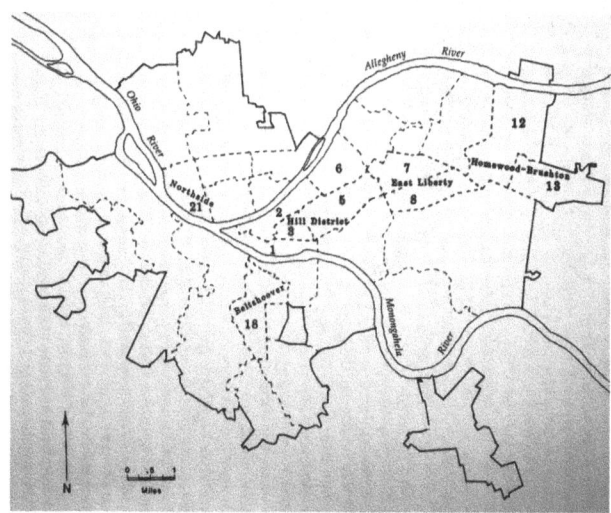

African American communities in interwar Pittsburgh.
Pittsburgh Department of City Planning.

Major black communities in western Pennsylvania.
Dennis C. Dickerson, *Out of the Crucible: Black Steelworkers in Western Pennsylvania, 1875–1980* (Albany: State University of New York Press, 1986), 38–39.

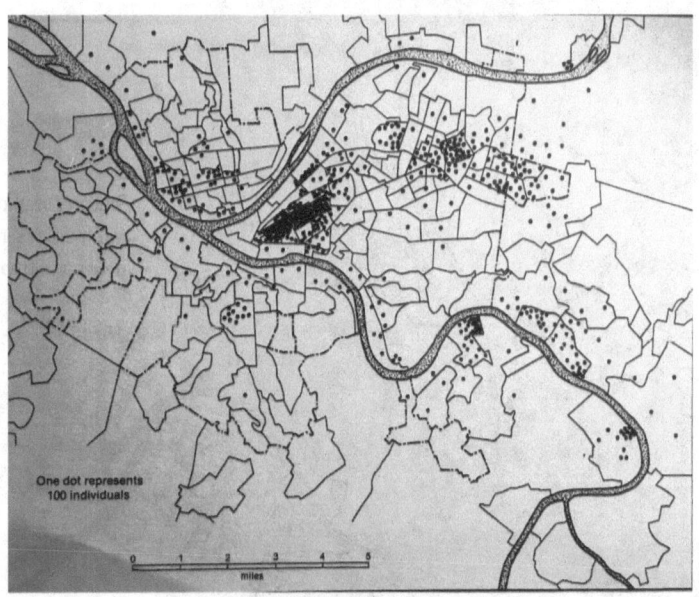

Concentration of African Americans in Pittsburgh by 1930.
Allegheny County Bureau of Social Research, 1933.

flues, leaking roofs, and broken window panes.[40] In his 1924 book, *Black America*, social critic Scott Nearing offered a similar analysis of the Hill: "The streets are ill-kept, dirty. The houses are dilapidated. Some of them even abandoned. Many of them are built of wood. Throngs of unemployed Negro workers stand gossiping at the principal corners. The whole community speaks of poverty, neglect and physical hardship."[41]

These conditions created a health crisis in the black community. Mortality rates for black Pittsburghers doubled between 1915 and 1917, and during the same period pneumonia deaths increased by 200 percent. In 1918 black infants died twice as often as white infants, and throughout the 1920s African Americans suffered disproportionately from tuberculosis and whooping cough.[42]

Black Community Life in Pittsburgh

With little incentive to stay in their crowded and unsanitary boardinghouses, migrants found psychological comfort and emotional release at church, night spots, and sporting events. The Ebenezer Baptist church in the Hill District saw its membership grow from fifteen hundred to three thousand between 1915 and 1926.[43] Although it catered to native blacks and OPs, its size and reputation initially attracted many incoming migrants eager to reestablish familiar religious customs. However, historian Dennis Dickerson notes that sermons at elite black churches often focused on molding migrants into reliable employees and respectable members of the community.[44] Throughout the 1920s, area employers supported black churches in this effort, donating money, land, and sometimes buildings. "Once these ties were established," Dickerson wrote, "an intricate and deferential relationship evolved between black churches and big business in the Pittsburgh vicinity."[45]

As their numbers increased, many migrants gradually left established churches and created so-called storefront churches where they practiced the emotional style of worship that characterized their native congregations.[46] From the outset, OPs and reformers perceived the boisterous and expressive storefront churches as a threat to the image of black respectability. Throughout the late nineteenth and early twentieth centuries, African American reformers preached Victorian moral values including sexual monogamy, thrift, sobriety, industriousness, and genteel public behavior both to uplift the black masses and to undermine white arguments that blacks were incapable of assimilating into the larger society.[47] For devotees of respectability, storefront churches reinforced crude antiblack stereotypes and distracted migrants from the task of becoming good urban citizens. In a 1930 study of black life in the Hill District, NUL research director Ira Reid maintained that "the spurious growth of 'store front' churches and irresponsible religious organizations is of dubious value. Because those churches lack ability and discipline, because their leaders usually lack the educational equipment necessary to lead and because the churches tend to make inroads on the well directed and ably led church organizations, those institutions are undesirable."[48]

Outside the church, migrants found an exciting array of clubs to enjoy along Wylie Avenue and Centre Avenue in the Hill. Popular establishments like the Harlem Bar, Bailey Hotel, and Crawford Grill nurtured the careers of some of the nation's most talented jazz musicians, including Lena Horne, Billy Strayhorn, and Roy Eldridge.[49] To the frustration of reformers, migrants also gambled, played dice, and frequented pool halls, taverns, and brothels.[50] One Urban League official complained about "the 'sap-head' Negro to whom money means just so much more 'Jakey' and 'Craps.'"[51] Reformers' concerns about the city's nightlife had racial, class, and gender elements. In order to counter racist stereotypes of hypersexualized black men and women, it was necessary that black women present themselves as chaste and virtuous and that black men display industriousness, reliability, and sobriety. Their presence at nightclubs undermined this effort.[52] Reformers' objections to prostitution and gambling were also grounded in a desire to slow the spread of sexually transmitted diseases and intraracial violence in the black community—both of which increased sharply during the early interwar period.[53] As part of their larger program to "adjust" migrant behavior, reformers encouraged white employers to fund the creation of parks and recreational centers where they could channel migrants into healthier leisure pursuits, including organized sports.[54]

In the late nineteenth and early twentieth centuries, steel firms, YMCAs, and settlement houses organized segregated baseball leagues to foster company loyalty among industrial workers and anchor migrants to the larger community. After work and on the weekends, black industrial workers gathered in parks and sandlots and played baseball on teams managed by black welfare workers employed in the personnel departments of area mills. The industrial baseball leagues built up the institutional apparatus of black sports in Pittsburgh and paved the way for black entrepreneurs to gradually gain control of it. Gus Greenlee, the owner of the Crawford Grill, founded the

The Ugliest, Deadest Town 33

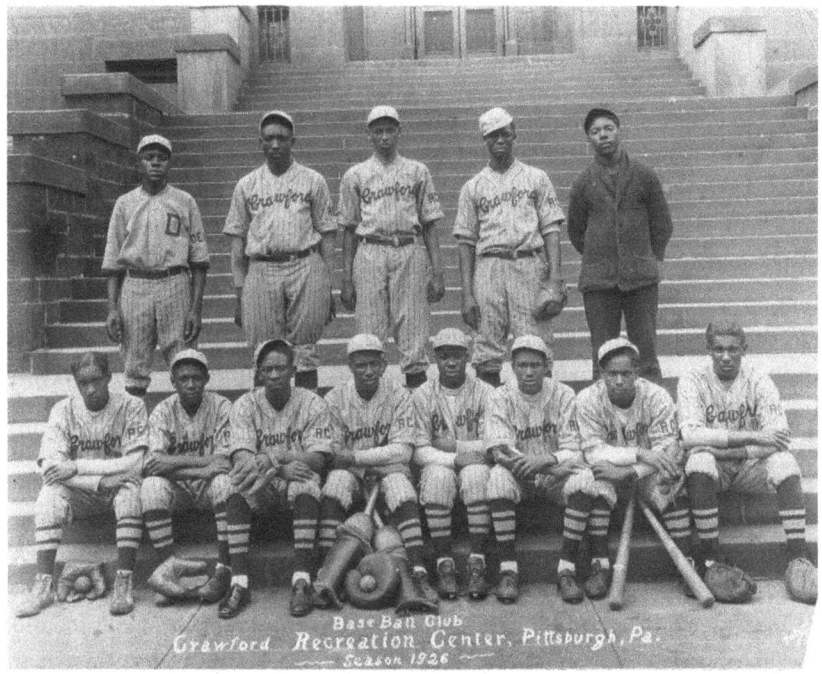

The Pittsburgh Crawfords, 1926.
Dorsey-Turfley Family Photographs, Detre Library and Archives,
Heinz History Center, Pittsburgh.

Pittsburgh Crawfords. Across the river, Cumberland Posey organized the Homestead Grays.[55]

As historian Rob Ruck notes, Pittsburgh became the center of black baseball during the interwar period. The Negro National League established its headquarters there, and the city's two teams, the Crawfords and Grays, won a combined twelve league championships and fielded some of the best players in the country, including Satchel Paige, Josh Gibson, Oscar Charleston, Smokey Joe Williams, and Buck Leonard.[56] Ruck demonstrates that black sporting life bridged regional and social divisions in the black community. Migrants and native blacks sat side by side in bleachers as they cheered on their favorite athletes. In the midst of the disruption of black communities caused by the Great Migration, Ruck writes that "Sport played a part in the re-formation by providing migrants and Pittsburgh-born blacks with teams and athletes that both groups could identify with."[57]

"Segregation Existed Right Here":
Racial Reaction in Pittsburgh

The growing black population alarmed white Pittsburghers. The Hill District went from 25 to 53 percent black between 1910 and 1930, and citywide African Americans went from 4.8 to 8.2 percent of the total population.[58] During the same period, the black population across sixteen major mill towns in western Pennsylvania increased from about twenty-nine thousand to seventy-four thousand.[59] The influx of African Americans in western Pennsylvania sparked a racial backlash by whites across the social spectrum that affected the entire black community. During the interwar period, Italians attacked black swimmers at the Highland Park pool; native whites developed a robust KKK presence across western Pennsylvania; middle- and upper-class whites insolated their neighborhoods and schools from black encroachment; white workers and employers adopted policies that limited upward mobility for black workers; and local police targeted young black men and women for juvenile detention and the city penitentiary.

Even when black Pittsburghers could afford to move out of the squalid neighborhoods of the inner city, local whites found ways of limiting their access to healthier environs. After the U.S. Supreme Court ruled municipal segregation unconstitutional in 1917, white homeowners began drafting restrictive covenants to prevent African Americans from moving into their neighborhoods. Often couched in terms of maintaining property values, restrictive covenants forbade the sale of homes to nonwhites. Moreover, during the New Deal years, federal policies meant to boost home ownership often deemed black communities uncreditworthy, and the Federal Housing Administration frequently insured mortgages containing clauses that restricted future sales to whites only. The combined force of poverty and racially restrictive policies facilitated the development of segregated communities in cities across the North.[60]

Segregated communities begat segregated schools. An 1881 law ended legal segregation in Pittsburgh's schools, but separate and unequal education nevertheless persisted. By the mid-1930s, the student population in the lower Hill's Watt Street School was about 2 percent white and 98 percent nonwhite. Rose Street School, McKelvey School, Moorehead School, and Herron Hill Junior High, among others, had similar disparities.[61] Black students attended poorly staffed schools in disrepair. One of the largest was in the dank and dimly lit basement of the AME Church on Wylie Avenue. In these unequal schools, black children, many undernourished, were often inattentive and on average took two years longer to complete the primary grades than their white counterparts.[62]

African American children and teens found few outlets for wholesome recreation after school. They traveled home through a community sorely lacking in basic government services; with the exception of the Centre Avenue YMCA, they had no playgrounds, parks, or pools available. The streets served as their playground, which made them easy targets for police who frequently patrolled the Hill. Juvenile delinquency rates for black Pittsburghers far outpaced those for native and foreign-born whites in the city.[63]

Black adults increasingly got swept into the criminal justice system as well, especially once the Great Migration commenced. Contemporary reports indicate police in the Hill had considerable discretionary power to arrest African Americans for virtually anything, including vague and highly subjective charges such as "suspicious behavior."[64] Blacks were also arrested for prostitution, gambling, drunkenness, and vagrancy. By 1926 NUL researcher Ira Reid found that black migrants represented over a third of the prisoners at Pittsburgh's Western Penitentiary. In his analysis of the social and economic backgrounds of these inmates, Reid called attention to how race-based restrictions on employment opportunities and educational resources contributed to high incarceration rates among African Americans.[65]

Like many black reformers, Reid's career touched multiple cities. He spent his childhood in the Steel City and later pursued a master's degree at the University of Pittsburgh. There, he and his classmate Abram Harris wrote master's theses highlighting the limited occupational mobility of black workers in the city.[66] Harris went on to teach at Howard University after graduating, and Reid became research director of the NUL in New York. In the 1930s, Reid and other NUL officials frequently traveled to Washington, DC, to lobby for the full inclusion of African Americans in New Deal work-relief projects.[67] Reid also returned to Pittsburgh several times, once in 1926 to conduct research for his study of prisoners and again in 1930 to undertake an assessment of the "social conditions of the Negro in the Hill." The latter study highlighted the damaging effects of racism on the black community, noting employers' refusal to hire black teachers and nurses in the city, the absence of convalescent homes for black women, violations of city housing ordinances by white landlords in the lower Hill, and discriminatory arrests of black men.[68]

Reid's research underscored the unjust treatment of African Americans by the law enforcement community, which in interwar western Pennsylvania included countless instances of racial profiling, at least two cases of police brutality, and two attempted mass deportations. In August 1923, a migrant in Johnstown, Pennsylvania, shot and killed several police officers, sparking reactionary elements in the white community. Members of the local Ku Klux Klan burned crosses throughout Johnstown, and the local mayor tried unsuccessfully to deport all African Americans and Mexicans from the town.[69] Ten years later, police in Industry, Pennsylvania, arrested over forty black migrants and forcibly shipped them to the West Virginia border, prompting a year-long legal battle with the Pittsburgh NAACP.[70]

The Johnstown and Industry incidents suggest the intensity of white racism in interwar western Pennsylvania. D. W. Griffith's *Birth of a Nation* helped inspire a revival of the KKK in the 1920s that spread outside the South to communities from California to Maine. In the midst of this resurgence, a substantial Klan presence emerged in western Pennsylvania. Klan chapters (called Klaverns) formed in Pittsburgh and its surrounding communities of Homestead, Connellsville, New Kensington, Altoona, Duquesne, Latrobe, Vandergrift, and elsewhere, and the number of members across western Pennsylvania ultimately reached about 125,000.[71]

Klaverns needed little cause to resort to violence. In 1926 the Pittscoal Company imported a host of southern blacks to work in its mines in Imperial, Pennsylvania (outside Pittsburgh). Fearing their newfound competition, white miners called on the support of local Klan members, who soon gathered outside the migrants' bunkhouse with the intention of driving them out of town. The migrants stood their ground, and a scuffle ensued that resulted in the injury of a white superintendent who came to the aid of the black workers.[72]

Many whites who were not part of the Klan still supported measures to keep African Americans away from them. In theaters across western Pennsylvania whites confined African Americans to balconies, and virtually no restaurants in downtown Pittsburgh served food to nonwhites.[73] "There were no *five and tens* that you could go into to get a lunch," the Reverend Harold Tolliver remembered. "And that sort of thing really impressed me, as I had come from Virginia. I found that sort of segregation existed right here in the North."[74] Even staff at the Pittsburgh Free Dispensary, a medical facility for the poor, segregated black patients.[75]

African Americans felt their second-class status in public transportation as well. The B & O Railroad frequently relegated black passengers to the rearmost luggage cars, and local taxi drivers often refused to stop for blacks until they had taken care of their white customers. In one instance a black woman with a sick child waited an hour before a taxi would take her to the hospital.[76]

"J&L was Jim Crowed": Migrants in the Steel Industry

Similarly, with few exceptions employers in the metals industry confined African Americans to the lowest-paying, least desirable positions available. The number of black employees in the industry grew rapidly during the early part of the interwar period. Across the Carnegie plants, the black workforce increased from about fifteen hundred to four thousand between 1916 and 1917. By 1923 African Americans comprised 20 percent of all industrial workers in the Pittsburgh area.[77] In 1918 Epstein found that 95 percent of black steelworkers were employed in unskilled positions.[78] This situation did not improve in the ensuing years. Studies in 1923 and 1929 showed almost no occupational mobility among Pittsburgh's black industrial workers.[79] The limited employment opportunities in Pittsburgh caught the attention of national black leaders. "Among the cities of the North," observed T. Arnold Hill of the NUL in 1928, Pittsburgh "has shown little progress in occupational opportunities, except in the iron and steel industries, and even here the tasks of Negro have not shown the promotion from unskilled occupations that might be expected."[80]

Over the first three decades of the twentieth century, native and foreign-born white workers also impeded black occupational advancement. Before the Great Migration, from about 1900 to 1915, African Americans in Pittsburgh competed for manufacturing jobs with eastern European immigrants from Slovakia, Lithuania, Serbia, and especially Poland. Native white foremen—usually of English, Scottish, Irish, or German ancestry—served as key intermediaries in this process. Often, they based their hiring decisions on prejudicial stereotypes of both groups, but in a perverse way this benefited eastern European applicants. As John Bodnar, Roger Simon, and Michael Weber explain, foremen preferred to hire Poles because they viewed them as a naturally docile and submissive people who could easily be controlled and would work under any conditions without complaint. "Give them rye bread, a herring, and beer, and they will be all right," one foreman remarked. By contrast, they often perceived African Americans, especially those from the South, as unreliable and unfit for the heavy demands of industrial labor.

This helps explain why black workers dispersed into occupations across the economic spectrum while Poles saturated the metals industry. By 1910, eastern Europeans no longer relied on native white foremen for jobs, as plant superintendents increasingly granted immigrants the authority to hire their kin and friends.[81]

When European immigration to the United States declined sharply during and after World War I, Pittsburgh's industrial firms began hiring considerable numbers of African Americans. But by then first- and second-generation immigrants had already gained numerical dominance over certain departments in local plants and had assumed control over some of the skilled and supervisory positions within them. At the Jones and Laughlin steel plant, for instance, Poles controlled the hammer shop while Serbs dominated the blooming mill. Eager to protect their gains, they militated against outside intrusion by black jobseekers. "After being allowed to implement kinship ties in gaining jobs," Bodnar et al. explain, "immigrants were unwilling to welcome later arrivals into their established enclaves."[82]

Harrison Gant facilitated one of the few exceptions to this pattern. During his childhood in Americus, Georgia, his father had taught him that "good manners and good behavior will take you further than money," and he carried this lesson with him to Pittsburgh. When he first started working in the boiler department at Jones and Laughlin, almost all the men there were Polish. But he gradually managed to earn the respect of his department foreman through his skill, reliability, and leadership qualities, and he eventually convinced him to begin replacing Polish workers with black workers. Within a few months almost everyone in the department was black.[83]

Still, white superintendents and foremen usually obstructed African Americans' advancement to better-paying positions. Several of the foremen Epstein interviewed claimed they did not promote African Americans for fear of reprisal from white workers, which did occur on occasion.[84] In the die casting department of the Westinghouse Electric and Manufacturing Company, white workers threatened to go on strike "if any Colored men were put regularly on the machines."[85] However, other officials Epstein spoke with pointed to the prejudice of the gang bosses themselves, "who oppose the Negro's doing better classes of work."[86] A superintendent at a Jones and Laughlin plant outside Pittsburgh refused to allow African Americans to work in his department.[87]

Arkansas migrant LeRoy McChester remembered encountering stiff occupational barriers in the North. He migrated to Gary, Indiana, in 1923 and spent the next ten years laboring at a steel plant there. When he moved to Pittsburgh in 1933, McChester discovered that "J & L was Jim Crowed," and he felt he ended up with a worse job than he had in Gary. "There wasn't no advancement," he complained. "You go in there rolling the wheel bar in the labor gang. You die with that same wheel bar in your hands."[88]

Over time white employers and workers came to see some positions as "black jobs" for which southern migrants were best suited. Typically these were the hottest and most physically demanding jobs in the mill, such as feeding blast furnaces and cleaning spilled metal from tapped open-hearth furnaces. During the winter months, when these tasks might have provided some respite from the cold, foremen often transferred African Americans to outdoor jobs and let white employees work near the furnaces.[89]

Black jobs were good enough for white workers when times got tough. Economic downturns in 1920–21 and 1924 affected all of Pittsburgh's industrial workers, but especially African Americans, whom employers often fired first and rehired last. According to one contemporary study, 17,224 blacks held industrial jobs in Pittsburgh in 1923, but during a recession the following year that number dropped to 7,636.[90] In 1924 the total number of black industrial workers in Pittsburgh declined by 19 percent, compared to only 0.4 percent for whites, and throughout the twenties African Americans averaged between two and four months of unemployment per year.[91]

Company officials laid off James Simmons three times during his tenure in the rolling mill of Lockhart Iron and Steel, often for arbitrary reasons. A Polish foreman he knew gave preferential treatment to workers that rented houses from him, while a superintendent hired and fired laborers based on how well they worked with Italians. As a result, Simmons kept a lookout for jobs to tide him over during layoffs. He found one of them at a spring mill in Coraopolis, Pennsylvania.[92]

Discriminatory hiring practices affected African Americans in the nonindustrial sector as well. Most employers refused to hire black women as typists, telephone operators, receptionists, and office secretaries, positions that became increasingly available to women in the 1920s. Consequently, during that decade almost 90 percent of employed black women in Pittsburgh worked as domestics for whites: cooking, cleaning, washing clothing, purchasing food, and caring for children.[93]

White employers also circumscribed the job options for native black Pittsburghers. Unlike migrants, local African Americans typically held service jobs as waiters, butlers, janitors, elevator operators, railroad clerks, and chauffeurs. The employment prospects for college-educated African Americans were even more limited. Black lawyers and dentists could only expect business from black, usually poor clients and patients; until 1922 no Pittsburgh hospital hired black nurses; and the Allegheny County School Board refused employment to black teachers until 1937.[94]

Varieties of Racial Resistance

In the midst of growing inequality, black Pittsburghers developed an array of tactics to promote their economic interests and safeguard their dignity. White reaction drew blacks together and mitigated their social and regional differences, but these differences nevertheless tended to affect how they dealt with the situation. In 1925 a small team of government researchers detected as much in their survey of African Americans across Pennsylvania.

> Pressure from the outside in the shape of segregation and discrimination has thrown all classes of Negroes closer together and made them feel that they have common interests and common grievances. . . . On the other hand, the large influx of Negroes from the South has brought with it the idea of a few Negro leaders dealing with the white population in matters of community welfare rather than common participation between the masses of the race.[95]

In Pittsburgh and cities across the North, African Americans adopted organizational positions from separatism and Marxism on the left to accommodation on the right. Integrationists in reform organizations like the Urban League and NAACP tended to fall somewhere in the middle.

During the 1920s, the black masses more readily identified with Marcus Garvey's Universal Negro Improvement Association (UNIA) than with either the NAACP or the Urban League. Garvey's appeals to race pride, his rejection of white society, and his promises to restore African greatness resonated with thousands of frustrated and marginalized black workers in urban centers. Garvey, a fiery and articulate immigrant from Jamaica, organized the UNIA in 1914 on a platform stressing pan-Africanism and black self-determination. Economic nationalism was central to Garvey's vision of racial advancement; he called on African Americans to establish and patronize black-owned businesses and form a separate, self-sustaining black economy.[96]

After the UNIA established its headquarters in Harlem in 1916, it soon gathered a large following in communities across the United States and Caribbean. At its peak in the early 1920s, the UNIA claimed it had four million members. Given its industrial prominence, western Pennsylvania became a major center of UNIA operations. Affiliates emerged in at least twenty towns across the region, including Aliquippa, Pittsburgh, Duquesne, Homestead, and Farrell. Garvey and his surrogates regularly delivered speeches in the Pittsburgh area, and in 1923 he denounced Johnstown officials for threatening to expel the migrant community.[97]

After hearing a Garvey speech in Pittsburgh, Georgia migrant Mathew Dempsey organized a UNIA branch in nearby Aliquippa, a steel town along the Ohio River that was home to fifteen hundred African Americans. Dempsey hoped the Aliquippa affiliate would help African American workers build the organizational strength needed to contest the discriminatory practices of the Jones and Laughlin steel firm and to protect the black community against company police and KKK members—who broadcast their presence in the town with burning crosses, parades, and antiblack speeches. Dempsey held regular meetings and drew about fifty members to the local affiliate. Steel firms closely monitored UNIA activity, which they deemed as subversive and dangerous, and they cooperated with the FBI in rooting out its organizers and driving it from the region. FBI agent R. B. Spencer and Jones and Laughlin police superintendent Harry Mauk were instrumental in identifying Dempsey as the principal organizer, and he and the other fifty members of the organization were ultimately fired. The Aliquippa UNIA disbanded shortly afterward.[98]

While the UNIA enjoyed support from the black masses, many college-educated African American leaders across the political spectrum opposed it. Garvey's calls for black separatism conflicted with the NAACP's efforts to promote integration. NAACP official Robert Bagnall unflatteringly characterized Garvey as a "fat and sleek" man with "small bright pig-like eyes and rather bull-dog-like face." He warned that the UNIA leader was "as adroit as a fencer in changing front, as adept as a cuttle-fish in beclouding an issue he cannot meet, [and] prolix to the *n*th degree in devising new schemes to gain the money of poor ignorant Negroes."[99] If unnecessarily mean, Bagnall's critique of Garvey nevertheless reflected the NAACP's concern that the Jamaican immigrant's promises of creating a black panacea in Africa distracted poor and working-class African Americans from the more realistic goal of integration. Ernest Rice McKinney, one of Pittsburgh's leading black leftists, shared Bagnall's misgivings and further argued that Garvey-style separation would prolong the economic marginalization of black communities.[100]

McKinney's involvement in social work and left-wing political activism underscores the intersections between the two and highlights the complexity of black activists in interwar northern communities. McKinney grew up in southern West Virginia in the late nineteenth century. His maternal grandfather, Lewis Rice, was a former slave who worked as a preacher and coal miner. McKinney remembered seeing Rice return from the mines one day on a stretcher, having sustained injuries while trying to organize black coal miners. McKinney's father worked in the mines for a time as well, but later he and McKinney's mother found work as teachers. They evidently inspired in him a love of reading, which in college fused with an organizational impulse that his grandfather had instilled. While attending Oberlin in the early 1910s McKinney worked with W. E. B. Du Bois to form a local NAACP chapter, and he joined the Socialist Party around the same time. His simultaneous involvement in these organizations demonstrated a commitment to racial integration and class solidarity that characterized much of his later work.[101]

McKinney moved to Pittsburgh shortly after graduating from college, and before and after World War I he served as a social worker for the Centre Avenue YMCA in the Hill as well as the Kingsley Settlement House in East Liberty. Over time, he increasingly blended political activism with social work. He helped establish the Pittsburgh NAACP, served as a contributing editor for A. Phillip Randolph's *Messenger*, wrote columns for the *Pittsburgh Courier*, and, in 1920, joined the Communist Party. McKinney's time in the party was relatively short. Frustrated with its political infighting and increasingly authoritarian leadership, he left it in 1926 to pursue other left-wing causes. On the eve of the depression he and A. J. Muste formed the Conference for Progressive Labor Action. Through this organization and its journal, *Labor Age*, McKinney promoted black involvement in industrial labor unions.[102] Later, during the mid-thirties, McKinney, Ben Careathers, William Scarville, and other black labor organizers played key roles in persuading black steel workers to join CIO unions in mill communities like Aliquippa, Pittsburgh, Homestead, and Clairton.[103]

Despite his increasing involvement in left-wing networks, throughout the interwar period McKinney supported the social work efforts of the local Urban League. He encouraged native black Pittsburghers to donate to the ULP in 1919, reminding them that it "worked for the interests of us all," and in the thirties he served with ULP members on committees formed to pressure the Allegheny County School Board to hire black teachers.[104] For their part, Urban Leaguers such as John T. Clark and William Hill found common ground with left-wing activists on the issue of black union involvement. Clark twice invited William Z. Foster, the radical labor organizer and two-time presidential nominee of the Communist Party, to speak to black workers in Pittsburgh on the benefits of labor unions.[105] In the late thirties, Hill worked with black communist Ben Careathers to form a chapter of the National Negro Congress in Pittsburgh and organize a massive labor rally that featured speakers from Vann to CIO labor leader Phillip Murray.[106]

These connections notwithstanding, in the 1920s leftists and social workers generally held different views on how to address racial inequality. Black radicals argued that racial inequality stemmed from the larger class struggle between workers and capitalists. Once workers recognized their common class interests and united in overthrowing the capitalist hierarchy, racial justice would follow. By contrast, reformers in the NUL, which formed in 1910, used social work methods to address problems related to black urbanization.[107] Operating from their headquarters in New York, NUL workers adapted for black migrants the sociological theories of immigrant assimilation developed at the University of Chicago.[108]

Led by scholars such as W. I. Thomas and Robert E. Park, the famed Chicago School offered models for understanding the poverty, disease, and moral degeneration of immigrant communities in American cities in terms of social and cultural forces rather than biological factors. The lives of rural peasants, their social institutions, folkways, and cultural mores, became fundamentally disorganized upon settling in American cities. The task of the reformer, then, was to help migrants adjust to their new urban environments. Social reorganization theory postulated that successive generations of immigrants gradually would build new social institutions to replace the old ones, move out of inner cities, gain better jobs, and assimilate into American society. The Chicago School challenged the idea, advanced by social Darwinists, that the "Slavic races" were innately inferior. Instead, it offered an optimistic program of gradual immigrant assimilation through enlightened guidance and adjustment work.[109]

The NUL built on the Chicago School model in leading a movement to reorganize black migrant life in urban communities. Its members developed vocational training programs, advocated for better housing and recreational outlets, and sponsored initiatives to improve health in black neighborhoods. Urban League researchers also conducted fact-gathering studies of migrants' living and working conditions, both to guide the league's reform agenda and to raise public awareness of racial inequality. In the midst of the Great Migration, Urban League affiliates formed in cities across the country, including Pittsburgh.[110]

In the Steel City, black and white leaders established the Pittsburgh chapter in 1918 to facilitate migrant adjustment. The ULP's charter members included prominent black leaders such as Vann and the Reverend G. B. Howard, pastor of the Central Baptist Church and former classmate of Booker T. Washington, as well as white philanthropists like Walter May, owner of the May Drug Company. White progressives helped establish the league as well, and foremost among them was Dr. Francis Tyson, an energetic young economics professor at the University of Pittsburgh. Tyson directed Epstein's thesis on black migrants and later participated in committees addressing racial discrimination in the city.[111]

In 1918 Tyson asked Eugene Kinckle Jones of the NUL to recommend a capable leader for the Pittsburgh affiliate. Jones dispatched thirty-four-year-old John T. Clark, who had served as the NUL's field secretary. Before drafting the ULP's reform agenda, which directed its actions for the next decade and a half, Clark read Epstein's study of the migrant community and surveyed the situation for himself.[112] The plan of action he ultimately laid out addressed what both he and Epstein saw as the most serious challenges confronting black Pittsburgh. "We are faced with the after effects of social problems arising out of living congestion, bad housing, irregular employment, delinquency, lowered health standards and the lack of sufficient accommodation in social institutions," Clark later explained. "Hence we now emphasize in our program, the kind of work which demands the greatest attention."[113] Guided by this utilitarian reform ethos, ULP staff strove to secure decent employment for black workers and improve housing, recreation, and health care in the black community. As they saw it, access to good jobs, quality affordable housing, and proper health care were *rights* that belonged to all citizens.[114]

During the latter part of the interwar period, the Pittsburgh NAACP (PNAACP) added a legal advocacy arm to the black reform effort that ably contested police brutality, segregation in public spaces, unlawful deportations, and discriminatory hiring practices. Through much of the early 1920s, however, the association struggled to gain a foothold in Pittsburgh. The situation did not improve until later in the decade when Reverend Augustus Jones helped reorganize the PNAACP and placed Homer Brown and Daisy Lampkin in leadership positions. Brown was a talented young lawyer and Lampkin an exceptional fundraiser and organizer. Together, they put the PNAACP on sound financial footing. By 1925 it had raised funds for the national branch's legal battles while managing several of its own projects in Pittsburgh. In the early thirties it became one of the NAACP's most active chapters, but for much of the twenties it contributed little to the ULP's campaigns to improve living conditions in black Pittsburgh.[115]

The *Pittsburgh Courier* joined the ULP in its campaign for better housing. The paper criticized white landlords in the lower Hill who charged high rents for dilapidated housing units, and it called for improvements to public sanitation in the black community. "The lack of proper housing conditions in Pittsburgh makes it unbearable for the Negro wage earner to live here," Vann wrote in 1926. "He is now being attacked by disease of nearly epidemic prevalence as a result of the neglected housing conditions."[116]

During the interwar period the *Courier* served multiple functions for the black community in Pittsburgh as well as for African Americans across the nation. As a Jim Crow watchdog, the paper aided the NAACP in its efforts to identify and resist racial injustice. It bolstered black pride through its positive coverage of the achievements of people of African descent, both historical and contemporary. And through its editors the *Courier* launched major campaigns to change the course of history: it crusaded for better housing in the twenties, called upon black voters to switch to the Democratic Party in the early thirties, and rhetorically linked fascism abroad with white supremacy at home during World War II.

Vann, who helped establish the *Courier* in 1910 and later built it into the nation's largest black weekly newspaper, was in several respects an archetypical black reformer. He was a college-educated migrant from the upper South who supported multiple reform organizations, including the ULP and PNA-ACP, corresponded with black leaders across the country, operated in several cities, and advanced an incremental program of racial activism aimed at a broadly conceived notion of citizenship. Vann was pragmatic and flexible, and during his career he changed political positions several times to promote both his own interests as well as the interests of his race.

Migrants and reformers benefited from and built on the institutional apparatus in the black community, both to fortify themselves against local white reaction and to adapt to changes in industrial capitalism and American political culture. Despite their differences, they came to Pittsburgh in pursuit of opportunity: opportunity for a political voice, a quality education, and a good job. Both groups encountered difficulties in this journey. Harrison Gant and

John T. Clark had to overcome their outsider status to gain acceptance among local blacks, and from white Pittsburghers they encountered racial antipathy that circumscribed their social and material lives. Yet they did not passively accept their lot. Migrants walked off the job to protest poor wages and working conditions, and they registered complaints with the ULP when white foremen discriminated against them.[117] Reformers in the ULP developed and advanced a reform agenda premised on an expansive vision of citizenship that included access to decent employment, housing, and health care—which is the subject of the next chapter.

NOTES

1. Harrison Gant, interview with Peter Gottlieb, August 23, 1974, Pittsburgh Oral History Project, Heinz History Center. For information about Clark, see Priscilla A. Dowden-White, *Groping toward Democracy: African American Social Welfare Reform in St. Louis, 1910–1949* (Columbia: University of Missouri Press, 2011), 118–19, 174–75, and Arthur J. Edmunds, *Daybreakers: The Story of the Urban League of Pittsburgh, the First Sixty-Five Years* (Pittsburgh: Urban League of Pittsburgh, 1999), 13–14.
2. Touré F. Reed, *Not Alms but Opportunity: The Urban League and the Politics of Racial Uplift, 1910–1950* (Chapel Hill: University of North Carolina Press, 2008), 29–30.
3. Dowden-White, *Groping toward Democracy*, 118–19, 174–75; Edmunds, *Daybreakers*, 13–14.
4. Laurence Glasco, "Double Burden: The Black Experience in Pittsburgh," in *City at the Point: Essays on the Social History of Pittsburgh*, ed. Samuel P. Hays (Pittsburgh: University of Pittsburgh Press, 1989), 73–75. For a discussion of similar class divisions in Philadelphia's black community, see Charles Pete T. Banner-Haley, "The *Philadelphia Tribune* and the Persistence of Black Republicanism during the Great Depression," *Pennsylvania History: A Journal of Mid-Atlantic Studies* 65, no. 2 (1998), 190–202.
5. Rob Ruck, *Sandlot Seasons: Sport in Black Pittsburgh* (Urbana: University of Illinois Press, 1993), 11.
6. Edmunds, *Daybreakers*, 13–14; Dowden-White, *Groping toward Democracy*, 118–19, 174–75.
7. Edna McKenzie, "Pittsburgh's Daisy Lampkin: A Life of Love and Service," *Pennsylvania Heritage* 9, no. 3 (1983): 9–12.
8. See Andrew Buni, *Robert L. Vann of the* Pittsburgh Courier*: Politics and Black Journalism* (Pittsburgh: University of Pittsburgh Press, 1974), 3–63.
9. For more on Lowndes, see Edmunds, *Daybreakers*, 38. For biographical information on R. Maurice Moss, see "Up through the Ranks to Urban League Exec," *New York Age*, February 11, 1956, R. Maurice Moss Papers, 1924–1931, box 5, folder 227, Urban League Records, University of Pittsburgh Archives Service Center. For additional information on where reformers lived, see Cora Jones, meeting announcement, February 28, 1930, box 2, folder 43, Urban League Records.
10. Ruck, *Sandlot Seasons*, 11–12.

11. Harold Tolliver, interview with Dennis Dickerson, October 9, 1974, Pittsburgh Oral History Project.
12. ULP survey, "The Migrant and the Church," box 5, folder 207, Urban League Records. Black preachers did not have to worry about overcrowding for very long. Preferring a more emotional and expressive brand of worship, migrants gradually began establishing their own churches, administered by southern-born preachers. For more on migrant religion in Pittsburgh, see Buni, *Robert L. Vann of the* Pittsburgh Courier, 56, Gottlieb, *Making Their Own Way*, 197, 202, Glasco, "Double Burden," 81, and Dennis Dickerson, "The Black Church in Industrializing Western Pennsylvania, 1870–1950," *Western Pennsylvania Historical Magazine* 64, no. 4 (1981): 329–44.
13. For instance, Vann criticized local black clergy members for their inattention to the ongoing struggles for decent hospitals, schools, and housing. "It is of far more benefit to Aframericans to have a physician instruct groups of prospective mothers in the proper care of themselves and their offspring than to hear a vapid discourse on the spirituals," he concluded in an editorial, "and every new sewer is worth a hundred sermons" (*Pittsburgh Courier*, August 21, 1926, 16; Buni, *Robert L. Vann of the* Pittsburgh Courier, 56). Some black preachers emerged as dedicated advocates for poor blacks. Harold Tolliver recalled that Reverend J. C. Austin of Ebenezer Baptist Church and other ministers established a league "to find housing for as many of the people as they could who were coming from the South, and who were being victimized with high rents in depressed areas that whites were vacating" (interview with Dennis Dickerson, October 9, 1974, Pittsburgh Oral History Project). Austin also supported local Universal Negro Improvement Association chapters, which briefly enjoyed widespread appeal among working-class blacks, and he invited members from the national organization to speak at his church. For more on the Garvey movement in Pittsburgh, see Joe W. Trotter, *River Jordan: African American Urban Life in the Ohio Valley* (Lexington: University of Kentucky Press, 1998), 120–21.
14. Ernest Rice McKinney, "Nature's Play," *Pittsburgh Courier* newspaper clipping, ca. May 1919, box 7, folder 291, Urban League Records,.
15. August Meier and Elliot Rudwick, *From Plantation to Ghetto* (New York: Hill and Wang, 1966), 194–271; Dennis C. Dickerson, *Out of the Crucible: Black Steelworkers in Western Pennsylvania, 1875–1980* (Albany: State University of New York Press, 1986), 30–32; Trotter, *River Jordan*, 95–97.
16. In 1922 John T. Clark, executive secretary of the Urban League of Pittsburgh, wrote an article about living and working conditions in Pittsburgh that was published in black newspapers throughout the South. In response to the article, thousands of prospective migrants wrote Clark asking for more detailed information about the city, including what the weather was like, where they might find affordable lodging, and the typical wages and working conditions of the mills. These letters highlight the agency of black southerners in strategically choosing the location and timing of their migration (John T. Clark Papers, reel 5, Carter G. Woodson Collection, Library of Congress).
17. James Simmons, interview with Peter Gottlieb, June 13, 1974, Pittsburgh Oral History Project.
18. Ben Irving, interview with Peter Gottlieb, July 31, 1974, Pittsburgh Oral History Project.

19. Bartow Tipper, interview with Dennis Dickerson, March 4, 1980, Pittsburgh Oral History Project.
20. Dickerson, *Out of the Crucible*, 31; Trotter, *River Jordan*, 95–96.
21. Ruck, *Sandlot Seasons*, 10.
22. Peter Gottlieb, *Making Their Own Way: Southern Blacks' Migration to Pittsburgh, 1916–30* (Urbana: University of Illinois Press, 1987), 65. By 1930, two-thirds of all black Pittsburghers were migrants. See Ruck, *Sandlot Seasons*, 10.
23. Abraham Epstein, "The Negro Migrant in Pittsburgh" (senior thesis, University of Pittsburgh, 1917), 24–27. William Hill, who worked for the ULP in the late 1930s, also discussed southern whites' efforts to prevent African Americans from traveling to northern communities. See "The Negro Wage Worker," in *The WPA History of the Negro in Pittsburgh*, ed. Laurence Glasco (Pittsburgh: University of Pittsburgh Press, 2004), 223–24.
24. Gottlieb, *Making Their Own Way*, 42.
25. Harrison Gant, interview with Peter Gottlieb, August 23, 1974, Pittsburgh Oral History Project.
26. Bruce M. Stave, "Pittsburgh and the New Deal," in *The New Deal*, vol. 2, *The State and Local Levels*, ed. John Braeman, Robert H. Bremner, and David Brody (Columbus: Ohio State University Press, 1975), 390.
27. Gottlieb, *Making Their Own Way*, 66.
28. Glasco, "Double Burden," 69–70.
29. Buni, *Robert L. Vann of the* Pittsburgh Courier, 23–24.
30. Harold Tolliver, interview with Dennis Dickerson, October 9, 1974, Pittsburgh Oral History Project.
31. Laurence Glasco notes that the Hill went from 25 to 53 percent black between 1910 and 1930. Despite a rising population, by 1930 black homeownership in the lower Hill remained miniscule, at only 1 percent. Poles and Italians in neighboring communities had much higher rates of homeownership. About 24 percent of the residents in Polish Hill owned their homes, and in Bloomfield, an Italian enclave, homeownership stood at 47 percent ("Double Burden," 79–80).
32. See Cora Jones, meeting announcement, February 28, 1930, box 2, folder 43, Urban League Records.
33. Buni, *Robert L. Vann of the* Pittsburgh Courier, 63.
34. Gottlieb, *Making Their Own Way*, 69.
35. Harrison Gant, interview with Peter Gottlieb, August 23, 1974, Pittsburgh Oral History Project.
36. Bartow Tipper, interview with Dennis Dickerson, March 4, 1980, Pittsburgh Oral History Project.
37. Gottlieb, *Making Their Own Way*, 69. Glasco notes that 99 percent of African Americans in the lower Hill rented their homes ("Double Burden," 79–80).
38. Epstein, "The Negro Migrant in Pittsburgh," 16–17.
39. Negro Survey of Pennsylvania, 1925, 36, 42, Department of Welfare, Commonwealth of Pennsylvania, box 7, folder 303, Urban League Records; Gottlieb, *Making Their Own Way*, 69.
40. Wiley A. Hall, "Negro Housing and Rents in the Hill District of Pittsburgh" (MA the-

sis, University of Pittsburgh, 1929), 19; Gottlieb, *Making Their Own Way*, 69. Also see Hill, "The Negro Wage Worker," 225.
41. Quoted in John Bodnar, Richard Simon, and Michael P. Weber, *Lives of Their Own: Blacks, Italians, and Poles in Pittsburgh, 1900–1960* (Urbana: University of Illinois Press, 1982), 197.
42. Epstein, "The Negro Migrant in Pittsburgh," 54–60; ULP health education brochure, 1919, box 6, folder 242, Urban League Records; Dickerson, *Out of the Crucible*, 58–59.
43. Dennis Dickerson, "The Black Church in Industrializing Western Pennsylvania, 1870–1950," *Western Pennsylvania Historical Magazine* 64, no. 4 (1981): 329–44.
44. Dickerson, "The Black Church in Industrializing Western Pennsylvania."
45. Dickerson, "The Black Church in Industrializing Western Pennsylvania," 388. Attendees at a 1923 convention of black Baptists in Pittsburgh agreed that migrants' "presence in our midst" created problems for northern blacks, and they called for welfare programs designed to "make them efficient and contented workmen and good, law-abiding citizens." See J. S. Morton, resolutions of the Baptist State Convention, October 23–27, 1923, box 5, folder 207, Urban League Records. During the same month, October 1923, several other prominent black clergymen in Pittsburgh convened an interracial meeting of reformers, professionals, and church officials to discuss ways to assist the migrant community and help the race achieve "economic efficiency." See Reverend W. Augustus Jones to Francis Tyson, October 30, 1924, box 5, folder 207, Urban League Records.
46. Gottlieb, *Making Their Own Way*, 198.
47. For a penetrating analysis of the "politics of respectability," see Evelyn Brooks Higginbotham, *Righteous Discontent: The Women's Movement in the Black Baptist Church, 1880–1920* (Cambridge, MA: Harvard University Press, 1993).
48. Ira Reid, *Social Conditions of the Negro in the Hill District of Pittsburgh* (Pittsburgh: General Committee on the Hill Survey), 17. White intellectuals sometimes expressed similar sentiments. H. L. Mencken, prominent editor of the *American Mercury*, described storefront churches as "extraordinarily stupid, ignorant, barbaric and preposterous," and he accused southern black pastors of expressing "ideas only fit for the jungle" ("The Burden of Credulity," *Opportunity*, February 1931). For Adam Clayton Powell's rebuttal of Mencken, which calls attention to white fundamentalists that lynched African Americans, see *Opportunity*, March 1931.
49. Glasco, "Double Burden," 75–76.
50. For a ULP account of prostitution and sexually transmitted diseases among migrant workers in Woodlawn (later renamed Aliquippa), a steel town outside Pittsburgh, see Bureau of Advice and Information, April 1920, box 2, folder 82, Urban League Records.
51. Gottlieb, *Making Their Own Way*, 194.
52. Black social welfare worker and left-wing political activist Ernest Rice McKinney articulated this perspective in a speech in 1931. "Every negro man is considered a potential rapist," he argued, "and the Negro woman as legitimate game. Any contact that might occur between the Negro man and the white woman is frowned upon as exposing the woman to great danger. Naturally enough, the object of such suspicion is ostracized or set apart." For this reason, he warned his audience to avoid reinforcing racial stereotypes in public. "Every accidental occurrence which comes to their attention to sustain the concepts they may entertain, only strengthens their belief that the concept

is a true one. In other words, the sight of a Negro dancing the Charleston on the street confirms their belief that they do dance; a Negro eating watermelon in public is a 'typical Negro', and so on" ("Psychology of Race," January 14, 1931, box 3, folder 124, Urban League Records).

53. For an illuminating study of the deleterious health conditions in black Pittsburgh, see Carolyn Leonard Carson, "And the Results Showed Promise . . . : Physicians, Childbirth, and Southern Black Migrant Women, 1916-1930," in *African Americans in Pennsylvania, Shifting Historical Perspectives,* ed. Joe W. Trotter and Eric Ledell Smith (University Park: Pennsylvania Historical and Museum Commission and Pennsylvania State University Press, 1997), 330-62. Andrew Buni notes that petty crimes in black Pittsburgh increased by 200 percent between 1915 and 1917 (*Robert L. Vann of the Pittsburgh Courier,* 73-74).
54. Gottlieb, *Making Their Own Way,* 130.
55. Ruck, *Sandlot Seasons,* 3-7.
56. Ruck, *Sandlot Seasons,* x-xii, 3-7.
57. Ruck, *Sandlot Seasons,* 6.
58. Glasco, "Double Burden," 80; Dickerson, *Out of the Crucible,* 39.
59. Dickerson, *Out of the Crucible,* 38-39.
60. Thomas Sugrue, *Sweet Land of Liberty: The Forgotten Struggle for Civil Rights in the North* (New York: Random House, 2008), 6, 52-53. Also see Meier and Rudwick, *From Plantation to Ghetto,* 236.
61. "State Will Probe Negro Teacher Ban," *Pittsburgh Press,* April 8, 1937; report of the legislative committee appointed pursuant to Resolution No. 27 of the House of Representatives of the General Assembly of the Commonwealth of Pennsylvania, session 1937-39, box 8, vol. 5, Homer Brown Collection, University of Pittsburgh Archives Service Center.
62. Buni, *Robert L. Vann of the* Pittsburgh Courier, 28.
63. Buni, *Robert L. Vann of the* Pittsburgh Courier, 29.
64. For information on arrests of African Americans in Pittsburgh between 1914 and 1917, see "The Negro Migrant in Pittsburgh," 48. Also see Buni, *Robert L. Vann of the* Pittsburgh Courier, 74.
65. About 97 percent of the black inmates were southern migrants. See Ira Reid, "A Study of 200 Negro Prisoners in the Western Penitentiary of Pennsylvania," 1927, box 10, folder 456, Urban League Records.
66. Glasco, "Double Burden," 76-77.
67. Harvard Sitkoff, *A New Deal for Blacks: The Emergence of Civil Rights as a National Issue,* thirtieth anniv. ed. (New York: Oxford University Press, 2009), 186.
68. See Reid, *Social Conditions of the Negro in the Hill District of Pittsburgh,* 11-16. For the faction's views, as well as Reid's rebuttals, see 9, 11, and 16.
69. "Johnstown's Mayor's Deportation Order Defeated," *Crisis,* November 1923. For the estimate of Johnstown's black population, see Richard B. Sherman, "Johnstown v. the Negro: Southern Migrants and the Exodus of 1923," *Pennsylvania History: A Journal of Mid-Atlantic Studies* 30, no. 4 (1963): 456.
70. For detailed discussions of the incident in Johnstown and the Industry deportation, see chapter 3.
71. Dickerson, *Out of the Crucible,* 64. For an engaging analysis of the emergence of the

Klan in western Pennsylvania, see John M. Craig, *The Ku Klux Klan in Western Pennsylvania, 1921–1928* (Bethlehem, PA: Lehigh University Press, 2014).

72. For more information on this incident, see Kathryn Gough to NAACP headquarters, April 16, 1926, NAACP Branch Records, pt. 1: G-190, Library of Congress.
73. For a time, a café in the basement of Rosenbaum's Department store appears to have been the only place downtown where African Americans could order food. See Dickerson, *Out of the Crucible*, 62. For an account of discrimination at Pittsburgh's Plaza Theatre, see A. B. Reynolds to William Pickens (NAACP field secretary), December 31, 1924, NAACP Branch Records.
74. Harold Tolliver, interview with Dennis Dickerson, October 9, 1974, Pittsburgh Oral History Project.
75. John T. Clark to James Stevenson (president of the Pittsburgh Free Dispensary), July 6, 1925, box 6, folder 279, Urban League Records.
76. John T. Clark to unknown recipient, August 29, 1923, box 6, folder 279, Urban League Records. In the same box and folder see report of informant, April 8, 1924.
77. Gottlieb, *Making Their Own Way*, 92.
78. Epstein, "The Negro Migrant in Pittsburgh," 21.
79. Glasco, "Double Burden," 76–77; ULP report, "Special Problems of Negro Workers in Pittsburgh," April 6, 1929, box 5, folder 245, Urban League Records.
80. T. Arnold Hill, transcript of WJAS radio broadcast, December 5, 1928, box 3, folder 126, Urban League Records.
81. John Bodnar, Michael Weber, and Roger Simon, "Migration, Kinship, and Urban Adjustment: Blacks and Poles in Pittsburgh, 1900–1930," *Journal of American History* 66, no. 3 (1979), 548–65. The quote from the foreman can be found on page 554.
82. Bodnar, Weber, and Simon, "Migration, Kinship, and Urban Adjustment," 565.
83. Harrison Gant, interview with Peter Gottlieb, August 23, 1974, Pittsburgh Oral History Project.
84. Epstein, "The Negro Migrant in Pittsburgh," 32.
85. Gottlieb, *Making Their Own Way*, 138.
86. Epstein, "The Negro Migrant in Pittsburgh," 32.
87. Dickerson, *Out of the Crucible*, 52.
88. LeRoy McChester, interview with Peter Gottlieb, July 9, 1974, Pittsburgh Oral History Project. Merril Lynch also remembered being confined to unskilled positions. During his working years in Pittsburgh, Lynch never held a skilled job. See Lynch, interview with Dennis Dickerson, August 22, 1974, Pittsburgh Oral History Project.
89. Gottlieb, *Making Their Own Way*, 99; Trotter, *River Jordan*, 100; Dickerson, *Out of the Crucible*, 51–52. Also see the account of ULP officer William Hill in "The Negro Wage Worker," 219–20, 229.
90. Glasco, "Double Burden," 76–77. The personnel records of the A. M. Byers mill in Ambridge, Pennsylvania, corroborate these findings. A sample of its employee files from 1919 to 1929 reveals that the layoff rate for black workers was almost 10 percent higher than for whites. I drew this information from a random sample that included seventy black and sixty white workers employed at the company between 1919 and 1929. Analysis shows that 41 percent of the black workers were eventually laid off at some point, compared to 33 percent of the white workers. My sample size is too small to draw general conclusions; I use it here to support the findings of larger studies. In 1987 Peter Got-

tlieb conducted a thorough analysis of the Byers records. In later portions of this book I rely on his findings, which he drew from a sample of 669 black employees. The A. M. Byers Company Personnel Records are housed at the University of Pittsburgh Archives Service Center.

91. Gottlieb, *Making Their Own Way*, 103; Trotter, *River Jordan*, 100.
92. James Simmons, interview with Peter Gottlieb, June 13, 1974, Pittsburgh Oral History Project.
93. Gottlieb, *Making Their Own Way*, 104, 108.
94. Glasco, "Double Burden," 83–84; Edmunds, *Daybreakers*, 59–63. Pittsburgh is located in Allegheny County.
95. Negro Survey of Pennsylvania, 1925, 78, Department of Welfare, Commonwealth of Pennsylvania, box 7, folder 303, Urban League Records. Urban Leaguer R. Maurice Moss added to this perspective in a 1931 lecture in which he complained about lower- and working-class black Pittsburghers' unwillingness to follow the lead of black elites. Although the league facilitated some programs to generate grassroots mobilization, in general its leaders took a hierarchical, top-down approach to race reform. "The Negro has advanced in ability to do anything the white man can do," he argued, "except to organize and be subordinate to a Negro superior. The feeling is too prevalent that a Negro cannot or should not have authority" ("Fanning the Flames," January 21, 1931, box 3, folder 124, Urban League Records).
96. Sugrue, *Sweet Land of Liberty*, 14–16.
97. Dickerson, *Out of the Crucible*, 79–81.
98. Dickerson, *Out of the Crucible*, 79–81.
99. Robert W. Bagnall, "The Madness of Marcus Garvey," *Messenger*, March 1923, 638–48. Also see W. E. B. Du Bois, "The Black Star Line," *Crisis*, September 1922, 210–14.
100. Pamela Twiss, "Ernest Rice McKinney: African American Appalachian, Social Worker, Radical Labor Organizer and Educator," *Journal of Appalachian Studies* 10, nos. 1–2(2004): 95–110.
101. Twiss, "Ernest Rice McKinney," 98.
102. Twiss, "Ernest Rice McKinney," 98–100.
103. Joe W. Trotter and Jared N. Day, *Race and Renaissance: African Americans in Pittsburgh since World War II* (Pittsburgh: University of Pittsburgh Press, 2010), 29–30.
104. Ernest Rice McKinney, "Nature's Play," *Pittsburgh Courier* newspaper clipping, ca. May 1919, box 7, folder 291, Urban League Records. For information on the special education committee, see steering committee minutes, March 14, 1932, box 2, folder 64, Urban League Records. In 1930, McKinney also served on the ULP's contact committee, a precursor to the special education committee (minutes, March 14, 1930, box 2, folder 43, Urban League Records).
105. The first time was in 1919 and the second was in 1926. See "Urban League Happenings," *Pittsburgh Courier*, April 1, 1919, and Edmunds, *Daybreakers*, 66.
106. "Phil Murray Urges Negro Workers to Join Great Steel Industry Union," *Pittsburgh Courier*, February 13, 1937.
107. The organization was originally called the National League on Urban Conditions Among Negroes, but it soon became the National Urban League.
108. For a penetrating analysis of how the Chicago School influenced the Urban League, see Reed, *Not Alms but Opportunity*.

109. Reed, *Not Alms but Opportunity*, 21–26.
110. Sugrue, *Sweet Land of Liberty*, 10.
111. ULP, promotional brochure and plan of work, March 1918, box 5, folder 235, Urban League Records; Edmunds, *Daybreakers*, 13–14, 29.
112. ULP, promotional brochure and plan of work, March 1918, box 5, folder 235, Urban League Records; Edmunds, *Daybreakers*, 13–14, 29.
113. ULP, 1924 annual report, 2, box 6, folder 246, Urban League Records.
114. Clark served as executive secretary of the ULP from 1918 to 1926. Shortly after his departure, ULP staff member Christina Jeffries became interim head until the board hired Alonzo Thayer to replace Clark. Thayer stayed only two years before he moved to Chicago. R. Maurice Moss succeeded him and stayed on for the remainder of the interwar period. See Edmunds, *Daybreakers*, 68–70.
115. William Pickens to Augustus Jones, December 8, 1924, and NAACP press release, "Pittsburgh Pastor Helps Reorganize Local NAACP," December 12, 1924, NAACP Branch Records; see also Walter White to Mrs. W. T. Poole, October 28, 1925, NAACP Branch Records.
116. Quoted in Buni, *Robert L. Vann of the* Pittsburgh Courier, 61; also see "Housing and Sanitation," *Pittsburgh Courier*, July 24, 1926.
117. The records of the A. M. Byers mill, for instance, reveal an extraordinarily high turnover rate. Occasionally, black workers also protested collectively. When the white workers at Westinghouse issued their petition stating that their whole department would strike if any black men were assigned to work with them, the department foreman, who wanted to avoid trouble, reassigned the black workers to another department. However, they refused to go and instead went to the ULP office to register a complaint. See Gottlieb, *Making Their Own Way*, 126–27, 135–38, and A. M. Byers Company Personnel Records, University of Pittsburgh Archives Service Center.

CHAPTER TWO

"A Healthy and Prosperous Race"

THE URBAN LEAGUE OF PITTSBURGH AND THE STRUGGLE FOR JOBS, HOUSING, AND HEALTH, 1915–1929

> I have plucked you from the skies
> Baby, for my paradise!
> Tiny fingers, God but knows
> How you antedate life's woes.
>
> Was it fair that you should be
> Peon to my misery,
> That one hour you might rest
> Cuddled solace on my breast?
>
> —Georgia Douglas Johnson, "Black Baby,"

Pittsburgh must have seemed strange to eight-year-old Nola Lindsey as she and her mother stepped off their train car at Union Station and confronted a boisterous terminal with dozens of people shuffling around her, lugging their belongings, and shouting to be heard above hissing locomotives and rolling carts. Nola grew up in Greensboro, North Carolina, but in 1923 her father moved to Duquesne, just outside Pittsburgh, for a job at the local Carnegie plant. When she and her mother joined him a year later, they entered a city eleven times the size of Greensboro. Union Station was the first point of entry for Pittsburgh's incoming migrants, and it showcased at once the promises and perils of the urban North. Drug peddlers, scam artists, and pimps patrolled the walkways in the terminal looking to sell fake insurance and stocks or persuade young women to work in the red-light district. They were probably around when Nola got there, but chances are Sadie Bond was as well.

Bond was the only black staff member of the local travelers' aid society, and like the peddlers and pimps she positioned herself at the terminal to intercept migrants entering the city. Travelers' aid societies formed in cities across the North in the late nineteenth and early twentieth centuries to assist European immigrants entering the United States. Later, they began assisting domestic migrants from the South as well. Bond's job was to reach black newcomers before the pimps did and to direct them to the Urban League of Pittsburgh (ULP), which would help them find lodging and employment.[1] In just the first three months of 1919 she aided 643 incoming migrants, over a third of whom were girls or women without jobs or money.[2]

Bond was part of a larger network of informal Urban League agents who, though not on its payroll, coordinated with league staff and assisted in its operations. ULP head John T. Clark convinced the society to hire Bond, and he helped secure positions for black welfare personnel in factories across the region, who in turn performed social service work in places beyond the league's reach. Additionally, black employees at the B & O railroad and other locations secretly documented instances of discrimination and disclosed the information to Clark.[3]

Bond's role represented the first part of an overall league program that aspired to improve every aspect of migrant life: their job prospects, leisure activities, shopping habits, housing conditions, and health care practices. Life in Pittsburgh and other northern cities presented serious challenges that labor agents in the South did not advertise to prospective migrants. Employers offered migrants only the lowest-paying and least desirable jobs, and local unions excluded them. Poverty and racially restrictive housing policies confined them to inner city slums in Chicago's South Side, New York's Harlem, Cleveland's East Side, and Pittsburgh's Hill District, where they lived in overcrowded and often unsanitary boardinghouses and tenements. In these conditions, preventable and treatable diseases killed blacks disproportionately in communities across the North.[4]

Reformers in the ULP secured jobs for incoming migrants and strove to expand their employment opportunities by lobbying unions and employers to drop discriminatory policies and open skilled positions to African Americans. They supported black prisoners at parole hearings and helped them find work and lodging upon release while assisting prostitutes and juvenile offenders in cases brought before the city morals court. Urban Leaguers also lobbied employers to fund better housing and worked with migrants to improve sanitation in poor neighborhoods. To save black lives, they sponsored community-wide health awareness campaigns to educate migrant families on the benefits of prenatal and obstetrical care and register babies with local medical facilities.

These programs improved everyday life for migrants and native black Pittsburghers, but they sometimes had uneven benefits. As I show in this chapter, the league's preference for recruiting, training, and placing married men who appeared responsible likely benefited migrants with some financial means and education more than the poorest, least-educated blacks. Urban Leaguers viewed reform through a middle-class lens that affected their perception of the migrant community and the path to racial advancement. They saw migrant folkways—their work patterns, religious customs, leisure habits, and medicinal practices—as part of the problem, and they worked to "adjust" migrant behavior accordingly. While this approach implicitly blamed migrants for racial inequality, reformers treated behavioral reform as just one in a series of strategies designed to subvert the logic of racial subordination and improve daily life for as many African Americans as possible. Despite their emphasis on adjustment, league staff made clear their view that racial prejudice caused much of the suffering in the black community. Therefore, as one ULP officer explained, every black Pittsburgher had a duty to fight unfounded racial stereotypes by demonstrating exemplary conduct in the workplace and in public.

> The stage has for years burlesqued Negro life, the Negro church, and Negro characteristics, so that it gives rise in the minds of whites, the question of the truth of this picturization. The action of one or more individuals when similar to the burlesques with which they are more familiar, causes those same whites to believe these concepts. Beware of the kind of conversation carried on before whites. . . . We all are in the position of being ambassadors to the Race, and as we conduct ourselves now, the future of our boys is determined.[5]

Although reformers viewed activism from a middle-class perspective, many of them were themselves southern migrants who experienced and witnessed the physical manifestations of racial injustice. Thus, as a ULP worker noted, the league facilitated employment, housing, and health programs with the hope that a "healthy and prosperous race will be built up and the high death rate greatly decreased."[6]

Historians of urban black history often dismiss the Urban League as a bourgeois organization whose members were preoccupied with their status in the black community and who did little to address structural inequality embedded in the political and economic system.[7] Urban Leaguers themselves acknowledged this failing, but they operated under difficult circumstances that both limited their range of options and informed their strategic approach to racial advancement. Although longtime Urban Leaguer Grace Lowndes believed "it is social and economic vandalism to give attention to the curing of ills rather than to insist upon the prevention of ravages in society," in the 1920s treating the source of black inequality was not easy.[8] Ethnic and native white industrial workers leveraged their numerical superiority to prevent migrants from entering more desirable departments in the city's mills, and reactionaries militated against their presence by forming Ku Klux Klan chapters across western Pennsylvania. Meanwhile local and state officials rejected social welfare legislation for the poor and working-class of any color, and they refused to pass laws protecting the growing black population against racial discrimination. The ULP may not have been equipped to significantly alter these conditions, but its social service efforts in the 1920s nevertheless provided crucial support for some of the most economically vulnerable members of the black community. The league's failures should not lead us to overlook its successes, even if modest.

Opening Employment Opportunities

In the midst of the Great Migration, African-American representation in the steel mills of Pittsburgh jumped from about 3 to 20 percent between 1910 and 1923.[9] Unlike Slavic and Italian workers, however, African Americans did not move up the employment ladder. European immigrants experienced prejudicial treatment from native whites, who derisively called them "Hunkies" and "Wops," but generally their access to apprenticeships and skilled positions remained open. Even local unions eventually welcomed foreigners among them.[10] When their numbers grew large enough, Slavs and Italians gradually gained control over certain departments in mills and managed to promote their own to skilled and supervisory positions. This pattern did not repeat for black workers. About 95 percent of them worked as common laborers in 1918, and most remained there through the 1920s.[11]

As the ULP's executive secretary, Clark labored to improve black employment prospects in the city. The league lobbied local and national labor leaders to open their ranks to black workers, and it forged alliances with executives in area steel firms. Like *Courier* editor Robert L. Vann, social worker

Grace Lowndes, and other reformers, Clark was a racial pragmatist. Operating under extraordinarily difficult circumstances, he valued tactics he saw as likely to foster incremental improvements in the everyday lives of black Pittsburghers. For the sake of racial advancement, interwar-era reformers adopted positions and created alliances across the political spectrum. In the short span from 1925 to 1932, for instance, they worked with and courted support from steel executives and organized labor, Republicans and Democrats, capitalists and socialists.

"A GREAT, BIG FAR-REACHING THING": THE ULP AND ORGANIZED LABOR

On a hot July afternoon in 1920, rumors of mass layoffs circulated among black workers at the Newport News Ship Drydock and Building Company in Virginia. Business had boomed during the First World War and the company's African American workforce had swelled to five thousand, but shortly afterward demand slackened. Although company managers denied the layoff rumors, the black workers nevertheless sent two representatives on a tour of several northern cities to find a suitable new home, if the need should arise. Richard Alexander and A. D. Cooke, mechanics with keen eyes and ready pens, canvassed black labor prospects in New York, Buffalo, Detroit, Chicago, and Cleveland. Their last stop was Pittsburgh, where Clark led them on a tour of the city. What they saw dismayed and disappointed them: poverty, squalid living conditions, and above all exploited and unorganized black workers. Alexander later wrote Clark that after seeing Pittsburgh he better understood "the labor problem as it affected colored men, . . . and I find that we have just begun what we have thought we had finished. This is a great, big far-reaching thing. And in your part of the country at least, it is only in its experimental stage."[12]

It was no doubt a point of frustration for Clark, who had supported black unionization since his arrival two years earlier but had little to show for it. Although he recognized that African Americans' exclusion from organized labor contributed to their economic marginalization, during his time in Pittsburgh he could not find a way to overcome the racial barriers erected by local white workers. In 1917 social researcher Abraham Epstein discovered that only two of the city's unions admitted black workers, the Hod Carriers' Union and Hoisting Engineers' Union. The rest excluded them either through clauses in their constitutions or, more often, by ritual practices. One union required its new initiates to repeat a pledge that they would not "introduce for membership into this Union anyone but a sober, industrious, WHITE person." The prognosis appeared grim to Epstein. "If the present policy of the American labor movement continues," he wrote, "the Negroes can depend but little upon this great liberating force for their advancement."[13]

A few months into Clark's tenure at the ULP, he began working to reverse this trend. In early February 1918 he held a meeting with local black workers to assess their involvement in and attitude toward area unions. Several men indicated that only two of the city's two hundred black plasterers had gained entry into the plasterer's union. Another workman he spoke with was a plumber who complained that over the past four years his union had denied entry to dozens of qualified black applicants. A cement mason made similar remarks and further noted that some contracting firms, such as Brown Brothers in Dormont, Pennsylvania, refused to extend contracts to unions with black members.[14]

Clark also wrote union officers in Pittsburgh and other cities to determine the extent of African American membership. Through these correspondences, he better understood the isolation of northern black workers. "In reply to your letter," went one typical response, "I beg to state that we have no negro plasterers in our association."[15] Another official cordially replied, "Am very glad to answer your communication, but wish to state that we have no colored men in our union at the present time." The official observed that the thirty-six members of his union were all white, and on a personal note he mentioned that in his ten years with the union no African American had ever been admitted.[16]

With "whites only" unionism entrenched in Pittsburgh, Clark pressed for change at the national level. A few months earlier, leaders in the American Federation of Labor (AFL) pledged their support for interracial unions and encouraged African Americans to join ranks with them. Seeking to capitalize on the opportunity to organize black workers, the National Urban League (NUL) arranged a meeting with Samuel Gompers and other AFL officials to take place on February 12 at the federation's headquarters in Washington, DC.[17] The black delegation included E. K. Jones and Robert R. Moton, who succeeded Booker T. Washington as principal of the Tuskegee Institute. When Clark learned about the scheduled conference, he sent Moton a report summarizing the results of his meeting with black workers as well as Epstein's findings on discriminatory unions in Pittsburgh. He informed Moton that these workers "seem to doubt the sincerity of the American Federation of Labor about their fair attitude toward the Negro," and on their behalf he urged Moton to stress to the AFL the importance of curtailing the exclusionary practices of locals.[18]

Moton took Clark's report with him to the meeting, using it to reference specific cases of discrimination, and a few days later he pressured Gompers to crack down on AFL affiliates. An "appeal to labor organizations from you," he wrote on February 20, 1918, "cannot but have a wholesome effect in changing . . . the attitude of individuals and organizations, North and South, towards colored labor." Pointing to the mutual disadvantages of a racially divided workforce, Moton explained that "there is no better time than at present to do this, not only for the help of colored labor but quite as much for the protection of organized labor."[19]

His appeal proved prophetic. A year later, black strikebreakers in Pittsburgh, Chicago, and other communities hastened the defeat of the Great Steel Strike of 1919. Both Clark and Vann discouraged strikebreaking. Clark refused to refer black workers to mills under strike. Vann, who shared Clark's commitment to fostering interracial unions, expressed support for the strike through the pages of the *Courier*.[20] Nevertheless, about six thousand black workers in the Pittsburgh area crossed picket lines. Needing the money and feeling mistreated by white workers, few of them had any reservations about taking vacated jobs at mills under strike.[21]

Clark continued lobbying for black unionization after the strike. He encouraged area unions to hire black labor organizers, and he sponsored events to educate black workers on the merits of interracial unions. Even so, the locals declined his request to hire black organizers and continued their policy of racial exclusion.[22] Although the AFL provided token support for inclusive unions, it rarely managed to democratize its affiliates. On the eve of the Great Depression, African Americans comprised less than 2 percent of all unionized workers.[23]

"STEADY RELIABLE MARRIED MEN": THE ULP AND THE BUSINESS COMMUNITY

On Wednesday morning, December 13, 1922, thousands of African Americans across the country noticed in their newspapers a short article proclaiming abundant employment opportunities in Pittsburgh for married southern black men willing to settle there. Prospective migrants from Savannah to Houston read with interest as the local Urban League head described good-paying jobs in the steel mills of western Pennsylvania, and over the next few weeks they flooded Clark's office with hundreds of letters seeking additional information about wages and working conditions, available housing, labor relations, and the climate. Reprinted in major black weeklies in the South and North, the article promised assistance to black men and their families who settled in the Steel City. In this seemingly innocuous column, Clark's stipulation that newcomers be "steady reliable married men" revealed elements of a larger strategy for obtaining full citizenship rights for the city's black community.[24]

While assessing the possibilities of organized labor, Clark garnered support from local employers. Here as elsewhere he appealed to employers' material interests to advance his racial agenda. Writing to Duquesne Steel Foundry executive E. A. Way in 1923, Clark distinguished between "the better type of Negro labor," who were reliable and hardworking, and the unreliable "bad ones."[25] The ULP provided job placement services for incoming migrants and worked to expand their range of employment options. In part, this required persuading white employers and officials that African Americans were integral to the larger community and worthy of equal citizenship rights. Hence Clark preferred to recruit craftspeople from the South likely to support this goal instead of migrants whose work traditions and cultural values might impede it—typically young unmarried men accustomed to holding temporary jobs during slack seasons on the family farm. In his letter to Way, Clark suggested he "employ an intelligent Colored man to work with your employment director." This person would have "close contact with the Negro laborer" and therefore could "weed out the bad ones and help to better satisfy the disgruntled ones."[26]

Clark's willingness to sacrifice "the bad ones" for what he saw as the greater good reflected his utilitarian outlook on reform work. Migrants' limited experience with industrial labor, coupled with their high turnover rates in the city's mills, made it more difficult for Clark to persuade employers to open skilled positions to black workers. Accustomed to the seasonal rhythms of agricultural labor in the South, where they often found temporary work between the busy times of planting and harvesting, few migrants had reservations about quitting a factory job after a few months. They also walked off the job to express their displeasure with prejudiced foremen who confined them to the hottest and most demanding positions in the mill.[27] But as Clark understood it, pursuing the greater interests of the black community required eliminating transients, importing "respectable" black workers, and providing them with the vocational training necessary to perform skilled industrial labor. Whatever merits it had, however, such a strategy tended to exclude the poorest and least-educated blacks.

Still, Clark's relationship with employers had practical benefits for many migrant workers. Appealing to their self-interest, he convinced managers at Lockhart Iron and Steel, the Pittsburgh Steel Company, the Pittsburgh Forge and Iron Company, and several Carnegie plants to hire black welfare workers. Clark informed employers that black welfare personnel could help migrants adjust to industrial labor and urban living, thereby reducing turnover rates and related costs for recruitment and training.[28] Yet he also understood that white workers and foremen often mistreated migrants, and he recognized the importance of placing trained professionals in the mills to address migrants' concerns and promote fairness on the shop floor. With limited resources at his disposal, Clark used welfare workers as Urban League emissaries to do social work in neighboring communities outside his reach, including Corapolis, Duquesne, Braddock, Clairton, and Homestead.

One such welfare worker was W. P. Young, a graduate of the historically black Lincoln University, whom Clark placed with the Lockhart Iron and Steel Company in the McKees Rocks district. Young soon established a rapport with Lockhart's black steelworkers and became the coach of their team in the Negro Industrial Baseball League.[29] As a liaison between migrant workers and steel managers, Young performed several functions that improved everyday life for black workers. The black turnover rate at Lockhart stood at about 25 percent per month. When Young linked this to the overcrowded, dark, and poorly ventilated conditions at the company bunkhouse, he convinced company executives to fund the construction of larger housing units and provide regular improvements to their amenities. Lockhart replaced the coal stoves with a steam heating system, outhouses with indoor toilets, and wooden cots with double-mattressed metal beds.[30] Young also persuaded Lockhart executives to build a free laundry facility for the wives of black steelworkers, and he organized a race relations committee to address discrimination in the McKees Rocks district.[31]

Welfare workers sometimes lived in company bunkhouses with black migrants, and they often spent time with them at community centers in the evenings. Through such close contact they became intimately acquainted with the lives of the men they oversaw. Grover Nelson, the welfare worker at the Carnegie plant in Homestead, was a regular at the local community center for black workers. Through his frequent dealings with them and advocacy on their behalf, Nelson gained the respect of black steelworkers and, according to one report, had "a great deal of influence for good over [them]."[32]

Building on several decades of welfare capitalism designed to foster company loyalty and undermine unions, area steel firms often constructed community centers for their black and white employees. The black community center in Homestead featured a billiard room, reading room, classroom, kitchen, and bathrooms. By providing healthy recreational outlets at the community centers and other locations, Nelson, Young, and other welfare personnel hoped to curb intraracial violence. Not infrequently, fights that led to serious injury or death broke out among black steelworkers over card or dice games. To address this situation, welfare workers developed community programs, managed company baseball teams, sponsored classes on black history, and organized choirs that sang "Negro folk song[s]."[33]

ULP officers collaborated with welfare workers during informal meetings as well as large conferences. In February 1920, the ULP joined with the Employers' Association of Pittsburgh to sponsor a two-day conference for black industrial welfare workers that included representatives from forty-seven different plants employing over 17,500 black workers. There, Jones, Young, Lowndes, and other Urban Leaguers gave talks that both underscored reformers' alliance with white employers and revealed how they obtained resources for the black community. Reformers prepared lectures on topics including black education, health, recreation, and northern legal norms, which they anchored to the theme of making black workers more reliable employees who could "demonstrate to capital . . . their determination to hold a permanent and indispensable position in Northern Industrial Life." These patronizing, business-friendly declarations often obscured Urban Leaguers' deeper concerns about structural inequality in urban black communities and about finding practicable solutions within a very restrictive political and social context. Beneath their rhetoric lay their expectations about what full citizenship entailed, including the rights to gainful employment, suitable housing, and adequate healthcare. Before departing, the conferees drafted resolutions calling on large firms to hire black welfare workers, nurses, and home visitors; to "promote as soon as possible the building of suitable houses for sale or rent to their married Negro employees"; and to support "shop training [and] extension classes for leisure time and instruction."[34]

By framing the industrial welfare program in terms of labor reliability, Clark spread the ULP's mission beyond the bounds of Pittsburgh at employers' expense and helped ensure that "the problems Negro workmen encounter[ed]" reached "the highest official through their Negro Industrial social worker."[35] Moreover, the league's programs encouraging sobriety, monogamy, reliability, hard work, and company loyalty had the added benefit of attracting funding from local industries. In 1923, for instance, the ULP garnered donations of $1,000 from both Carnegie Steel and the Jones and Laughlin Company as well as contributions of $500 from the National Tube Company and Standard Sanitary Manufacturing.[36] Prior to 1927, when the ULP became a participating member of the city welfare fund, the league could not have continued operating without the financial support of employers. Clark's fundraising campaigns enabled him to build up the ranks of the ULP—he hired six staff members in 1918 with the $8,000 he raised that year—and develop important programs to address the pressing practical problems that the majority of black Pittsburghers faced every day.[37]

PROMOTING THE BLACK MIDDLE CLASS

Along with their other functions, industrial welfare conferences gave Clark an opportunity to meet with his network of agents and coordinate their activities. As he communicated with Young, Nelson, and other welfare personnel, he likely felt some satisfaction at having placed them in their occupations. He later boasted that the league overcame employers' reservations regarding hiring black officials and that now "11 of the large industrial plants have each employed from 1 to 3 capable Negroes in their employment and welfare departments."[38] Although the ULP placed primary emphasis on meeting the needs of migrants, it also worked to expand employment opportunities for black professionals. Clark helped persuade the local travelers' aid society to hire Bond to oversee the arrival of southern black migrants at Union Station in downtown Pittsburgh, and he convinced the Public Health Nursing Association to hire Jeannette Washington to administer to the needs of poor blacks in the Hill District and other neighborhoods.[39] Additionally, league staff lobbied against the exclusion of black teachers in Pittsburgh's schools. No law precluded their employment, but in practice the Allegheny County School Board never hired black teachers—even though African Americans made up more than half the student population in several Hill District schools.[40]

The league promoted the growth of the black middle class, and Clark's annual reports suggest he was proud of his limited success in this regard. Although teaching jobs remained closed to African Americans in Pittsburgh until 1937, Clark persuaded local schools to admit a trained black teacher as a home and school visitor to help struggling black students succeed, and he opened doors to professional-level positions in industry, nursing, and social work.[41] Still, the ULP directed most of its resources to programs for poor black migrants. As Clark indicated in 1924, the organization aspired "to develop machinery to meet the incoming southerner, find safe lodgings, help locate for them the best available jobs and attempt to interest those who came into contact with these new citizens, in understanding them."[42] ULP staff additionally advocated for young black women held before the city morals court as well as black inmates during their parole hearings, and they sponsored improvements in sanitation and heath in disease-ridden neighborhoods.[43]

Further, Clark's efforts to promote professional opportunities facilitated the growth of a valuable body of research on migrant problems. The league partnered with the NUL to sponsor a fellowship program that awarded competitive scholarships for college-educated African Americans to earn advanced degrees in economics, social work, or sociology at the University of Pittsburgh. Throughout the 1920s, league fellows composed masters' theses that shed light on structural inequality in the city, and the data they compiled informed many of the ULP's community initiatives.[44]

Urban Leaguers had long felt that collecting and disseminating reliable quantitative information could help expose racial injustice and gain white allies. "The Urban League turns [on] the light of scientific inquiry in order to point the way to the establishment of a more equitable social order nearer to the oft evoked ideals of Democracy," one black editorialist commented.[45] The ULP's fellowship program also helped launch the careers of several distinguished scholars, most notably Ira Reid and Abram Harris. After earning their master's degrees, Reid moved to New York to direct research operations for the NUL and Harris accepted a faculty position at Howard University in Washington DC.

In 1930, Reid returned to Pittsburgh to head a massive new study titled "The Social Conditions of the Negro in the Hill District of Pittsburgh."[46] The ULP supported Reid and his team of twenty paid and unpaid researchers as they compiled data on African Americans in the Hill; moreover, ULP head R. Maurice Moss served as a key adviser on the project and helped revise the original manuscript.[47] Upon completing his report, Reid submitted it for review to the General Committee on the Hill Survey, an interracial group of over fifty leaders from various social agencies charged with preparing the document for publication. Soon, however, debates arose in the committee over Reid's presentation of certain information. A group of whites wanted the study to report on conditions in the Hill "without stressing racial

Black delegates to the National Urban League's industrial welfare conference, held in Pittsburgh in 1920.
Urban League Collection, box 10, folder 541,
University of Pittsburgh Archives Service Center.

feeling," and they sought to modify Reid's overt references to racial discrimination and segregation—especially his discussion of the Allegheny County School Board's refusal to hire black teachers. However, the African American members of the committee and their white allies insisted the racial components remain. Consequently, when published in 1930, the study shed light on serious economic and social inequities in Pittsburgh. Reid found disproportionately high death rates in the two wards of the Hill District, a total absence of convalescent homes for black women, no hospitals that would hire black nurses or doctors, lack of upward mobility for black industrial workers, violations of city housing codes by white landlords in the lower Hill, and discriminatory arrests and prosecution of black men, among other racial injustices.[48]

Housing and Health

Black migrants' poor employment prospects contributed to their disproportionate representation in the Western Penitentiary, located on Pittsburgh's

North Side. Local police targeted African American teenagers and young women as well. Along with its other services, the ULP provided support services for black inmates on parole and young women arrested for prostitution.

Prostitution had become a highly profitable enterprise in Pittsburgh, and a successful pimp at Union Station could lead newly arrived migrant women to one of over two hundred brothels in the Hill District. It may have offered a source of employment outside domestic work, but it also exposed young women to health risks and trouble with the criminal justice system. In 1918, city officials created a morals court to administer punishment to young women accused of prostitution as well as juveniles who committed minor offenses. Clark sent Lowndes to the court to advocate for African American women, secure reduced sentences for them when possible, and keep them out of the prison system. Lowndes and a few volunteers managed over a thousand cases in 1924 alone.[49]

While serving in the morals court, Lowndes also headed the league's neighborhood unit program, which built grassroots support for improving sanitation in black neighborhoods. For good reason, ULP staff saw housing and health as critical issues. The overcrowding and poor sanitation in the African American community was a lethal combination. Mortality rates for black Pittsburghers doubled between 1915 and 1917, and during the same period pneumonia deaths increased by 200 percent. The year Clark arrived in Pittsburgh, more than 2 out of every 10 black children died in infancy, 530 black adults died of pneumonia, and another 100 perished in the influenza epidemic that swept through the city.[50] An alarmed Vann wrote that "the Negro wage earner . . . is now being attacked by disease of nearly epidemic prevalence as a result of the neglected housing conditions."[51]

Clark made this connection as well, and he called for an effort "to obtain more sanitary houses for Negroes to live in," houses that were "less congested [and] unhealthy." Here and in other programs, Clark rhetorically linked his racial agenda to the interests of the white community to obtain the funding and support necessary to execute his plans. "Health and sanitation are of vital interest to Negroes and to Pittsburghers," he declared.[52] Urban Leaguers tacitly recognized that demanding racial justice for its own sake had less appeal among potential white donors than practical arguments tied to their economic interests and community harmony. Hence Clark and others framed calls for better housing and sanitation in terms of safeguarding community (i.e., white) health and fostering a more stable workforce.[53] On these grounds, Clark conveyed to industries "the basic necessity for building family homes" for their black employees; he obtained funding for his health education campaigns; and in 1921 he helped convince the city council to spend $81,000 to build a public bathhouse in the lower Hill District.[54]

With industry dollars to pay for staff, office space, and printing material, Clark developed several programs to confront the health crisis. He charged Lowndes with the task of establishing neighborhood units in the Hill District and other black neighborhoods where poor and working-class women could meet regularly to discuss environmental problems and sponsor events to address them. By 1930, she oversaw sixteen units ranging between twenty and thirty members. Sitting with Lowndes and other ULP staff, African American women from different geographic and social backgrounds discussed ways to improve sanitation in their houses and neighborhoods and assist the neediest families among them. They launched campaigns to raise money for educational scholarships for black children, brought medical specialists to their neighborhoods to give talks on health and sanitation, and sponsored initiatives to clean up their streets. Under Lowndes, the neighborhood unit program fostered a sense of civic pride, forged community ties, and helped address the health crisis.[55]

League women also led a home economics outreach initiative among migrant families. As part of the ULP's larger campaign to improve black health, Clark sent home economics workers on a door-to-door campaign to educate migrant families about proper hygiene and good nutrition, inquire about their health and housing conditions, make medical referrals when necessary, and "help them become more desirable citizens."[56] In February 1919 alone they visited eighty-three houses.[57] These encounters revealed class divisions as well as racial solidarity. Given the implications of their visit, some migrants resented the intrusions of the home economics workers. And league women sometimes contrasted what they called "the more intelligent class" of African Americans, usually native Pittsburghers who kept "respectable homes," with southern migrants whose homes were dirty.[58]

Social welfare workers' predilection for making these moralistic distinctions, their insistence on the correctness of their views and implicit rejection of migrant folkways, and their inability to rectify on a structural level the sources of racial inequality have led many historians to overlook the ways they improved everyday life in their communities. Even if it was presumptuous, going door to door in depressed neighborhoods to visit migrants from distant states was not easy. Although ULP staff reports indicate migrants usually received them civilly, any unsolicited visit could end with verbal

A Healthy and Prosperous Race 69

Grace Lowndes (seated second from left) at a neighborhood unit meeting in Schenley Heights, Pittsburgh.
Arthur J. Edmunds, *Daybreakers: The Story of the Urban League of Pittsburgh* (Pittsburgh: Urban League of Pittsburgh, 1983), 41.

abuse or a door slammed in their face. At a minimum, Urban Leaguers had to overcome migrants' suspicion that they were like other local scammers who went door to door selling fake insurance and stocks. One home economics worker commented in May 1919 that "the newcomer here [is] very skeptical and cautious of help offered.... [But] when we have really convinced them of our sincerity, which is usually brought about by some assistance rendered, they are very appreciative." Beneath their bourgeois goals of molding migrants into good middle-class citizens, home economics workers understood that teaching migrants how to improve home sanitation and obtain affordable nutritious food in an urban environment could possibly save lives. Committed to the well-being of migrants and the uplift of the black masses, league women crossed regional and class barriers "to prove to [migrants] that we are their friends and are working for real constructive and adjustment work."[59]

In the black neighborhoods of Pittsburgh, disease and death found their calling. Mortality rates increased alarmingly across the city's black community, as African Americans suffered disproportionately from bronchitis, pneumonia, and other illnesses.[60] Infants and unborn children proved especially vulnerable. By 1923, the rate of still births for black Pittsburghers climbed to 7.4 per 100 live births, compared to 3.5 for whites. The experience of Bishop and Emma Phifer, whose son died in infancy and daughter had tuberculosis, was common among black Pittsburghers. Alarmed by the grim health statistics and perplexed by what he saw as a lack of concern among middle and upper-class whites, in 1924 a white ULP board member, Edwin May, published a searing article that criticized "Mr. Pittsburgh" for firing blacks in disproportionate numbers and confining them to the city's slums. "If in the overcrowded [Hill] district there arises an epidemic," he warned, "it will not stop short of your comfortable home on Squirrel Hill."[61]

To mitigate the situation, the league launched health programs that introduced migrants to modern medical practices, educated them about preventative measures, and provided free health screenings for adults and babies. It also established and coordinated a health care network with local medical facilities and referred sick patients for care. Yet reversing black mortality rates was a daunting task. Compounding the health problems emerging from inadequate housing, migrants often valued their traditional medicinal beliefs and homemade remedies over modern medical practices, which they regarded with suspicion. "The Negro," Epstein observed, "not only because of his ignorance but perhaps even more because of his inclinations to voodooism and superstition, feels an aversion to the hospital, where he thinks the knife and the 'black bottle' are frequently used." *Courier* columnist George Schuyler added that black faith healers "are more dangerous to the health of a community than a whole battalion of chiropractors or osteopaths. They . . . are often the cause of sending to the grave people who could have survived through proper medical attention."[62] Although afflicted with tuberculosis, one couple refused treatment at a medical facility because they feared "that white people wanted to take their children off and experiment on them."[63] Their concerns had merit, as the infamous Tuskegee experiments later demonstrated. Harrison Gant, who migrated to Pittsburgh in 1916, remained skeptical of modern medical practices decades later. "I didn't believe in doctors," he pointed out, "[and] I still don't, I'll be honest with you. . . . The same thing that can cure yah can kill yah." He recalled that in Georgia his parents made their own medicine, "and I'll say right now . . . [they] were the best doctors I ever met."[64]

In order to overcome these suspicions and reduce infant mortality, the ULP educated migrant women on the importance of prenatal care and obstetrical services. Supplementing the information its home economics workers provided at neighborhood unit meetings and home visits, the league regularly sponsored health education weeks and baby shows. During its Negro

Health Campaign in 1918 it distributed twenty-thousand health brochures, brought in prominent black doctors to give talks on proper health care, provided free physical and dental examinations, and partnered with thirty-one black preachers, who delivered sermons that discussed the health problems confronting the community.[65]

The ULP's "Better Baby" contests also provided vital health information. In 1921 the league sponsored three baby shows—in the Hill District, East Liberty, and North Side—that featured "exhibits of all kinds," according to a ULP report. The events included movies, informational literature, and guest lectures by black and white health professionals, "all of which was for the purpose of directing the attention of the colored mothers of Pittsburgh to better care of their children." Eager to show off their babies, learn ways to keep them alive and healthy, and possibly win one of the available prizes (such as strollers and high chairs), over a thousand mothers and friends attended, and they brought 368 babies, who received health screenings and were registered with health centers across the city.[66] Jeannette Washington, Pittsburgh's first black nurse, administered the screenings alongside black physician Marie Kinner.[67]

When Washington first aspired to become a nurse several years before, she attended Mercy-Douglas Hospital School of Nursing in Philadelphia because no school in Pittsburgh would admit her, and when she returned to the city with her RN degree in hand, area hospitals refused to hire her.[68] Even the city's staff of public health nurses was all white. Taking up her case in September 1922, Clark explained to city officials that many migrant women had reservations about seeing white health practitioners. Given the severity of the health problems in the black community, he convinced the city to hire Washington.[69]

Kinner faced the twin burden of being black and female. Upon graduating from Howard University Medical School, Kinner set up a private practice in Pittsburgh. Yet she found that many African Americans had reservations about seeing a female doctor, and consequently her practice suffered. To supplement her income, she obtained a second job with Planned Parenthood in Pittsburgh's North Side. Despite her busy schedule Kinner helped plan and administer the ULP's health campaigns and "Better Baby" shows, and she played a central role in increasing attendance at well-baby clinics.[70]

In addition to running education campaigns, according to historian Carolyn Carson, the ULP "established a widespread health-care network for poor blacks of which it was the center. Mutually beneficial relationships existed between several city hospitals, clinics, dispensaries, social agencies, and the Public Health Nursing Association."⁷¹ The league had contacts in the social service offices of Columbia Hospital, Allegheny General, St. Francis, Passavant, West Penn, Mercy, and Magee Women's Hospital, among others, and it used this network to direct migrants to appropriate healthcare facilities and ensure they received proper care.⁷² The story of the Baker family is instructive. Robert and Camilla Baker lived in a home in the lower Hill District with their six children and several boarders, according to a ULP Health Committee report:

> Family discovered by our Home Economics Worker. They keep a large number of male lodgers and live in a conjested [sic] condition. The family showed evidence of tuberculosis, the worker suggested that they be examined, and as a result one child was sent to Crescent and another to the Bedford Avenue T.B. League. Entire family has had the Wasserman Test, and they are willing to follow any suggestions. ⁷³

Ultimately, during the 1920s the league helped alleviate the health crisis in the black community. Black mortality rates declined every year from 1918 to 1923, despite the influx of migrants into neighborhoods with fixed housing capacities. Although health improved citywide, between 1920 and 1925 infant mortality decreased twice as rapidly for blacks as they did for whites. Moreover, the ULP brought thousands of migrants into the medical system through its heath education programs and clinical networks. In 1915 only 13 percent of pregnant black women had a physician deliver their babies, preferring midwives instead, but by 1931 more than half opted for a medical professional.⁷⁴

Urban Leaguers and the Spectrum of Black Activism

The ULP alleviated the symptoms of racial inequality in the 1920s, but it did little to treat the source. By the eve of the Great Depression black Pittsburghers remained locked in unskilled positions and excluded from organized labor. Although their neighborhood sanitation and health improved, they still suffered disproportionately from high infant mortality rates and from illnesses associated with poor housing.⁷⁵

The league's limited success in improving black life largely owed to the difficult environment in which it operated. ULP staff set up shop in Pitts-

Better Baby Show, ca. 1930, with Jeannette Washington, Pittsburgh's first black nurse, standing in the bottom right corner.
Historic Pittsburgh Image Collection, 8III.539B01.UL, University of Pittsburgh Archives Service Center.

The grim reaper in Pittsburgh.
Wilbert Holloway, editorial page, *Pittsburgh Courier*, September 4, 1926.

burgh in the midst of profound disruptions in the black community brought about by the Great Migration. Southern migrants exacerbated housing shortages and sparked a white backlash that affected native black Pittsburghers as well as newcomers. Formed to help migrants adjust to and stay in the city, the league struggled to gain support from a local black community that in general wished migrants would leave. The ULP's financial records from the 1920s indicate that donations from African Americans supplied only about 10 percent of its annual budget. Clark and his staff had little choice but to reach out to the white community to make up the difference. Before 1927, when the league joined the city welfare fund, a precursor to the United Way, it relied upon support from local philanthropists and industries. Even then, the fledgling organization barely managed to survive the periodic economic downturns of the 1920s. For two months in 1924, its staff worked without pay.[76]

Urban Leaguers' initial dependence on white employers has led some historians to write them off as bourgeois accommodationists of the Booker T. Washington mold. In the early twentieth century Washington came to embody gradualism and accommodation, while W. E. B. Du Bois represented a vigorous insistence on full equality for blacks. Yet between "freedom can wait" and "freedom now" lay a range of perspectives and ideologies. Home economics workers looked with disfavor on the religious customs and leisure habits of migrants, but more often their writings and actions suggested an understanding of and sympathy for their struggles and the ways white racism exacerbated them. Although Clark facilitated programs to indoctrinate migrants with the gospel of reliability, temperance, and company loyalty, both he and his industrial secretary, Tom Barton, continued pressing for black unionization, much to the displeasure of white business owners on the ULP's executive board.[77] Their frustrations peaked in 1926 after Clark had invited the prominent communist and AFL organizer William Z. Foster to meet with black steelworkers. Although the records are not clear about what happened afterward, the board apparently pressured Clark to resign from his position at the ULP.[78] "I was very sorry to learn of the Pittsburgh situation," E. K. Jones wrote to Clark, seeking to console his friend. "I would appreciate your letting me know whether you have any preference as to the place you should like to locate."[79]

By then Clark's reputation as a capable community organizer had spread beyond Pittsburgh, and shortly after his resignation he received and accepted an offer to head the Urban League affiliate in St. Louis, where he continued advocating for working-class African Americans for the next two decades.

For instance, in the early 1930s Clark supported the organization of the International Laborers and Builders Corporation when city officials commenced construction of a black hospital in the heart of St. Louis's African American community without hiring any skilled black workers. The newly formed union of almost three hundred African Americans pressured contractors to include nonwhites on the construction project.[80]

In 1934 Clark also traveled to New York to help the NUL organize its workers' council program to unify black workers and integrate unions. Clark drew up the plans for the program, and soon workers' councils formed in cities across the country, including Pittsburgh.[81] As one NUL official later explained, Clark was "probably the first man in the League to come to grips with the problems of the black worker and organized labor."[82]

Rigid categorizations of reformers obscure more than they clarify. Several ULP staff who worked closely with employers in the 1920s joined the industrial labor movement in the mid-1930s. Other reformers worked with black communists in forming the National Negro Congress. Pittsburgh NAACP head Homer Brown became one of Pennsylvania's first black congressmen, and he used his position to establish black workers' right to join unions. Vann, once a stalwart Republican, helped persuade thousands of black Pittsburghers to abandon the GOP and vote for Franklin Roosevelt.

These changes were set in motion by the onset of the Great Depression in 1929. The economic devastation that followed exacerbated several of the problems working-class blacks encountered in the 1920s, including high unemployment and poverty, while creating new opportunities for cooperation between black reformers and workers, racial organizations and unions, and African Americans and the state. A ULP report on April 6, 1929, foreshadowed these developments: "It may be evident from such an index to the situation . . . that group meetings of Negroes are very necessary [and that] they be gradually educated to the point where concerted action for the common good is a more easy matter."[83]

In these turbulent waters full of peril and opportunity, the ULP's executive board struggled to find a suitable replacement for Clark. His immediate successor, Alonzo Thayer, held this post only two years before joining the Chicago Urban League. It was not until 1930 that the board hired a committed leader in R. Maurice Moss, who subsequently guided the league through the depression and Second World War. Together with longtime staffers like Lowndes and capable new members such as Harold Lett and William Hill, Moss took on the Herculean task of confronting the economic crisis in Pittsburgh's black community and adapting strategically to new political circumstances.[84]

NOTES

1. Lindsey eventually earned a high school diploma, one of few migrants who did so. Afterward, like most employed black women in the Pittsburgh area, she worked as a domestic in the home of a white family. See Nola Lindsey, interview with Dennis Dickerson, September 4, 1975, Pittsburgh Oral History Project, Heinz History Center. For information on Sadie Bond's role at the travelers' aid society, see traveler's aid worker report, ca. 1920, box 6, folder 244, Urban League Records, University of Pittsburgh Archives Service Center. In the same box and folder see also "Colored Travelors [sic] Aid Worker Back at Union Station," ca. 1922, and historical sketch of the Urban League, ca. 1922.
2. Arthur J. Edmunds, *Daybreakers: The Story of the Urban League of Pittsburgh, the First Sixty-Five Years* (Pittsburgh: Urban League of Pittsburgh, 1999), 42.
3. Black urbanization alarmed local whites, who responded with unwritten policies to keep African Americans away from downtown restaurants, in the balconies of movie theaters, and in the rearmost cars of trains. Clark kept abreast of these developments through secret informants located in key positions in the city. One of them was a night caller for the B & O Railroad, who catalogued instances of racial discrimination and reported them to Clark. In September 1925, for instance, he observed two guards direct a group of black passengers to board one of the last two coaches, which had been set aside for them. When one of the black men objected the officers threatened to arrest him. On another occasion Clark's informant reported that "two colored ladies applied for parlor chair seats and were told that colored people were sold parlor chair seats under no circumstances" (Edmunds, *Daybreakers*, 58). Armed with this information, Clark pressured B & O officials to curtail the discriminatory practices of their employees. Writing Joseph P. Taggert, the company's assistant general passenger agent, Clark condemned the "legally unfair treatment of Negro passengers through the B. & O. station" and implored him to take "definite" measures to safeguard the rights of all passengers, hinting that "serious trouble might result" if he did not. For Clark's correspondence with Taggart, see Clark to Taggart, September 25, 1925, and August 29, 1925, box 6, folder 279, Urban League Records.
4. Peter Gottlieb, *Making Their Own Way: Southern Blacks' Migration to Pittsburgh, 1916–30* (Urbana: University of Illinois Press, 1987), 66–70; Thomas Sugrue, *Sweet Land of Liberty: The Forgotten Struggle for Civil Rights in the North* (New York: Random House, 2008), 6.
5. A ULP program attributes this speech, delivered on January 21, 1931, to R. Maurice Moss, but the transcription is credited to Thomas E. Barton. The conflicting attribution likely resulted from an administrative error. However, the layout of the program, which summarizes the speech and provides a biographical sketch of Moss, suggests that Moss probably delivered the speech. See "Fanning the Flames," box 3, folder 124, Urban League Records.
6. Historical sketch of the Urban League of Pittsburgh, ca. 1922, box 6, folder 244, Urban League Records.

7. For example, see Nancy J. Weiss, *The National Urban League, 1910–1940* (New York: Oxford University Press, 1974), Gottlieb, *Making Their Own Way*, 7, Kimberly Phillips, *Alabama North: African-American Migrants, Community, and Working-Class Activism in Cleveland, 1915–1945* (University of Illinois Press, 1999), 157, and Touré F. Reed, *Not Alms But Opportunity: The Urban League and the Politics of Racial Uplift, 1910–1950* (Chapel Hill: University of North Carolina Press, 2008), 196.
8. Edmunds, *Daybreakers*, 48.
9. Gottlieb, *Making Their Own Way*, 90–92. Social researcher Abraham Epstein observed similar growth in his survey of twenty Pittsburgh industries. He noted that between 1915 and 1917 the number of black workers grew from 2,550 to 8,325 ("The Negro Migrant in Pittsburgh" [senior thesis, University of Pittsburgh, 1917], 7).
10. See William Hill, "The Negro Wage Worker" in *The WPA History of the Negro in Pittsburgh*, ed. Laurence Glasco (Pittsburgh: University of Pittsburgh Press, 2004), 219–20. Hill wrote this essay in the late 1930s.
11. Epstein, "The Negro Migrant in Pittsburgh," 21; Laurence Glasco, "Double Burden: The Black Experience in Pittsburgh," in *City at the Point: Essays on the Social History of Pittsburgh*, ed. Samuel P. Hays (Pittsburgh: University of Pittsburgh Press, 1989), 76–77; Ira Reid, *Social Conditions of the Negro in the Hill District of Pittsburgh* (Pittsburgh: General Committee on the Hill Survey, 1930), 52–54. For additional accounts of occupational stagnation, see ULP, "Special Problems of Negro Workers in Pittsburgh," April 6, 1929, box 5, folder 245, Urban League Records, LeRoy McChester, interview with Peter Gottlieb, July 9, 1974, Pittsburgh Oral History Project, and Merril Lynch, interview with Peter Gottlieb, August 22, 1974, Pittsburgh Oral History Project.
12. Richard Alexander to John T. Clark, August 24, 1920, box 3, folder 89, Urban League Records.
13. Epstein, "The Negro Migrant in Pittsburgh," 37, 39.
14. Mechanics meeting transcripts, February 5, 1918, box 3, folder 149, Urban League Records; Guichard Parris and Lester Brooks, *Blacks in the City: A History of the National Urban League* (Boston: Little, Brown and Company, 1971), 138–39.
15. Albert A. Wilko, secretary of OPIA Local 9, to John T. Clark, March 1, 1918, box 3, folder 150, Urban League Records.
16. Robert Stuber, secretary of Plasterers Union 105 in Reading, PA, to John T. Clark, March 4, 1918, box 3, folder 150, Urban League Records.
17. Parris and Brooks, *Blacks in the City*, 135–37; Robert R. Moton to John T. Clark, March 1, 1918, box 3, folder 149, Urban League Records.
18. Parris and Brooks, *Blacks in the City*, 135–37.
19. Robert R. Moton to Samuel Gompers, February 20, 1918, and Robert R. Moton to John T. Clark, March 1, 1918, box 3, folder 149, Urban League Records. In the same box and folder, also see Eugene Kinckle Jones to John T. Clark, February 28, 1918, and Eugene Kinckle to Samuel Gompers, February 20, 1918.
20. Gottlieb, *Making Their Own Way*, 158–63. Even before the Great Steel Strike of 1919, Vann argued that black workers ultimately hurt themselves by acting as strikebreakers. Like Clark, he called upon them to join unions alongside whites whenever possible. Short of that, he suggested African Americans form independent unions. As Vann explained it in a 1916 editorial, black workers must "organize themselves into a substantial union of their own . . . and thus get control of their own labor. We now stand di-

vided, disorganized" (Andrew Buni, *Robert L. Vann of the* Pittsburgh Courier: *Politics and Black Journalism* [Pittsburgh: University of Pittsburgh Press, 1974], 69).
21. Gottlieb, *Making Their Own Way*, 158-63. Hill also discussed the widespread refusal among black industrial workers in Pittsburgh to participate in the strike ("The Negro Wage Worker," 222). For a detailed analysis of the Great Steel Strike, see David Brody, *Steelworkers in America: The Nonunion Era* (Cambridge, MA: Harvard University Press, 1960), 233-62.
22. See John T. Clark to Vernon Fletcher, secretary of the United Brotherhood of Carpenters and Joiners, July 1, 1920, and Vernon Fletcher to John T. Clark, August 2, 1920, box 3, folder 149, Urban League Records. Clark invited the prominent communist and AFL organizer William Z. Foster to speak to black workers in 1919 and 1926. After the second meeting, alarmed white philanthropists on the ULP's executive board apparently called for Clark's resignation. For more information, see "Urban League Happenings," *Pittsburgh Courier*, April 1, 1919, and Edmunds, *Daybreakers*, 66.
23. Harvard Sitkoff, *A New Deal for Blacks: The Emergence of Civil Rights as a National Issue*, thirtieth anniv. ed. (New York: Oxford University Press, 2009), 19; August Meier and Elliot Rudwick, *Plantation to Ghetto* (New York: Hill and Wang, 1966), 242.
24. "Pittsburgh Wants Men with Families," *New York Amsterdam News*, December 13, 1922; letters to John T. Clark, 1922-23, reel 5, John T. Clark Papers, Carter Woodson Collection, Library of Congress. For additional information on Clark's article and responses to it, see John T. Clark to W. A. Harbison, December 20, 1922, box 3, folder 89, Urban League Records. Vann echoed Clark's concern that the unreliability of some migrants would hurt the race as a whole by damaging blacks' reputation among area employers; see "A Bad Start, Boys," *Pittsburgh Courier*, September 29, 1916, and Buni, *Robert L. Vann of the* Pittsburgh Courier, 72.
25. John T. Clark to E. A. Way, vice president of Duquesne Steel Foundry, May 8, 1923, box 3, folder 89, Urban League Records.
26. John T. Clark to E. A. Way, May 8, 1923, box 3, folder 89, Urban League Records.
27. The turnover rate at the A. M. Byers mill in nearby Ambridge was astonishing. In 1923 alone, the company made 1,408 separate hires just to sustain an average of 228 migrant workers (A. M. Byers Company Personnel Records, University of Pittsburgh Archives Service Center).
28. John T. Clark to E. A. Way, May 8, 1923, box 3, folder 89, Urban League Records; Edmunds, *Daybreakers*, 30; I. W. Ratto to John T. Clark, June 11, 1920, box 3, folder 89, Urban League Records. In the same box and folder also see John T. Clark to E.L. Parker, an official for the Columbia Steel and Shafting Company, September 10, 1920. For information on firms that employed black welfare workers, see Dennis C. Dickerson, *Out of the Crucible: Black Steelworkers in Western Pennsylvania, 1875-1980* (Albany: State University of New York Press, 1986), 105.
29. Edmunds, *Daybreakers*, 30.
30. Dickerson, *Out of the Crucible*, 108.
31. Edmunds, *Daybreakers*, 30.
32. Dickerson, *Out of the Crucible*, 109.
33. Dickerson, *Out of the Crucible*, 110.
34. Edmunds, *Daybreakers*, 32-33.

A Healthy and Prosperous Race   79

35. This quote is from an early draft of Clark's annual report for 1923 (box 6, folder 246, Urban League Records).
36. Dr. Francis Tyson, a ULP board member and economics professor at the University of Pittsburgh who advised Epstein's thesis on black migrants, probably played a role in facilitating this program. The ULP's annual contribution to this scholarship was modest. Its budget records from 1930 indicate it contributed $266.10 out of its total budget of almost $20,000. See budget records, box 2, folder 49, Urban League Records. For more on the ULP's fellowship recipients see its 1930 annual report, box 6, folder 246, Urban League Records. Master's theses produced by Urban League fellows at the University of Pittsburgh include Abram Harris's "The New Negro Workers in Pittsburgh" (1924), Ira Reid's "The Negro in Major Industries and Building Trades of Pittsburgh" (1925), Floyd Covington's "Occupational Choices in Relation to Economic Opportunities of Negro Youth in Pittsburgh" (1928), and Wiley Hall's "Negro Housing in the Hill District of Pittsburgh" (1929).
37. Traveler's aid worker report, ca. 1920, "Colored Travelors [sic] Aid Worker Back at Union Station," ca. 1922, ULP historical sketch, ca. 1922, box 6, folder 244, Urban League Records. For information on Jeannette Washington, see ULP's annual reports from 1923 and 1924, box 6, folder 246, Urban League Records, and Edmunds, *Daybreakers*, 59–61.
38. ULP, 1924 annual report, box 6, folder 246, Urban League Records.
39. ULP, 1924 annual report, box 6, folder 246, Urban League Records.
40. ULP, 1924 annual report, box 6, folder 246, Urban League Records.
41. For more on the league representative in the morals court, see responsibility of court worker, March 3, 1926, box 2, folder 52, Urban League Records. In the same box and folder see Grace Lowndes to "Mr. Stanton," ca. 1924, box 2, folder 52, Urban League Records. For information on the league's support for black inmates at their parole hearings, see Joseph McGill to John T. Clarke, April 13, 1924 and George Yervis to John T. Clark, May 4, 1924, box 2, folder 45, Urban League Records.
42. ULP, 1924 annual report, box 6, folder 246, Urban League Records.
43. Dickerson, *Out of the Crucible*, 115.
44. Edmunds, *Daybreakers*, 30.
45. Editorial, *Opportunity*, May 1932.
46. Ira Reid, *Social Conditions of the Negro in the Hill District of Pittsburgh* (Pittsburgh: Published by the General Committee on the Hill Survey), 13.
47. Reid, *Social Conditions of the Negro in the Hill District of Pittsburgh*, 5.
48. Reid, *Social Conditions of the Negro in the Hill District of Pittsburgh*, 11–16.
49. For information on Lowndes and the morals court, see the following items in the Urban League Records: historical sketch of the Urban League of Pittsburgh, ca. 1922, box 6, folder 244, John T. Clark, draft of speech, "Annual Report of the Work of the Urban League of Pittsburgh for 1924," ca. January 1925, box 6, folder 246, and Grace Lowndes to "Mr. Stanton," ca. 1924, box 2, folder 52. For information on prostitution in Pittsburgh, see Alex Pittler, "The Hill District of Pittsburgh—A Study in Succession" (master's thesis, University of Pittsburgh, 1930), 48–51.
50. Epstein, "The Negro Migrant in Pittsburgh," 54–60; ULP health education brochure, 1919, box 6, folder 242, Urban League Records; Dickerson, *Out of the Crucible*, 58–59.

51. Robert L. Vann, editorial, *Pittsburgh Courier*, December 18, 1916; see also Buni, *Robert L. Vann of the* Pittsburgh Courier, 61.
52. Edmunds, *Daybreakers*, 15.
53. For example, see ULP board member Walter May's comments on poor health in the Hill District in "Pittsburgh's Sorely Cripple Arm," *Pittsburgh First*, September 20, 1924, box 6, folder 242, Urban League Records.
54. For information on Clark's 1918 agenda and his efforts to secure a public bathhouse, see Edmunds, *Daybreakers*, 46–47, 55.
55. ULP, 1930 annual report, box 6, folder 246, Urban League Records.
56. Home economics workers operated with the goal to "teach economic cooking [and] thrifty housekeeping by conservation of food, clothing and fuel to the women whereby they can save a part of the man's savings" (Home economics worker report, February 1919, box 2, folder 80, Urban League Records).
57. Home economics worker report, February 1919, box 2, folder 80, Urban League Records.
58. Home economics worker report, March 1919, box 2, folder 80, Urban League Records.
59. Home economics worker report, May 1919, box 2, folder 80, Urban League Records. For another ULP complaint about local scam artists preying on migrants, see "Committee on Home & Community Work: Digest of Home Economics Work to Date," March 3, 1926, box 2, folder 52, Urban League Records.
60. In 1918, about 530 African Americans died of pneumonia, and another 100 perished in the influenza epidemic that swept through the city. See Epstein, "The Negro Migrant in Pittsburgh," 54–60, ULP health education brochure, 1919, box 6, folder 242, Urban League Records, and Dickerson, *Out of the Crucible*, 58–59. According to Dickerson, in 1924 black Pennsylvanians succumbed to pneumonia at a rate of 268.89 per one hundred thousand, a substantially higher rate than the white rate of 140.31.
61. ULP health committee report, "Phifer Family," March 1920, box 2, folder 82, Urban League Records; Walter May, "Pittsburgh's Sorely Cripple Arm," *Pittsburgh First*, September 20, 1924, box 6, folder 242, Urban League Records.
62. Epstein, "The Negro Migrant in Pittsburgh," 58; George Schuyler, "Views and Reviews," *Pittsburgh Courier*, January 2, 1926.
63. ULP health committee report, "Phifer Family," March 1920, box 2, folder 82, Urban League Records.
64. Harrison Gant, interview with Peter Gottlieb, August 23, 1974, Pittsburgh Oral History Project.
65. Carolyn Leonard Carson, "And the Results Showed Promise . . . : Physicians, Childbirth, and Southern Black Migrant Women, 1916–1930," in *African Americans in Pennsylvania, Shifting Historical Perspectives*, ed. Joe W. Trotter and Eric Ledell Smith (University Park: Pennsylvania Historical and Museum Commission and Pennsylvania State University Press, 1997), 331; also see ULP, "Pittsburgh's Second Annual Negro Health Education Campaign," 1919, box 6, folder 242, and program of health activities, 1929, box 2, folder 51, Urban League Records.
66. ULP press release, July 6, 1921, box 6, folder 244, Urban League Records.
67. Carson, "And the Results Showed Promise," 341–42; also see "Urban League of Pittsburgh Holds Better Baby Contest," *Pittsburgh Courier*, June 14, 1924.
68. Area hospitals sometimes even denied admission to black patients, notes historian Andrew Buni. When they did admit black patients, hospital staff treated them in segre-

gated sections of the facility. This, along with the absence of employment opportunities for black medical professionals, prompted Vann to draw up the charter for a black hospital. Throughout the interwar period Vann used his paper to campaign for the Livingstone Memorial Hospital and solicit donations. According to Buni, Vann's biographer, the project never garnered the level of support necessary to carry it through, even after the Federation of Jewish Philanthropies donated an old building in the Hill. Nevertheless, Vann continued supporting this idea until the end of his life (*Robert L. Vann of the* Pittsburgh Courier, 66).

69. Edmunds, *Daybreakers*, 59–61.
70. Edmunds, *Daybreakers*, 59–61.
71. Carson, "And the Results Showed Promise," 339.
72. ULP letter to area hospitals, 1925, box 2, folder 51, Urban League Records.
73. ULP health committee report, "Baker Family," 1920, box 2, folder 82, Urban League Records.
74. By 1925, black infant mortality had declined to 132 deaths per 1,000 births. Despite these gains, it remained disproportionately high into the thirties. For instance in 1934 the black infant mortality rate was 77.8%, compared to 51.5% for whites. See Carson, "And the Results Showed Promise," 335–42, 354, and ULP, 1925 annual report, box 6, folder 246, Urban League Records.
75. Carson, "And the Results Showed Promise," 335–42, 354, and ULP, 1925 annual report, box 6, folder 246, Urban League Records.
76. Edmunds, *Daybreakers*, 7.
77. Edmunds, *Daybreakers*, 36.
78. According to Edmunds, NUL public relations director Guichard Parris said that the ULP board forced Clark to resign because of his labor advocacy (*Daybreakers*, 66). The *Pittsburgh Courier* was silent on the subject of Clark's departure. Only a short, five-sentence blurb appeared noting that Clark was leaving Pittsburgh to direct the Urban League affiliate in St. Louis. Vann, who had previously served on the ULP Board and personally knew its members, may have thought it judicious to leave out the reasons for Clark's departure. See "Local Urban League Head to St. Louis," *Pittsburgh Courier*, July 17, 1926.
79. Priscilla Dowden-White, *Groping toward Democracy: African American Social Welfare Reform in St. Louis, 1910–1949* (Columbia: University of Missouri Press, 2011), 119.
80. Parris and Brooks, *Blacks in the City*, 248–49.
81. The league announced this new program in an open letter dated April 19, 1934. For Clark's role, see Parris and Brooks, *Blacks in the City*, 248–51.
82. Edmunds, *Daybreakers*, 66.
83. ULP "Special Problems of Negro Workers in Pittsburgh," April 6, 1929, box 5, folder 235, Urban League Records.
84. For changes in the ULP's leadership, see Arthur Edmunds, *Daybreakers*, 77, and "Local Urban League Heads Are Renamed," *Pittsburgh Courier*, January 24, 1931. At the ULP's annual meeting in 1931, Moss laid out the strategic approach the organization would adopt to reduce black unemployment, illness, and delinquency. He suggested the league had been too focused on curative measures and proposed redirecting its energies toward treating problems at their source. If young black women could be reached in their homes and neighborhoods before they turned to prostitution, Moss reasoned, there

would be no further need of a morals court worker. He therefore pulled Grace Lowndes from the morals court so she could devote her full attention to forming and enhancing neighborhood improvement groups in the Hill District and elsewhere. Moss likewise redirected the ULP's home and school visitor, who had previously worked with at-risk children, to "vocational guidance and student aid." The league even scaled back its work as a job placement agency to focus more on vocational training for semiskilled positions. Outside whatever strategic merit they may have had, these measures were at least partly driven by financial considerations. Like other organizations during the Depression the ULP experienced budget reductions—from $17,184 in 1930 to $15,071 in 1932—that forced it to cut back on its services ("Local Urban League Heads Are Renamed," *Pittsburgh Courier*, January 24, 1931; for budget information, see ULP annual reports for 1930 and 1932, box 6, folder 246, Urban League Records).

CHAPTER THREE

"The Weapons of Legal Defense"
THE PITTSBURGH NAACP AND THE CRIMINAL JUSTICE SYSTEM, 1924–1934

Joe Williams felt the sting of cold air on his face as he gazed at the bleak January landscape passing his view. Alongside about thirteen other black migrants, he sat huddled in the open bed of a government truck rumbling slowly southward on state route 18 toward the West Virginia border. The weather had been unmerciful. It was just warm enough that rain, instead of snow, pelted their heads and soaked their clothing, and the inclement conditions did little to improve the moods of the armed patrolmen watching them from the front of the truck. Williams wondered helplessly about his wife Mildred, who he had last seen in jail about fourteen hours earlier. Despite his earnest pleas, the nearby guard refused to say anything about her. Indeed, during the entire drive his captors divulged only that they planned to take the migrants to a place "from which they would never return."[1]

Just the previous night, on January 20, 1933, Williams had been a free man. He migrated from Georgia a few years earlier and settled in Midland, Pennsylvania, a steel town west of Pittsburgh where he and Mildred meant to build a life together. On Friday evening, after a week of taxing physical labor at the Crucible Steel plant, Joe took his wife to a house party in the nearby town of Industry, located in Beaver County.[2] Over fifty African Americans attended the gathering, and like Williams most of them had migrated north in search of economic opportunity. They danced, gambled, told stories, ate chitterlings, and drank moonshine, unaware that nearby outside a team of local police officers had assembled for a mass arrest. Sometime after 10:00 p.m., the officials suddenly kicked in the door. Wielding billy clubs and revolvers, they herded the frightened guests into a single room and demanded a payment of $2.50 from each. Police immediately released the few who could pay the fee and hauled off the rest, about thirty-nine men and seven women, to the Beaver County jail on charges of disorderly conduct.

The migrants spent that night sleeping on the concrete floor of the prison, and the next day police crammed the women into a Ford sedan and loaded the men in three large trucks that belonged to the Beaver County Bridge Department. Without giving their captives a word of information about where they intended to take them, six armed officers climbed onto the truck beds while department employees started the engines and began driving.

As the trucks crawled through southwestern Pennsylvania, the migrants —hungry, tired, and cold—could do little but sit on the hard floor and wait. Some did not even have a coat to insulate them from the chill, and none received food or water during the six-hour drive. Even passing bodily fluids proved a harrowing experience. As a migrant urinated by the side of the road during a stop, a nearby guard frightened him for sport by firing his revolver into the air. The captives endured these humiliations in silence, remembering the warning they received earlier that anyone who tried to escape would be shot.

Finally, after they had gone over a hundred miles, they drew to a stop at a spot a few miles from the West Virginia border. With guns in hand, the policemen ushered their captives from the trucks. Williams then listened as a guard told him and the other migrants that they had been paroled out of Pennsylvania, and that if they ever returned they would be sentenced to two years in the Beaver County workhouse. With that, the trucks drove off, leaving the migrants standing there in the January rain—stiff, wet, and bewildered.[3]

On Monday morning, January 23, Homer Brown received an urgent telegraph from Walter White, the head of the NAACP. Brown had served as president of the Pittsburgh branch of the NAACP (PNAACP) since 1925, and during that time he had made a name for himself as an effective courtroom litigator and civil rights advocate. White's telegraph informed Brown of the migrant abduction and charged him to look into the matter immediately.[4] Brown commenced at once with an investigation into a case that, unbeknownst to him, would drag on for the next eleven months. During that time, he harnessed the resources of the association and worked every legal angle he knew in the pursuit of justice for Williams and the other migrants.

The Pittsburgh branch's role in what came to be called the "shanghai case" reflected its larger mission in the community. While PNAACP staff contested discrimination and pursued civil rights in the Steel City, they also strengthened the Urban League's social safety net by providing effective legal advocacy that buffered the black community against a racially biased criminal justice system. When Pittsburgh police arrested African Americans for insisting on their right to swim in a public pool, or local patrolmen abused unarmed black men, or county detectives illegally deported unsuspecting migrants, the PNAACP intervened to provide legal representation and pursue justice.

This chapter contributes to a growing body of historical scholarship on crime and punishment in the United States by examining how the Jim Crow carceral regime operated in northern cities during the interwar period.[5] Black Pittsburghers long recognized the attributes of what we today associate with mass incarceration and discriminatory policing. They saw the heavy police presence on their streets, witnessed their neighbors getting arrested for unclear reasons, and heard about the disproportionate representation of blacks in the local prison. In Pittsburgh, the criminal justice system operated in concert with the city's other forms of racialized social control. The economic practices, political culture, and social norms of the Steel City effectively exploited people of color for their labor in the factories while confining them to the margins of public life by denying service to them in downtown restaurants, containing them in the inner city, and locking them up in local jails. Urban Leaguers worked to mitigate the material deprivation that arose from this social order, and the NAACP fought for justice through the courts of law and public opinion. Ultimately, while reformers succeeded admirably in bringing attention to unequal justice, the experience of working with ambivalent public officials convinced many of them to shift focus to the political arena.

Prostitutes, Juvenile Justice, and the Morals Court

The criminal justice system had a troubled history in the black community even before the Great Migration, and it touched the lives of adults and children. With schools that had little to offer and homes that were overcrowded, black teens took to the streets. Since the Hill District did not have a playground, they had few alternatives to poolrooms and saloons, and their mere presence in such places invited attention from local police, who could arrest them "on suspicion."[6] These factors help explain the high rates of juvenile delinquency among black Pittsburghers. As early as 1906 they accounted for 14.9 percent of the cases brought before the juvenile court, although at the time African Americans comprised only 3.5 percent of the city's population.[7]

Along with the other services it provided, the local Urban League mediated between black juveniles and white officials, particularly in connection with the morals court. In 1918 city leaders created this institution for juveniles detained for minor offenses and young women accused of prostitution. The ULP sent its representative, Grace Lowndes, to meet with black detainees, investigate the charges against them, and work with court officials to secure reduced sentences when warranted.[8] Lowndes and a few volunteers managed 1,010 cases in 1924 alone.[9] It was a challenging task, as Lowndes indicated in an undated letter to a colleague. She noted that since the fates of first offenders depended on her investigation of the case and subsequent recommendation to the court, "the worker some times [sic] finds herself in a queer position with client, if he or she happens not to be pleased with the final result."[10]

Two-thirds of the cases Lowndes managed in 1924 dealt with young black women between the ages of twenty and twenty-three.[11] Police arrested many of them for prostitution, which had become a lucrative business in Pittsburgh. A successful pimp at Union Station could usher a young migrant woman to one of over two hundred brothels in the Hill District. Social researcher Alex Pittler documented the presence of these establishments in the lower Hill in 1929 while conducting research for his master's thesis on changing residential patterns in the area brought about by the Great Migration. He looked disapprovingly on a community teeming with brothels, speakeasys, dope dens, gambling halls, and pool rooms—all of which he chronicled in a section titled "Vice."[12]

Pittler drew from the urban ecology research model pioneered at the University of Chicago to highlight the deleterious changes under way in the Hill as a result of the influx of southern migrants. Framed in this way, the migrants became uncivilized invaders—"people of lower economic and cultural levels," as he called them—who displaced the local population and caused the moral and physical degradation of the community.

> In the initial stage of invasions there is a resistance offered the invaders.... The occupants try to withhold further intrusion but do not suc-

ceed.... Dissatisfied with living among these people who bring with them their modes and manners of life and often produce socially disreputable conditions through carelessness and neglect, all the "select" residents are impelled to move from this neighborhood. In this way the whole district is transformed into a socially deteriorated area.[13]

Pittler implied that poverty, drug use, intraracial crime, and prostitution resulted from migrants' backward cultural customs and poor decision making. He did not mention that local foremen confined black men to the lowest-paying and most expendable positions in the mills, that area unions closed their doors to African Americans, that white employers denied secretarial and administrative jobs to black women, or that the poor black neighborhoods of the Hill lacked basic government services and institutional support. ULP workers recognized more readily than Pittler the impact of structural inequality on black living conditions. With black Pittsburghers shunned from much of the white community and denied assistance from the city and state governments, the league tried to provide a social safety net, meager though it was.[14]

There are gaps in the records on the league's role in the morals court, but surviving accounts indicate that Lowndes buffered young black women against both an unforgiving legal system and the worst elements of impoverished communities. While prostitution offered black women a source of income outside domestic work, it also increased their risk of contracting one or more of the sexually transmitted diseases overspreading the Hill. Sex workers could also face physical abuse from pimps displeased with their financial performance as well as from jealous or dissatisfied customers. If arrested, prostitutes who slipped through Lowndes's net spent time in the city penitentiary. According to one ULP report:

> Girls who perchance are brought before the law for one offense, upon investigation by our worker, are in many instances saved from Houses of Correction and Reform which might tend to have evil influences upon them, and are placed in other institutions which are an assistance to these unfortunate girls, and a medium through which they can make a new start in the right direction.[15]

A charming and gregarious woman, Lowndes ingratiated herself in circles across the social gamut, from white justices in the austere morals court to prostitutes and migrant women in the slums of the lower Hill. Her service in the morals court launched a twenty-six-year career with the ULP, from 1918 until her retirement in 1944, during which she facilitated its neighborhood unit program, headed its home economics (later civics) department, and edited its newsletter, the *Informer*.[16]

Lowndes's parents were freeborn blacks from the South Carolina Sea Islands who moved onto the mainland to teach slaves. They frequently switched between standard English and the Gullah dialect common on the Sea Islands, and the habit rubbed off on their daughter. In the early twentieth century Lowndes joined thousands of African Americans in the northward migration. She initially settled in Pittsburgh and worked as a dressmaker, but wishing to start her own business, she enrolled in a costume design school in New York City. She arrived in the Big Apple with soaring hopes for the future, but when administrators saw she was an African American they told her that her position at the school and room at the YWCA was no longer available. Lowndes wept on the street corner as she grappled with the reality that Jim Crow followed her to the North, but she soon dried her tears and strode back in the school insisting upon her rights. The administrators backed down, and when Lowndes returned to Pittsburgh sometime later, she did so with a degree in hand.[17]

Lowndes's dressmaking shop in the Hill District was successful, and she climbed into elite society within the African American community. She socialized with other members of the black middle class at her home in the upper Hill (Schenley Heights), which overlooked the lower Hill where many migrants lived. Yet she never forgot that she herself was a migrant, and in dealing with prostitutes and other delinquents at the morals court she demonstrated sensitivity and care.[18] A lifelong advocate of contraception, she expressed concern about young women who had to "face 'the miracle of life' without the proper preparation or protection."[19]

Lowndes worked daily with Judge Tensard DeWolf in the morals court, and like the welfare workers in the city's mills she eased the effects of racial inequality for poor blacks. When he stepped down from the bench in 1924, DeWolf informed Clark that "Miss Lowndes has been invaluable in the assistance given. It is no exaggeration to say that it would have been impossible for me to have handled your people and their problems the way I desired without such cooperation."[20]

"At the Point of a Gun": Racial Profiling in Western Pennsylvania

Police targeted black adults even more vigorously than juveniles. A 1918 study revealed that white police patrolling black neighborhoods had wide discretionary powers. The vast majority of black Pittsburghers arrested between 1914 and 1917 were charged with petty offenses such as disorderly conduct, suspicious behavior, drunkenness, running or visiting gambling houses, prostitution, and vagrancy.[21] In one case, following the murder of a Jewish merchant in the Hill District on November 27, 1916, police swept through the area and indiscriminately arrested two hundred black men on charges of vagrancy.[22]

African Americans in western Pennsylvania risked widespread white backlash if they stood up to local police. In August 1923 an intoxicated migrant in the Johnstown district, east of Pittsburgh, shot a patrolman who had attempted to arrest him. Later that night a company of police officers and county detectives tracked down the man at a shed, where he had barricaded himself, and in the ensuing gunfight he killed three of them before they fatally shot him. Whites reacted almost immediately when they heard about the incident. Members of the local Ku Klux Klan burned crosses throughout the district, and Johnstown mayor Joseph Cauffiel ordered the deportation of all African Americans and Mexicans who lived in the district for less than seven years, which amounted to more than three thousand people.[23] Several hundred took heed and left soon afterward, but most remained, prompting the mayor to warn that "if the rest of them don't get out soon I will arm the police and send them . . . to walk the Negroes out of town at the point of a gun." Johnstown's chief of police and other local officials supported Cauffiel in this initiative.[24]

He encountered resistance soon after, however, when James Weldon Johnson of the NAACP pressured Pennsylvania governor Gifford Pinchot to intervene. With a Republican primary election looming, Cauffiel may have hoped to gain votes with his stance against the Johnstown migrant community. In any case, he never carried out his decree, and the public condemnation he received from Pinchot and the NAACP damaged his bid for reelection: he came in fourth.[25]

Discriminatory policing nevertheless persisted throughout the region. By 1926, African Americans made up a third of the inmates at the Western Penitentiary (outside Pittsburgh) while constituting only about 8 percent of the

Steel City's total population.[26] In his study of that prison, Urban League researcher Ira Reid drew correlations between the high incarceration rates of African Americans and their limited access to education and gainful employment. Most of the black inmates he surveyed had under four years of education and more than a quarter could not read or write.[27]

The ULP provided legal assistance to migrants during their parole hearings and helped them rejoin society upon release. "I want you to know, you are not helping a criminal in helping me," Joseph McGill wrote to Clark in April 1924, upon learning the ULP had reviewed his case and agreed to furnish a lawyer to represent him before the pardon board. McGill served eleven years at Western Penitentiary after a jury convicted him of involuntary manslaughter. With no friends or family for support, he turned to the league. Another inmate, George Yervis, wrote Clark a month later requesting he send someone to serve as a sponsor at his parole hearing, which he said was "indispensable in order that I may be liberated from here at the expiration of my minimum sentence."[28] Around the same time Clark persuaded his friend Homer Brown, then a young lawyer who had just taken over the PNAACP, to provide free legal representation for a migrant prisoner named Peter Brooks.[29]

The PNAACP's Formative Years

Brown inherited an organization in shambles. The PNAACP was initially received with great enthusiasm by the public when it formed in 1915 to protest the screening of *Birth of a Nation* and to lobby for antilynching legislation, but the affiliate soon bogged down in internal disputes and lost the confidence of Pittsburgh's black community. Over the next six years it barely managed to stay in existence. When the Reverend J. C. Austin took over as its president in 1921, he bemoaned that "this organization comes into my hands just about as Christ found Lazarus after the fourth day of his death, not only dead, but buried."[30] Austin could not resurrect the affiliate, and in 1924 NAACP field secretary William Pickens declared it "about as dead as can be."[31] The turning point did not come until later that year when Reverend Augustus Jones helped reorganize the branch and placed Homer Brown and Daisy Lampkin in charge.

Like many reformers in the Steel City, Brown was not a native Pittsburgher. He was born in Huntington, West Virginia, in 1896 and attended college at Virginia Union from about 1914 until he graduated in 1918. Following a brief stint in the U.S. Army, in 1921 Brown enrolled at the University of Pittsburgh Law School. Once he earned his law degree in 1923, he established a legal practice with his old classmate, Richard F. Jones, and shortly afterward accepted leadership of the PNAACP.[32]

Daisy Lampkin was also an outsider. Born in Washington, DC, around 1884, she committed herself at an early age to the struggle for racial justice and gender equality. After moving to Pittsburgh in 1909, she participated in the women's suffrage movement while contributing to local civil rights organizations. Her skill at fundraising soon became apparent when she won a cash award for selling the most subscriptions to the *Courier*, which she used to buy stock in the company. With her share of the company increasing, in 1929 Robert L. Vann made her the vice president of the *Pittsburgh Courier*—a post she held until her death in 1965. In the late twenties and early thirties, Lampkin also used her fundraising prowess to aid the NAACP, first for the Pittsburgh branch and later as regional field secretary for the national office. She continued climbing the ranks of the association in the ensuing years. In 1935 the NAACP promoted her to national field secretary, and twelve years later she became the first woman to serve on the association's board of directors.[33]

Working together, Brown and Lampkin helped put the PNAACP on sound financial footing. A year after they took over, the organization could support the national branch's legal battles while directing several of its own projects in the Steel City. In 1930 it raised $1,000 toward the NAACP's $200,000 fundraising drive before any other branch in the country. Its 1,149 members ultimately gave more than twice that amount before the drive ended—far exceeding the monetary contribution of the branch in Philadelphia, a city with a black population four times the size of Pittsburgh's.[34]

National officers took note of this as well, and perhaps consequently the NAACP held its twenty-second annual convention in Pittsburgh from late June to early July 1931. The slate of speakers featured several of the organization's highest officers, including Robert Bagnell, Joel Spingarn, and William Pickens as well as founding members like W. E. B. Du Bois and Mary White Ovington. The convention also included talks by an eclectic mix of outside dignitaries ranging from Norman Thomas, the leader of the U.S. Socialist Party, to Thomas Dunn, president of the Chamber of Commerce. Clarence Darrow, the famous civil rights lawyer who provided the legal defense for Dr. Ossian Sweet in 1925, also lent his voice to the occasion. Before large audiences that sometimes exceeded five thousand people, the speakers highlighted the prevalence of racial discrimination across the United States and

Homer Brown (seated in the center), ca. 1945.
Historic Pittsburgh Image Collection, 1996.69.146,
University of Pittsburgh Archives Service Center.

Daisy Lampkin (left) in the *Pittsburgh Courier* office, December 1945.
Teenie Harris Archive, Carnegie Museum of Art, Pittsburgh.

proposed ideas to combat the problem, which occasionally contradicted each other. Du Bois had become convinced that civil rights alone would not be enough to relieve the black masses from the crushing weight of discrimination and poverty, and in his speech before the convention he advocated for a kind of economic self-segregation in which urban blacks shop exclusively at black-owned stores and cooperatively buy and produce goods. Bagnall was among the speakers who rejected this proposal. "Race segregation must be destroyed or the Negro is doomed. . . . It is folly to think he can develop a self-sufficient little world within the greater world."[35]

Brown and Lampkin had reason to look beyond these disputes and consider with satisfaction how far their organization had come since they had taken over at the end of 1924. The convention's presence in Pittsburgh reflected the growing strength and reputation of the local branch. By the early thirties, it had developed the talent and institutional resources necessary to contest racial segregation at public pools, police assaults of unarmed black men, and extralegal deportations.

The Highland Park Pool

A month after the NAACP convention, on August 5, 1931, several black teenagers and young men went to Pittsburgh's Highland Park public pool to escape the summer heat. Eicel Norwood and his friends imagined an afternoon of swimming and fun, but they had barely dipped their toes in the water before they found themselves surrounded and outnumbered by a large group of hostile Italians who preferred to keep the pool "whites only." Norwood and his friends had no choice but to flee when the Italians attacked, and a few harrowing moments later they stood panting outside the pool gates: wet, humiliated, and bruised. Norwood bore the brunt of the assault and required medical attention. The next day, four black men approached the pool and began protesting the incident. The pool's manager promptly called the police to remove them, and when authorities arrived, they watched as a gang of whites stormed out of the pool and attacked the protesters. After giving the mob time to batter its victims, the police arrested all four black men on charges of disorderly conduct and inciting a riot.[36]

The situation escalated as the month progressed. Local blacks refused to surrender their right to use the pool, and the Italians proved equally determined to keep them out. One of the most dramatic events occurred on August 20, when a dozen African Americans approached the pool and saw a large group of whites patrolling the outer perimeter with sticks and rocks in hand, along with another carful in the parking lot armed with shotguns. The ensuing standoff ended like the previous altercations, with the arrest of all the African Americans involved.[37]

PNAACP staff devoted their full attention to defending the arrested protesters and opening the pool to blacks. Brown first took the matter to the director of public safety, who supervised the police force. However, when the director refused to provide police protection for black swimmers or even to curtail the discriminatory arrests, Brown and his colleagues organized a mass protest meeting. On August 10 thousands of black Pittsburghers gathered at the Bethesda Presbyterian Church to hear speeches by Brown, Lampkin, Reverend J. F. Jenkins, and other black leaders, who condemned segregation at the pool and circulated a petition calling for the removal of the police officers and pool officials who failed to perform their duty.[38] With local elections just a few months away, PNAACP officials used the meeting to consolidate black voting power and pressure local incumbents to take action. Like Robert L. Vann would do in 1932, Brown weighed his strategic options and reasoned that political pressure offered the best hope for redress, even if slim. "Our political leaders here have been . . . slow to assist us," Brown complained in a letter to Roy Wilkins, then assistant NAACP secretary, "[and] have in some instances flatly refused."[39]

Brown's letter reflected a sense of political powerlessness shared by many black Pittsburghers in the years leading up to the Democratic Party's takeover of the Steel City during the New Deal period. Before Vann's political campaign for Roosevelt rallied black voters and alarmed the GOP, local Republicans had little political incentive to pursue racial justice. In 1931 white intransigence was too strong and black political unity and voting strength too limited for politicians to take meaningful stands against discrimination. Though Brown could not desegregate the pool, he did successfully defend the black swimmers arrested for trying to use it. Throughout the month of August, as police arrested more would-be black swimmers, Brown rushed to their aid. Standing before Magistrate Charles Papale at the Number 6 Police Station, the gifted attorney secured the release of nine African Americans on August 7, three more on August 12, and another sixteen on August 20.[40]

The Highland Park pool remained segregated for another two decades, but the efforts of the PNAACP laid the groundwork for future protest and litigation work that would eventually democratize it. In 1948 the ULP and progressive whites led a protest march outside the pool, and in response, over

The Weapons of Legal Defense

The Highland Park pool in one of the first photographs of it after it was desegregated in 1952, taken by Teenie Harris sometime between 1952 and 1955.
Teenie Harris Archive, Carnegie Museum of Art, Pittsburgh.

600 local white residents staged an aggressive counterdemonstration—compelling concerned local authorities to dispatch 160 police officers to keep the peace. Four years later, in 1952, a team of black lawyers filed a lawsuit against the City of Pittsburgh for failing to protect the rights of black swimmers, and the court ruled in favor of the black plaintiffs and ordered the city to desegregate the pool.[41]

Racial Violence and Police Brutality

Just a few years after the Highland Park incident, in September 1934 a daylong race riot between African Americans and Italians on Larimer Avenue resulted in six serious injuries and over eighteen arrests. The combatants fought with guns, clubs, razor blades, and ice picks, and by the time police restored order several people had been shot while others suffered serious head injuries. In both the Highland Park and Larimer Avenue cases, police officers disproportionately targeted African American participants. Although Italians made up 90 percent of the Second Precinct, where the riot occurred, two-thirds of the people arrested in connection with the incident were black.[42] Two of the detainees, Nat Dickerson and Henry Eason, claimed police threatened "to blow their brains out" for their role in the riot.[43]

Black Pittsburghers had long recognized that the criminal justice system targeted them over other groups for the workhouse and local prisons. But they also faced physical danger from Pittsburgh policemen. On at least two occasions in 1933, local officers assaulted unarmed black men. Following a domestic dispute on July 13, police arrested both John Smith and his wife, Viola Smith. George Lewis, a lodger living with the Smiths, demanded an explanation for the arrest of Viola, who he believed did nothing wrong. But the officers, growing increasingly irritated with their questioner, refused to reply. When Lewis persisted in his objections, one of the patrolmen suddenly bludgeoned him so hard that he crumpled to the ground and lay stunned. With Lewis prostrate before them, the officers first handcuffed him and then began beating him. By the time they tired from the exertion, nearby witnesses said Lewis looked like a "mass of blood." The victim spent that night in the hospital receiving treatment for his wounds. The next day, police arrested him for "interfering with the officers" and imposed a $25 fine. Since Lewis could not pay the fee, authorities sent him to the workhouse.[44]

In most instances, northern African Americans like Lewis could not expect justice from the criminal justice system. Aside from overworked public defenders, their best hope for redress came from local black reformers who might take up their case. Just two months before the assault on Lewis, William Alexander lost control of his vehicle while driving in Pittsburgh, and he had the bad luck of slamming into a patrol wagon. Alexander immediately tried to explain what happened to the vehicle's occupant, officer Edward Sweeny. Without pausing to listen, Sweeny knocked him to the ground and placed him under arrest. When Homer Brown and his PNAACP colleague, attorney Joseph Givens, learned the details of the arrest they decided to prosecute Sweeny for aggravated assault and battery. The evidence they placed before the jury convinced it of Sweeny's guilt, and consequently the court suspended him from duty for six months and forced him to pay for both the court costs and the repairs to Alexander's car. Brown and Givens must have been pleased. It was the sixth case the PNAACP had won in the last ten months. But if Brown's faith in the efficacy of litigation work reached a high in June 1933, it received a sobering check by November, when his legal prowess proved no match for white intransigence.⁴⁵

The Limits of Litigation: The "Shanghai Case"

On the Monday morning of January 23, 1933, Walter White opened a copy of the *New York Herald-Tribune* and read a story captioned "Fifty Negroes Expelled by Pennsylvania Town." The column described in detail the abduction of dozens of migrants and their subsequent deportation to the West Virginia border. White immediately telegraphed Brown, and with that, the NAACP's involvement in the matter began.

The surviving records related to this case demonstrate the capacities for compassion and bigotry among whites in interwar northern communities, the efficacy and limitations of the PNAACP, and the difficulties of taking on a local law enforcement community determined to protect itself from outside investigation. Over the course of 1933, the association gathered key information, attracted press attention to the case, lobbied the governor and state attorney general to act, and helped build public pressure on Beaver County officials to prosecute those responsible for the deportation. When the case effectively closed in November, Brown and his colleagues felt more certain than ever that black America's best chance for real justice lay in its acquiring political power.

By the time Brown received White's telegraph on Monday morning, the deported migrants, about forty-six total, had scattered in multiple directions. With assistance from Joseph Givens, Brown began the difficult task of piecing together the details of the incident and determining the whereabouts of the victims. In addition to ensuring that they got home safely, he needed to collect their testimony in order to begin building a case against their captors. Through several long-distance phone calls, he learned that after the bridge department trucks drove off Saturday evening, about half the migrants headed for Morgantown, West Virginia, while the others traveled a few miles north to Waynesburg, a coal town close to the border.⁴⁶

The haggard and wet migrants must have seemed a pitiable sight in Waynesburg, for local officials immediately gave them shelter, food, and beds in the town jail. On Sunday morning, Judge A. H. Sayers paid for the migrant women to take a bus north to the nearby town of Washington, a stopover on the route back to Beaver County, while the men walked there. Sayers notified Washington authorities of the migrants' situation ahead of their arrival, and he also wrote a letter to Governor Gifford Pinchot urging him to take action on what he saw as a grievous injustice committed in his district. In Washington, Sheriff Frank Krepps provided food and lodging for the men in the town jail, and a local woman, Catherine Hall, lodged the women at her house. By the next morning, Krepps had secured enough money to pay for all of them to take a bus back to Beaver County.[47] Joe Williams and his wife, Mildred, finally returned to their home in Midland, three days after their ordeal began.

On Tuesday, Brown and Givens drove to Midland and Industry to gather testimony from the first group of migrants that had returned home. (Those who initially headed to West Virginia eventually turned around and made it back to Beaver County as well, but not until midweek.) The NAACP lawyers spent several hours speaking with Williams and the other deportees before traveling to the county capital of Beaver to meet with the local district attorney.[48] At that time, neither they nor the migrants knew how deep the deportation conspiracy went.

The compassion that white officials in southwestern Pennsylvania displayed in their dealings with the migrants contrasted sharply with the unremorseful obstinance of their colleagues in Beaver County. Beaver district attorney Anthony De Castrique informed Brown and Givens that he had looked into the matter and found no indication of wrongdoing. Brown felt perplexed. The abductees' testimony offered compelling evidence that county officials acted outside normal legal parameters, but De Castrique refused to submit the case before a grand jury. Following the meeting, Brown and Givens drove over an hour back to Pittsburgh. They had had a busy day, and Brown still had more work to do. After commutes to and from Beaver County, interviews with migrants in two different towns, and a frustrating meeting with a local DA, he sat in bed as he wrote a detailed summary of his findings to send to Walter White.[49] Brown's report served as the most reliable, comprehensive account of the incident for the next six months, and both the NAACP's public relations team and *Courier* staff drew from it in subsequent stories about the abduction.[50]

Over the next few weeks, the *Pittsburgh Press*, *Waynesburg Messenger*, and *Pittsburgh Courier* uniformly expressed outrage over the treatment of the migrants. On January 28, for instance, the *Courier* called attention to the incident in a front-page headline that read "Police 'Shanghai' 50 . . . Urge

Governor to Probe Abuse."⁵¹ Meanwhile, White arranged a meeting with Governor Gifford Pinchot so that Brown could lay the facts before him. Pinchot agreed to meet Brown, along with a small group of state NAACP representatives, on February 1.⁵²

At White's request, *Courier* editor Robert L. Vann accompanied Brown to the meeting. Over the past decade, Vann had turned his newspaper into a powerful tool of racial advocacy and political mobilization, and White understood that the editor's presence at the meeting added considerable weight to Brown's message. The delegation may have persuaded Pinchot to take substantive action; soon after the meeting, the governor ordered Pennsylvania attorney general William Schnader to launch a special investigation into the deportation case.⁵³

Seeking to build on this momentum, Brown met with Schnader a few weeks later to discuss his plans for the investigation. The attorney general offered a sobering assessment of the situation. Schnader could not assume any prosecutorial powers in this case unless the presiding judge of Beaver County, Frank E. Reader, requested a special investigation from the state attorney general. Without that request, Schnader could investigate but not prosecute the officials in question. Brown recognized immediately the fragile state of affairs. "Unless this action is taken by a presiding Judge," he confided to White, "an investigation would be futile."⁵⁴

Schnader wrote to Judge Reader after meeting Brown and asked him to request a special investigator. Perhaps hoping the matter would quiet down over time, Reader waited three weeks before denying Schnader's request. Since De Castrique expressed willingness to investigate the alleged deportation, Reader said he did not see a need to request a special investigator. Seeming to accept this logic and its ominous implications with perfect equanimity, Schnader reassured Walter White that he would appoint a special deputy attorney general to assist De Castrique in his investigation.⁵⁵ The news frustrated Brown. He met De Castrique just a month and a half earlier and knew the DA would not prosecute his colleagues in the Beaver County law enforcement community. Even so, Brown resolved to exhaust every possible option. "I don't want to stop until we go to the limit," he declared to White.⁵⁶

Schnader subsequently assigned attorney John D. Meyer of Pittsburgh to investigate the deportation case, but it took Meyer months to conduct his investigation, and he refused to communicate his progress to the PNAACP, whose members had so eagerly pursued justice for the deportees.⁵⁷ As May, June, and July passed with almost no word about the case, the story gradually fell off the public radar. Brown could do little but wait for Meyer to conclude his investigation, so he and the PNAACP worked on other cases.

Then, in late August, having reviewed the evidence and testimony Meyer gathered, Schnader submitted to Governor Pinchot a blistering report that condemned the actions of a number of Beaver County officials involved in the deportation. Almost overnight, the story returned to the spotlight. In detailing the circumstances of the arrest and deportation, Schnader's report revealed that, along with a host of police constables and state troopers, several of Beaver County's leading officials assisted with the deportation, including the chief of Beaver County detectives, a justice of the peace, the county commissioner, and the deputy warden of the Beaver County jail.[58] The complicity of so many officials may help explain why De Castrique had refused to act. Like Beaver County's presiding judge, who months earlier had declined to request a special investigation, De Castrique frequently worked with the officials involved in the deportation and may have felt bound to protect them out of professional courtesy.

Even if the deportation had not occurred, the circumstances surrounding the mass arrest merited investigation. The detective who obtained the warrant to search the home of Virginia Heath, where the party occurred, claimed he did so because Heath's neighbors complained about her. But when pressed for names, he could not recall any of the complainants. Additionally, the officers who arrested the migrants on charges of disorderly conduct later admitted that when they entered Heath's house the large majority of guests were simply talking and laughing. The testimony related to the deportation itself seemed equally troubling. Beaver County commissioner Howard Hunter claimed he organized the deportation to avoid the expense of housing the migrants in jail. For his part, the deputy warden of the Beaver County jail, Hamilton Brown, said he offered a choice to the prisoners: if they agreed to leave Pennsylvania, he would release them from prison. Although the deputy warden claimed the deportees agreed to these terms, when questioned all forty-six of them denied having done so. Schnader concluded his report with the assertion that "those responsible for the deportation are, in my opinion, chargeable with the common law offence of kidnapping, and a charge of conspiracy to do an unlawful act could also be sustained."[59]

In the weeks following the report, local papers condemned the deportation and called for the prosecution of the officials involved, but De Castrique refused to act.[60] By early September even Governor Pinchot grew frustrated. In a scathing letter to De Castrique, he asked "whether you are going to continue to close your eyes to your plain duty or whether you are going to submit the case immediately to a Grand Jury for proper action?"[61]

De Castrique opted for the former. The DA correctly calculated that if he held out long enough the prosecution fervor would fade away. Frustrated, Brown and Walter White urged the governor to take further action, but in reply Pinchot explained what they already knew. Without a written request from the presiding judge of Beaver County, the attorney general could not supersede the DA. "I shall again call the matter to the attention of Mr. de Castrique," Pinchot promised, "but that is the extent of my ability to help." And with that, the governor absolved himself of any further responsibility.[62]

Making matters worse as far as the PNAACP was concerned, in an interview with the *Pittsburgh Press*, Vann announced his plans to take over the prosecution of the Beaver County officials. "We expect no co-operation from the Beaver County District Attorney or from anyone else there," Vann told the reporter. Since the victims came from states outside Pennsylvania, Vann maintained that the case fell under federal jurisdiction, "and that is where we will take it."[63]

Vann's promises of unilateral action upset Brown. Strategically, Brown worried that this would provide an additional excuse for Pinchot and Schnader to withdraw from the case. Personally, Brown felt that Vann had discredited the local association. Ever mindful of promoting the PNAACP, and by extension himself, he informed Walter White that "Mr. Vann did not consult with me about this article and it certainly gives the people here the idea that we are laying down on the job." As head of the national branch, White moved carefully when dealing with internal disputes among activists in other cities. "In reply to your personal letter," he wrote Brown, "I really don't know what to advise. Do you not know Vann well enough to go to him frankly and discuss this situation with him?"[64]

Indeed, Brown and Vann did not often collaborate, which seems strange considering their commonalities. Both men grew up in the upper South—Vann in Ahoskie, North Carolina, Brown in Huntington, West Virginia—and went to college at Virginia Union as well as law school at the University of Pittsburgh. In Pittsburgh, they likewise divided their efforts between their legal practices and racial advocacy.

When they shared a long train ride to Harrisburg back in late January, Brown likely discussed with Vann the details of his investigation in order to prepare him for their upcoming meeting with Pinchot. By the time Vann sat down for an interview with a reporter in September, he knew how much effort Brown had put into the case. Whether motivated by personal ambition or genuine concern for the abductees, Vann lacked the sensitivity to include Brown in his plans. Brown was not the only person to express frustration over Vann's tendency to act unilaterally—and occasionally impulsively. Three years later, George Schuyler of the *Courier* commented on "his impatience at certain times and his Indian flares of anger that sometimes cause him to fly off the handle and take drastic action that he probably later regrets."[65] In any case, Vann briefly followed up on his pledge to pursue federal action on the abduction case, but his efforts yielded no results and he soon turned his attention to his new position in Washington, DC, as special assistant to the attorney general.[66]

Adding to Brown's frustration, by October the PNAACP had spent a considerable portion of its annual budget on a fight that increasingly seemed unwinnable. In January, February, and March the branch paid $126.70 for three trips to Beaver County, two trips to Harrisburg, and three long-distance telephone calls. Although the national office contributed $48 against the balance, Brown informed White that "we do not have sufficient funds in the treasury . . . to warrant any further expenses in this Beaver County matter." Like reformers in the ULP, Brown and his colleagues confronted severe financial constraints that forced them to make difficult choices about resource allocation. In the summer of 1933, racial altercations broke out again at the Highland Park pool, and the PNAACP posted bond for the black defendants and provided legal representation. It also launched successful court cases against segregation at a local school and the assault of a black man by a Pittsburgh police officer. While Brown felt his branch could not spend any more money on the case, he did not want to give up on it, either. "I want to see that we do everything possible in this Beaver County matter," he informed White in October.[67]

At the national office's expense, Brown proposed one final effort to bring the migrants' captors to justice. He would draft a petition demanding Judge Reader request a special prosecutor and then travel to Harrisburg to persuade attorney general Schnader to sign it. "I can not see how Schnader can refuse to join in our petition," Brown wrote, "if he is at all sincere as he says he is willing to cooperate."[68] Unfortunately, Brown overestimated Schnader's commitment to the case. The attorney general declined to join the petition, which left it without the key signature Brown desired. Judge Reader probably would not have changed his position either way, but without Schnader's support the effort seemed futile. Brown nevertheless submitted the petition, and as he expected Reader ignored it. At this point Brown felt he had exhausted every legal means available to seek justice for the deportees.[69] The officials in Beaver County colluded in committing a crime and then followed a uniform policy of mutual protection against outside agitators.

As 1933 slipped into 1934, Pinchot turned his attention to his reelection bid, Brown and the PNAACP moved on to other issues, and the public gradually forgot about the deportation story. Ultimately, only one person connected with the event faced formal charges: Virginia Heath, who hosted the party. After she pled guilty to possession of alcohol, the county court sentenced her to sixty days in prison and imposed a fine of $100.

The criminal justice system failed to hold its agents accountable for the unlawful arrest and deportation of forty-six American citizens. As for the money police collected at the party, no record was found of its having been deposited either with the Beaver County Jail or the courthouse. It seems possible that the officers simply kept if for themselves.[70] Worse still, when the migrants returned to their homes in Beaver County they discovered their employers had replaced them with white workers—which might have motivated the abductions in the first place. More than a few locals in Midland and Industry saw the migrants as outsiders who took precious jobs from whites during a time of depression.

For Brown, the abduction case revealed the futility of seeking judicial solutions without political leverage. "This is a case which shows that political solidarity and power through the ballot is one of the most effective weapons in the matter of legal defense," he explained.[71] Brown used the established legal channels, and they failed to produce justice. The bitter experience contributed to a growing conviction among black reformers that African Americans had to use their collective votes to gain greater representation in seats of power and force change from within. The *Pittsburgh Courier*'s campaign for Franklin Roosevelt, which occurred just a few months before the Industry abductions, illustrates this development.

NOTES

1. The most reliable information on this case comes from Homer Brown's initial report, dated January 24, 1933, and from state attorney general William Schnader's report, dated August 24, 1933. Both reports can be found in the NAACP Branch Records, pt. 1: G-190, Library of Congress.

2. Census information on Joe Williams reveals that he and Mildred separated sometime later in the 1930s. By 1940, he was married to a woman named Dora and had three children.
3. See Homer Brown, report, January 24, 1933, and William Schnader, report, August 24, 1933, NAACP Branch Records.
4. See "Fifty Negroes Expelled by Pennsylvania Town," January 23, 1933, *New York Herald-Tribune*; Walter White to Homer Brown, January 23, 1933, NAACP Branch Records.
5. For examples of recent studies examining the carceral state, see Rebecca M. McLennan, *The Crisis of Imprisonment: Protest, Politics, and the Making of the American Penal State, 1776–1941* (Cambridge: Cambridge University Press, 2008), Kali N. Gross, *Colored Amazons: Crime, Violence, and Black Women in the City of Brotherly Love, 1880–1910* (Durham, NC: Duke University Press, 2006), Cheryl D. Hicks, *Talk with You like a Woman: African American Women, Justice, and Reform in New York, 1890–1935* (Chapel Hill: University of North Carolina Press, 2010), David M. Oshinsky, *Capital Punishment on Trial: Furman v. Georgia and the Death Penalty in Modern America* (Lawrence: University Press of Kansas, 2010), Robert Perkinson, *Texas Tough: The Rise of America's Prison Empire* (New York: Metropolitan Books, 2010), Khalil Gibran Muhammad, *The Condemnation of Blackness: Race, Crime, and the Making of Modern Urban America* (Cambridge, MA: Harvard University Press, 2010), Heather Ann Thompson, "Why Mass Incarceration Matters: Rethinking Crisis, Decline, and Transformation in Postwar American History," *Journal of American History* 97, no. 3 (2010): 703–34, Talitha L. LeFlouria, *Chained in Silence: Black Women and Convict Labor in the New South* (Chapel Hill: University of North Carolina Press, 2015), and Jeffrey S. Adler, "Less Crime, More Punishment: Violence, Race, and Criminal Justice in Early Twentieth-Century America," *Journal of American History* 102, no. 1 (2015): 34–46. Also see Douglas A. Blackmon, *Slavery by Another Name: The Reenslavement of Black People in America from the Civil War to World War II* (New York: Doubleday, 2008), Michelle Alexander, *The New Jim Crow: Mass Incarceration in the Age of Colorblindness* (New York: New Press, 2010), and Bryan Stevenson, *Just Mercy: A Story of Justice and Redemption* (New York: Spiegel and Grau, 2014).
6. Andrew Buni, *Robert L. Vann of the* Pittsburgh Courier: *Politics and Black Journalism* (Pittsburgh: University of Pittsburgh Press, 1974), 29; Arthur J. Edmunds, *Daybreakers: The Story of the Urban League of Pittsburgh, the First Sixty-Five Years* (Pittsburgh: Urban League of Pittsburgh, 1999), 25.
7. Buni, *Robert L. Vann of the* Pittsburgh Courier, 29.
8. Responsibility of court worker, March 3, 1926, box 2, folder 52, Urban League Records, University of Pittsburgh Archives Service Center.
9. John T. Clark, draft of speech, "Annual Report of the Work of the Urban League of Pittsburgh for 1924," ca. January 1925, box 6, folder 246, Urban League Records.
10. Grace Lowndes to "Mr. Stanton," ca. 1924, box 2, folder 52, Urban League Records. The most likely recipient of this letter was William H. Stanton, who served as a board member of the ULP at the time.
11. John T. Clark, draft of speech, "Annual Report of the Work of the Urban League of Pittsburgh for 1924," ca. January 1925, box 6, folder 246, Urban League Records.
12. Social researcher Alex Pittler identified 169 brothels and 44 assignation (or "call")

houses in the Hill. Assignation houses, according to Pittler, required patrons to make an appointment in advance. I group them together here ("The Hill District of Pittsburgh—A Study in Succession" [master's thesis, University of Pittsburgh, 1930], 48–51).
13. Pittler, "The Hill District of Pittsburgh," 5.
14. In his report for 1924, Clark complained that "we come face to face daily with the serious lack of institutional facilities for Negroes or available to Negroes." These shortcomings hindered the ULP's efforts in "building Negro citizenship." Clark called for more nurseries for black infants, convalescent homes for invalids, a government-subsidized home loan corporation to help African Americans keep up with their payments and avoid foreclosure, homeless shelters, and social service agencies (draft of annual report for 1924, ca. January 1925, box 6, folder 246, Urban League Records).
15. ULP historical sketch, ca. 1922, box 6, folder 244, Urban League Records.
16. Edmunds, *Daybreakers*, 36–42 and 67.
17. Edmunds, *Daybreakers*, 38.
18. Edmunds, *Daybreakers*, 38.
19. Grace Lowndes to "Mr. Stanton," ca. 1926, box 2, folder 52, Urban League Records.
20. Quoted in Edmunds, *Daybreakers*, 38. Lowndes held DeWolf in similar regard, commenting in a letter to him upon his departure that he was the "soul of the Morals Court" (ca. 1924, box 2, folder 52, Urban League Records). In the same box and folder see also "Duties of the Morals Court Worker," ca. 1922.
21. According to Abraham Epstein, between 1914 and 1917 police arrested a total of 4,679 African Americans for petty offenses and 187 for major offenses including larceny, assault, homicide, and rape ("The Negro Migrant in Pittsburgh," [senior thesis, University of Pittsburgh, 1917], 48).
22. Buni, *Robert L. Vann of the* Pittsburgh Courier, 74.
23. "Johnstown's Mayor's Deportation Order Defeated," *Crisis*, November 1923. For the estimate of Johnstown's black population, see Richard B. Sherman, "Johnstown v. the Negro: Southern Migrants and the Exodus of 1923," *Pennsylvania History: A Journal of Mid-Atlantic Studies* 30, no. 4 (1963): 454–64.
24. "Johnstown's Mayor's Deportation Order Defeated," *Crisis*, November 1923; telegram from Walter White to Frank R. Steward, September 19, 1923, NAACP Branch Records.
25. Sherman, "Johnstown v. the Negro," 460–62.
26. About 97 percent of the black inmates were southern migrants. See Ira Reid, "A Study of 200 Negro Prisoners in the Western Penitentiary of Pennsylvania," 1927, box 10, folder 456, Urban League Records.
27. Reid, "A Study of 200 Negro Prisoners in the Western Penitentiary of Pennsylvania," 1927, box 10, folder 456, Urban League Records.
28. Joseph McGill to John T. Clark, April 13, 1924, and George Yervis to John T. Clark, May 4, 1924, box 2, folder 45, Urban League Records.
29. John T. Clark to Lucy D. Iams, April 1, 1924, box 2, folder 45, Urban League Records. In February 1920, Clark wrote to Magistrate John A. Fugussi to request the release of an inmate held for vagrancy, promising that he would "assume the responsibility for obtaining work for this man and seeing to it that he properly deports himself while in Pittsburgh" (February 11, 1920, box 2, folder 82, Urban League Records).
30. J. C. Austin to Mary White Ovington, February 11, 1921, NAACP Branch Records.

31. William Pickens to Robert L. Vann, September 22, 1924, NAACP Branch Records.
32. See the biographical article about Brown entitled "Races: Ablest," *Time Magazine*, June 5, 1939, box 2, folder 24, Homer Brown Collection, University Pittsburgh Archives Service Center.
33. Edna McKenzie, "Pittsburgh's Daisy Lampkin: A Life of Love and Service," *Pennsylvania Heritage* 9, no. 3 (1983): 9–12.
34. NAACP press release, May 10, and June 2, 1930, NAACP Branch Records. The PNA-ACP's membership rolls for 1930 offer insights into the class makeup of the organization. They indicate that few members lived on Wylie Avenue or Centre Avenue, which were primarily occupied by migrants and working-class blacks, while many resided on streets in the upper Hill, a haven for middle-class blacks.
35. "NAACP Given Keys to City," *Pittsburgh Courier*, July 4, 1931.
36. Daisy Lampkin to Walter White, August 11, 1931, and Homer Brown to Roy Wilkins, August 28, 1931, NAACP Branch Records.
37. Highland Park pool report, enclosed in letter from Homer Brown to Roy Wilkins, August 28, 1931, NAACP Branch Records.
38. "No Swimming, No Votes, Edict," *Pittsburgh Courier*, August 15, 1931.
39. Homer Brown to Roy Wilkins, August 28, 1931, NAACP Branch Records; "N.A.A.C.P. Has Been Active in Swimming Pool Fight," *Pittsburgh Courier*, September 5, 1931; "Bonsall Refuses to Act in Pool Case," *Pittsburgh Courier*, September 22, 1934.
40. Homer Brown to Roy Wilkins, August 28, 1931, NAACP Branch Records; "N.A.A.C.P. Has Been Active in Swimming Pool Fight," *Pittsburgh Courier*, September 5, 1931; "Bonsall Refuses to Act in Pool Case," *Pittsburgh Courier*, September 22, 1934.
41. Joe W. Trotter and Jared N. Day, *Race and Renaissance: African Americans in Pittsburgh since World War II* (Pittsburgh: University of Pittsburgh Press, 2010), 86–88.
42. "Six Hurt in Pitt Riot," *Baltimore Afro-American*, September 22, 1934.
43. "Guns Blaze as People Avenge Insult to Girl," *Pittsburgh Courier*, 22 September 1934.
44. "Complaints against Police," July 14, 1933, box 6, folder 253, Urban League Records.
45. "Police Assault," May 29, 1933, NAACP Branch Records; "Pittsburgh Cop Held for Cruel Attack," *Philadelphia Tribune*, June 15, 1933.
46. Homer Brown to Walter White, January 23–24, 1933, and Homer Brown report, January 24, 1933, NAACP Branch Records; "Fifty Negroes Expelled," *New York Herald-Tribune*, January 23, 1933.
47. See Homer Brown report, January 24, 1933, and William Schnader report, August 24, 1933, NAACP Branch Records. Also see "State Orders Probe of Shanghai Charge," *Pittsburgh Press*, January 27, 1933.
48. Homer Brown to Walter White, January 23–24, 1933, and Homer Brown report, January 24, 1933, NAACP Branch Records; "Fifty Negroes Expelled," *New York Herald-Tribune*, January 23, 1933.
49. Homer Brown to Walter White, January 23–24, 1933, and Homer Brown report, January 24, 1933, NAACP Branch Records; "Fifty Negroes Expelled," *New York Herald-Tribune*, January 23, 1933.
50. For example, see "Police 'Shanghai' Fifty," *Pittsburgh Courier*, January 28, 1933, and NAACP press release, February 3, 1933, NAACP Branch Records.
51. "Police Shanghai Fifty," *Pittsburgh Courier*, January 28, 1933; "State Orders Probe of

The Weapons of Legal Defense

Shanghai Charge," *Pittsburgh Press*, January 27, 1933; "Pinchot to Continue Probe into Abduction of Negroes," *Waynesburg Messenger*, February 3, 1933.
52. Walter White to Homer Brown, February 1, 1933, and NAACP press release, February 3, 1933, NAACP Branch Records.
53. "Pinchot to Continue Probe into Abduction of Negroes," *Waynesburg Messenger*, February 3, 1933; Walter White to Homer Brown, February 1, 1933, NAACP Branch Records.
54. Homer Brown to Walter White, February 22, 1933, NAACP Branch Records.
55. William Schnader to Walter White, March 23, 1933, NAACP Branch Records.
56. Homer Brown to Walter White, February 25, 1933, NAACP Branch Records.
57. For example, see Homer Brown to Walter White, April 18, 1933, and Walter White to Gifford Pinchot, April 25, 1933, NAACP Branch Records.
58. William Schnader, report, August 24, 1933, NAACP Branch Records.
59. William Schnader, report, August 24, 1933, NAACP Branch Records.
60. For instance, see "6 Beaver Officials Facing Prosecution in Kidnaping of 46," *Pittsburgh Press*, August 27, 1933.
61. "U.S. Has Charges Prepared in Beaver Jail 'Kidnappings,'" *Pittsburgh Press*, September 1, 1933.
62. Homer Brown to Walter White, September 15, 1933, and Gifford Pinchot to Walter White, September 20, 1933, NAACP Branch Records.
63. "U.S. Has Charges Prepared in Beaver Jail 'Kidnappings,'" *Pittsburgh Press*, September 1, 1933.
64. See Homer Brown to Walter White, September 6, 1933, and Walter White to Homer Brown, September 8, 1933, NAACP Branch Records.
65. George Schuyler to Percival Prattis, October 19, 1936, box 12, folder 20, Percival Prattis Collection, Mooreland-Spingarn Research Center, Howard University.
66. See Buni, *Robert L. Vann of the* Pittsburgh Courier, 199–201.
67. See Homer Brown to Walter White, May 17, 1933, and October 6, 1933, NAACP Branch Records.
68. Homer Brown to Walter White, October 6, 1933, NAACP Branch Records.
69. See Walter White to Homer Brown, November 14, 1933, and memorandum regarding long distance telephone call from Homer Brown to Walter White, November 14, 1933, NAACP Branch Records.
70. William Schnader, report, August 24, 1933, NAACP Branch Records.
71. Homer Brown speech, excerpts, June 1933, box 2, folder 22, Homer Brown Collection.

CHAPTER FOUR

"The Ranks of This New Army"

THE *PITTSBURGH COURIER* AND THE FIGHT FOR POLITICAL POWER AND NATIONAL RECOGNITION, 1929–1933

"Old Hoover messed me up good," Harrison Gant remembered. After migrating to Pittsburgh in 1916, the native Georgian found work in the boiler department at the Jones and Laughlin steel plant and began building a life in the city. He married a woman named Nellie sometime around 1923, and a year later she gave birth to their daughter Ruby. Like so many other black workers, Gant found himself locked into a position as an unskilled laborer. Yet he worked steadily through the twenties and managed to save some money. In 1930, he lived with his wife and child in a home on Wylie Avenue in the lower Hill District, and they had taken in four boarders to help reduce their rent. With the money he saved, Gant planned to quit his job at Jones and Laughlin and start a local grocery store. Then the effects of the depression began to take hold. Plants started shutting down or reducing operations; work grew increasingly scarce; shifts got shorter. By around 1932, Gant worked only three days a week, and all of his lodgers lost their jobs and could not pay their share of the rent. "Well, I couldn't tell these folks to move," he explained. "If you're alright with me when you got everything, you're alright with me when you got nothin'."[1]

Gant had seen some hard times since coming to Pittsburgh, but the depression introduced him to new levels of human suffering. He bitterly recalled seeing people sleeping under bridges and in bushes and even "layin' on the street like hogs." Gant believed in the virtues of hard work and personal responsibility, but the economic forces operating in the early thirties overwhelmed even the hardiest individualists. "What you gonna do?" he asked. "You ain't got two cents.... [Then] Duquesne cut off your light and gas. Even cut off water from your house. How in the devil did them people think you could pay them rent when there wasn't a job to be had?!"[2]

With his business plans thwarted, his shifts reduced, and his sense of urgency growing, Gant welcomed any ideas that might improve his financial situation and help him keep food on the table for his family. Like urban African Americans across the nation, he felt frustrated with the Republican Party and implicitly blamed its leaders for causing the depression. But as a Pittsburgher in the autumn of 1932, Gant had something most northern blacks did not: a steady, persistent voice offering a way to gain control over his life. By then, the *Pittsburgh Courier* had emerged as one of the largest black weeklies in the nation, and its presence was ubiquitous on Wylie Avenue and across the Hill District. On his way to the mill, Gant probably passed several newsstands carrying the latest edition of the paper, heard newsboys shouting "Pittsburgh Courrrier!" on street corners, and saw people reading it on their front stoops, in barber shops, and local diners. If not a subscriber, Gant likely read the *Courier* enough to know that it had turned Democratic late in 1932 and devoted every issue since then to urging black Americans to abandon the GOP and vote for Franklin Roosevelt in the upcoming presidential election.

In this setting, Gant may have joined five thousand other black Pittsburghers at a campaign rally for Roosevelt at Forbes Field on October 19, 1932. There, in the crisp autumn air, an African American women's band played the "Star-Spangled Banner" for an audience of around thirty-five thousand people. If Gant attended the rally, he might have spotted Robert L. Vann among the bowed heads. Vann published and edited the *Courier*, and like the other African Americans at the stadium he had come to support a Democrat for president. Although few took note of it at the time, the event heralded one of the most dramatic political realignments in American history.[3]

African Americans had overwhelmingly supported the Republican Party since the Civil War, but between 1932 and 1936 they moved rapidly into the Democratic camp. About 70 percent of black voters cast their ballots for Herbert Hoover in his bid for reelection in 1932. Four years later, roughly the same proportion voted for Roosevelt.[4] Black Pittsburghers were among the first to jettison the GOP and stake their fortunes with the Democrats, a development that Vann and his *Courier* staff helped to bring about. In 1932 Vann defected to the Democratic Party and used his influential newspaper to persuade black voters to support Roosevelt. "I, for one, shall join the ranks of this new army of fearless, courageous, patriotic Negroes who know the difference between blind partisanism and patriotism," he declared in September.[5] When the results came in, Pittsburgh emerged as one of just three major cities where FDR won a black majority.

Since its formation in 1910, the *Courier* had played a vital role in the black community as a source of racial pride, a Jim Crow watch dog, and an agent for political change. In interwar Pittsburgh, the majority group placed arbitrary limits on the possibilities of black lives and daily assaulted their dignity—and sometimes their bodies. Like the Urban League of Pittsburgh (ULP) and the Pittsburgh NAACP (PNAACP), the *Courier* offered the black community some shelter from this inhospitable racial climate. It bolstered African Americans' pride by publishing positive accounts of black life and by celebrating major achievements of black historical figures; it insisted on the biological equality of all races and fought against demeaning portrayals of blacks in the press and popular culture; it raised consciousness among African Americans about the major issues they faced; and through its reform campaigns it urged them to work together, vote, and take control of their destinies.

Despite the *Courier*'s importance, scholarly perceptions of it often parallel those of the Urban League. In a major monograph on black migrants in Pittsburgh, the index lists the *Courier* in terms of its "ambivalence toward migrants" and directs readers either to instances of the paper making a patronizing remark about migrants or to an example of discord between middle-class black Pittsburghers and the migrant community.[6] Similarly, the authors of a book on race and ethnicity in Pittsburgh explain that they did not draw from the immigrant press or the *Courier* because they "were essentially middle-class ventures that had little to say about the concerns and behavior of working people."[7] Likewise, an article on the *Courier*'s national Double V campaign argues that the newspaper had an underlying conservative agenda of restraining the radicalism of black workers.[8]

Andrew Buni's biography of Vann follows a similar trajectory. Buni depicts Vann as an insincere self-promoter who took editorial positions primarily to enhance his political stature and increase the *Courier*'s circulation. Like scholars who emphasize how Urban Leaguers enhanced their social status at the expense of working-class blacks, Buni regards with skepticism the motives behind Vann's reform initiatives. "As Vann gained personal recognition and began the process of political aggrandizement," Buni notes, "he left behind his idealism and something of his decency. Protective of his newly acquired honors, he increasingly steered a course between obstacles to his career, which caused him to change party allegiance on two separate and dramatic occasions."[9]

This chapter offers a different interpretation by maintaining that Vann and the *Courier* must be understood in the context of the larger black reform community active during the interwar years. Facing overwhelming racial hostility and viewing radicalism and separatism as untenable strategies, reformers worked within the system to pursue limited but achievable goals. We have seen how ULP staff alleviated the physical outcomes of discrimination and how PNAACP activists contested discriminatory policing. Alongside the members of these institutions, *Courier* staff worked toward a broad vision of citizenship that included access to basic social services, public accommodations, decent housing, gainful employment, and adequate health care as well as civil rights. Additionally, Vann believed that full citizenship both featured and required political empowerment.[10]

Vann's campaign for Roosevelt illustrates the *Courier*'s larger role in the community as a political mobilizer and demonstrates the pragmatic means by which reformers pursued citizenship. For Vann, this pragmatism included a willingness to trade loyalty for empowerment, to change positions and alliances in order to extract concessions from white America. In a 1912 editorial, for instance, he exhorted black Pittsburghers to register to vote so that "when we are approached for our ballot, we . . . may ask: *What shall we receive in return for our support*[?]"[11]

Throughout his life, Vann maintained that African Americans could best promote their interests by organizing into a cohesive voting bloc that could sway elections and consequently pressure the major parties to take their concerns seriously. He insisted that black voters should never stay with a party that does not serve their interests. Instead, he articulated a theory of a liquid vote whereby black voters would move from one party to the other in order to best promote racial advancement.[12]

In 1932 Vann had a unique opportunity to practice his theory. He owned and edited a leading black newspaper, and he lived and operated in a crucial state. Pennsylvania had more African Americans of voting age than any other northern state, and nationally only New York surpassed it in electoral points.[13] But Republicans had dominated Pennsylvania politics since the Civil War, controlling power from county seats to the state legislature and the governor's mansion. The last Democratic presidential candidate to win the state was James Buchanan in 1856.[14] GOP leaders understood this, and their landslide victories in the state led them repeatedly to pass over Vann for meaningful patronage appointments and generally to ignore the concerns of black Pennsylvanians. This pattern repeated itself at the national level, where a series of Republican presidents from Warren G. Harding to Herbert Hoover showed little regard for their African American constituents. Thus Vann, whose frustrations with the GOP mounted over the course of the 1920s, was well positioned to wrest concessions from Democratic leaders eager for any opportunity to take Pennsylvania from the Republicans.

Vann subsequently engaged in backroom negotiations with powerful Democrats in which he promised to deliver the black vote in Pennsylvania and possibly win the state for Roosevelt, with the understanding that the party would provide a significant number of patronage jobs for African Americans.[15] Operating from a reform ethos tailored to the bleak racial realities of early twentieth-century America, Vann used his influence over the black vote as leverage to gain support from Democrats and force them to take racial issues more seriously than they might otherwise.

Vann's Formative Years: The Shaping of a Reform Outlook

Vann's childhood and early adolescence in Harrellsville, located in Hertford County, North Carolina, helped shape his reform outlook. His mother worked as a domestic for a wealthy family, and during Vann's first ten years he lived in close association with the community's white aristocracy. He remembered fondly the special attention paid to him by Molly Askew, the mistress of the sprawling Askew plantation. She attended to his education while his mother, a light-skinned African American favored by the family, toiled in the kitchen or completed some other household chore. As Vann received guidance from the local gentry and played games with his white friends, he also saw white overseers and black farmhands at work in the Askew's fields. During these years Vann developed Victorian sensibilities that gradually fused with his sense of racial identity and his observations of the southern caste system.[16]

Vann was born out of wedlock in 1879 and never knew his biological father, but when he was ten his mother married a man who opened up to him a new range of experiences. Ignorant and unpolished, the man presented a sharp contrast to the genteel whites Vann knew since birth, and he compelled the boy to perform all manner of manual labor. Vann learned to split rails, plow fields behind an ox, hoe cotton and corn, cure tobacco, trap opossums, and "everything else that the plow boy of a poor Negro farmer would have to know." Vann's brief autobiographical essay makes clear that he disliked his stepfather for forcing this work on him at such a young age. Subconsciously, this resentment may have stemmed from the stepfather's role in exposing a sheltered boy to the harsh realities of life for southern black men and introducing him to the possibility that he might share a similar fate.[17]

Vann's six years of arduous labor in the fields sharpened his resolve to gain an education and escape the life of the poor black sharecropper. He did not receive payment for his toils with his stepfather, but he did earn money on the side while working in a local post office. By age sixteen he accumulated enough to enroll in Waters Training School in nearby Winton, North Carolina, where by several accounts he demonstrated a considerable work ethic and determination to excel. Vann graduated from Waters in 1901 at the top of his class, and not long after he set his sights on Virginia Union University in Richmond. There his vistas expanded. He discussed the finer points of racial uplift with like-minded classmates such as Eugene K. Jones, who would later head the National Urban League (NUL); he studied the accommodationist philosophy of Booker T. Washington; he wrote for the school newspaper; and he developed a reputation as a skilled orator while a member of the college debating team.[18]

Living conditions for African Americans in Vann's home state and across the South deteriorated during this time. Near the turn of the twentieth century, Vann witnessed the collapse of a Fusionist alliance of Republicans, Populists, and blacks in North Carolina and the ascendance of white-supremacist Democrats. In 1898 the chairman of the Democratic Party in Hertford explained to his constituents that "this is a white man's State, and white man's government" and he promised to "drive from power the haters of Anglo-Saxon blood and forever consign them to graves of dishonor and shame." During the state elections that year, Democrats in Winton threatened to murder the leaders of local Populists responsible for organizing black voters, and elsewhere across the state they resorted to intimidation to dissuade black voting. Through these tactics Democrats gained power, assuming county seats and positions in the state legislature, and they set the stage for future victories. An intimidated black electorate stayed home during the gubernatorial election of 1900. In Hertford, which was half black, Democratic candidate Charles B. Aycock won a landslide victory of 1,436 to 429.

Just two years earlier the Republican gubernatorial nominee won the county by more than 560 votes. Once in office, Aycock implemented a series of measures that further disfranchised the state's African Americans.[19]

It is difficult to know for certain what role Molly Askew and the other white elites of Harrellsville played in this development, but C. Vann Woodward's classic assessment of Jim Crow's emergence elsewhere in the South would suggest that Vann's former mentors safeguarded their class interests by using race baiting to divide poor whites and blacks and encourage segregationist fervor.[20] Civic minded and politically engaged, Vann undoubtedly followed these developments closely and recognized how they would hinder his personal ambitions. In 1903 he applied to and was accepted at the Western University of Pennsylvania, later renamed the University of Pittsburgh.[21] Vann said goodbye to his mother in Hertford shortly after and boarded a train for Pittsburgh.

The Emergence of the *Courier*

While at Pitt, Vann wrote for the school's newspaper, the *Courant*, and eventually rose to the position of editor. Vann also honed his oratorical skills by joining the school's debate team; he came in second place at a regional debating competition against other universities.[22] After earning a bachelor's degree in 1906, Vann enrolled in the University of Pittsburgh's law school and remained there until he passed the Pennsylvania bar examinations in 1909.[23]

Vann's involvement with the newspaper that would make him a nationally known figure began later that year when racial barriers pushed him to find a calling outside his legal practice. When he passed the bar examinations, he became one of only five African American attorneys in the entire city. But almost no whites hired black attorneys, and Vann even struggled to attract black customers. Hoping to limit the racial bias of white juries, many African Americans preferred to hire white attorneys when they could afford it.[24]

Looking for ways to supplement his income and pursue his passion for journalism, in late 1909 Vann partnered with a small group of investors, headed by Edwin N. Harleston, who wanted to establish a local newspaper that catered to the city's black population. With Vann's legal assistance, in early 1910 they formed the Pittsburgh Courier Publishing Company and began running the paper's first editions. During the early years of its existence, the four-page weekly sold for five cents and only covered local news. Vann served as the paper's legal advisor and editor, and he received payment in the form of company shares of stock. Over the next five years, as the original investors died, sold their stock, or moved on to other pursuits, Vann gradually gained control of the company.[25]

Yet Vann struggled with the responsibilities of running both a law office and a newspaper, so in 1914 he hired Ira Lewis, a stenographer by training, as managing editor to handle the *Courier*'s day-to-day operations. Lewis's meticulous nature and measured approach to financial management helped the young paper make good use of its limited funds. For instance, he began recruiting talented staff writers who helped generate interest in the paper and increase its circulation. Wilbert Holloway served as the *Courier*'s political cartoonist; John L. Clark covered local news in his Wylie Avenue section; Julia Bumbrey Jones wrote society gossip columns in Talk O' the Town and Julie's Soliloquy; Ernest Rice McKinney offered political commentary in It Is My Opinion; and W. Rollo Wilson wrote a lively sports section.[26]

The *Courier* grew rapidly during the early years of the Great Migration. Its circulation increased from five thousand to twelve thousand between 1915 and 1920, and by 1926 it reached twenty-two thousand. By then, the paper had begun publishing local and national editions and hiring out-of-town correspondents to contribute stories, including Joel Rogers and George Schuyler. Together, Schuyler and Rogers accounted for much of the *Courier*'s growth over the remainder of the decade. Schuyler frequently traversed the South to do investigative reporting. His shocking exposés of black living and working conditions—coupled with his satirical opinion column, Views and Reviews—attracted a national following. During his travels, Schuyler also developed branch offices for the *Courier* and increased its reach by soliciting subscriptions from African Americans in far-flung communities. Meanwhile, Rogers undertook research in Africa and published regular features on the importance of African kingdoms to Western history. His weekly piece, Your History, buttressed black pride and dignity at a time when the white press seemed interested only in covering stories of black crime.[27] Like Nettie, the fictional character in Alice Walker's *The Color Purple*, many African Americans learned about their heritage through Rogers's column. "Africans once had a better civilization than the European," she wrote to her sister, Celie. "I get this from reading a man named J. A. Rogers."[28]

In addition to employing some of the most talented journalists in the country, the paper regularly featured exclusive essays from national black leaders like W. E. B. Du Bois and Marcus Garvey, and through it NAACP

Robert L. Vann, ca. 1935.
Pennsylvania Department, P5846,
Carnegie Library of Pittsburgh.

head Walter White published a serialized novel entitled *Fire and Flint*.[29] By 1932, the *Courier* had expanded to a twenty-page format that featured contributions from over eighteen columnists, and it had about eighty thousand subscribers across forty-eight states plus the Caribbean, Canada, and the Philippines.[30] That local subscriptions accounted for less than a quarter of its circulation indicates that the *Courier* had a significant national following—especially when considering how newspapers were often shared among relatives in a household, coworkers in a break room, or patrons in a barber shop.[31]

While Lewis handled much of the business and managerial work for the *Courier*, Vann provided the editorial energy and spearheaded some of its most controversial, popular, and innovative campaigns, as his staff later recalled. Although Schuyler routinely criticized Lewis and other "old guard" *Courier* staff members, he praised Vann's editorial courage. "I am personally acquainted with all of the editors in Aframerica and it seems to me that Vann

Newspaper boys standing outside the *Courier* office on Centre Avenue.
Teenie Harris Archive, Carnegie Museum of Art, Pittsburgh

***Courier* staff at work in the editorial department, ca. 1945.**
Teenie Harris Archive, Carnegie Museum of Art, Pittsburgh

Typesetters, one of several kinds of African American technicians employed by the *Courier*.
Urban League Collection, box 10, folder 522, University of Pittsburgh Archives Service Center

The *Courier*'s printing press, which required several operators and maintenance men.
Urban League Collection, box 10, folder 522, University of Pittsburgh Archives Service Center.

is by long odds the ablest of the lot," he wrote to his friend and colleague Percival Prattis. "I know that he has been more willing than the others to experiment."[32] Prattis, who served under Vann in the late 1930s as the editor of the *Courier*'s city edition, echoed Schuyler's sentiment: "I have always thought about the *Courier* as a leading Negro journal not only because it managed to open doors and blaze trails but it managed to, in case after case, do so many things FIRST."[33] The *Courier*'s war correspondent, Frank Bolden, likewise recalled how the paper's campaigns set standards in the industry: "What I give the *Courier* credit for was that they were always in the forefront fighting for civil rights. The other papers would follow us, but they didn't initiate it. For instance, we didn't have to follow the *Defender*, or the *Afro-American*, or the *Norfolk Journal and Guide*. They follow us."[34]

Shaping Racial Discourse

As the *Courier* grew, Vann and his staff gained experience mobilizing public opinion around issues that affected African Americans locally and nationally. Before their campaign for FDR in 1932, they crusaded for better housing and health care, pressed for the unionization of black workers, and called attention to discriminatory hiring and promotional practices in the industrial sector. The *Courier* also joined Pittsburgh's black reform community in contesting racist depictions of African Americans in popular culture and mainstream newspapers. They understood well how native and foreign-born whites across the country continued to base their perceptions of African Americans on novels by Thomas Dixon, films by D. W. Griffith, and "coon songs" by Fred Fisher. By perpetuating crude stereotypes of people of color, the products of mass culture rationalized racial discrimination. For this reason, reformers like Vann worked to decry and delegitimize these forms of cultural expression.

In 1931, the *Courier* led a campaign to have the *Amos 'n' Andy* show removed from the air. First broadcast in 1928, the radio show featured two characters, Amos Jones and Andy Brown, voiced by white actors Freeman Gosden and Charles Correll, who journeyed from a farm in Georgia to Chicago, where they started a taxi company. For Vann, the characters' crude dialogue degraded African Americans and reinforced negative racial stereotypes. Over a six-month period in 1931 he campaigned to remove the show from the air. His national petition decried the show as "detrimental to the self respect and general advancement of the Negro" and called for a million signatures. The *Courier* regularly published updates on the petition, indicating the names of signers from each state, whom it praised as "100% Negro Americans." By August Vann had obtained 325,000 signatures, but neither the NAACP nor the other major black newspapers joined him. The campaign undoubtedly would have benefited from their support. Even so, it had garnered almost seven hundred thousand signatures by the time Vann ended it in late fall. Though its ratings declined somewhat, *Amos 'n' Andy* continued to be broadcast.[35]

Along with popular culture, the white press helped perpetuate the stereotypes that undergirded racial discrimination. At their best, local papers in Pittsburgh ignored positive achievements in the black community and focused instead on lurid accounts of black crime. At their worst, they openly expressed racist sentiments. On April 17, 1933, Florence Fisher Parry, an opinion writer for the *Pittsburgh Press*, wrote an article that rankled more than a few black leaders. Writing about the nationally famous Scottsboro trials, which concerned a group of black teens accused of raping a white woman in Alabama, Parry explained that southern blacks were like helpless children in need of protection, guidance, and, when necessary, punishment by their white guardians. Instructive for her was Claude G. Bowers's popular book on Reconstruction, which portrayed the period as a "tragic era" when an overbearing North encouraged former slaves to turn on their old masters and wreak havoc upon a prostrate South. Then as now, Parry explained, southern whites had to take emergency measures to restore the proper racial order and protect white women against lustful black men. "Because of their overwhelming numbers and their need of being wisely controlled, the Negro people of the South require a discipline unlike that which is administered in the North," she pointed out in a thinly veiled justification for mob violence and lynching.[36]

The Scottsboro case provided a national platform for white supremacists like Parry to broadcast their views on race and justice. Her article provoked an immediate response from black leaders in Pittsburgh, including PNAACP head Homer Brown. "We are hot under the collar about the ... articles in the Pittsburgh Press written by Mrs. Florence Fisher Parry," he wrote Walter White, executive secretary of the association's national office. Brown considered organizing a widespread boycott of the *Pittsburgh Press*, but he worried that the national chain running the paper would counter by cutting the NAACP out of its coverage.[37]

Considering the spotty racial record of local newspapers, Brown had legitimate concerns about antagonizing a national syndicate. At least several times a week the *Pittsburgh Press* published cartoons depicting African Americans as ape-like buffoons with grossly distorted features, and it commonly referred to them as "darkeys."[38] Less than a year after Parry's article surfaced, the *Pittsburgh Post-Gazette* published a front-page story featuring an unflattering caricature of an ignorant black southerner calling on Franklin Roosevelt for assistance, with the caption reading "Phone Call to President Saves Darkey's Cotton Soil." In response, Brown wrote a bitter letter to the *Gazette*'s editor that summarized his views of the white press in general.

> I should like to call your attention to the fact that on numerous occasions when matters concerning outstanding achievement among our people have been given to your paper for publication, you have seen fit to either not publish the article at all or to give the article the most limited amount of space in the most obscure parts of the paper.... You would, of course, do our race and our country an estimable favor if you would *use your paper in disseminating news rather than articles of contempt and ridicule.*[39]

The ULP joined the *Courier* and the PNAACP in the effort to combat damaging stereotypes and shape racial discourse. It regularly showed films and brought in outside speakers to provide information on issues affecting African Americans in Pittsburgh and throughout the country. For instance, social worker W. P. Young delivered a lecture on the history of black workers in Pittsburgh, while Ernest Rice McKinney gave a talk titled "The Psychology of Race."[40] McKinney pointed out that whites used their unfounded conceptions of African Americans as grounds for curtailing their economic, social, and political freedom. In particular, he argued that racial stereotypes were rooted in "economic fear ... that negroes will, through securing better, high-paying, more dignified jobs, attain a measure of independence and of self-assurance which will be dangerous to the dominance of the white group."[41] The social scientific research sponsored by the ULP furnished African Americans and their allies with additional evidence to use in their efforts to combat the rhetoric and logic of white supremacy. Master's theses and large-scale social surveys produced under league direction pointed to structural, not biological inequities that caused joblessness and poverty in black neighborhoods.

As in New York, Chicago, Philadelphia, and Washington, DC, the black community in Pittsburgh created a vital space for New Negro intellectual discourse where African Americans fleshed out questions concerning modernity, mass culture, and urbanization. In addition to the considerable body of research that came out of the ULP's fellowship program, the *Pittsburgh Courier* provided a forum through which national black leaders expressed a range of positions and philosophies on complex social issues. The paper also worked actively to raise self-esteem in black communities and promote positive black representation in the media.

For Vann, racial pride and solidarity served as the foundation of political unity. As editor of the *Courier*, he made a special effort to publish inspiring accounts of black accomplishments in the city and across the country, and in the process he helped thousands of African Americans feel proud of their history. African American parents across the country could open the *Courier* on Saturdays to Joel A. Rogers's column and read to their children stories about black heroes in America and Africa. In other sections readers could find articles celebrating the accomplishments of famous contemporary African Americans such as Duke Ellington, Paul Robeson, and Joe Lewis. The *Courier* also promoted black internationalism through its positive coverage of Haiti, Ethiopia, and Liberia.[42]

Vann and Brown understood that racist stereotypes in the white press and popular culture underwrote racial subordination.[43] Thus when Florence Fisher Parry's article appeared in 1933, Vann wasted no time in launching a vigorous counterattack. The April 22 edition of the *Courier* featured three articles blasting Parry's defense of the South. For instance, a column on the front page called for a boycott of the *Pittsburgh Press*. "We simply refuse to buy and pay for daily insults written by Mrs. Parry," the piece read. "We refuse to buy a paper which permits our group to become the target of a misinformed, biased, and openly prejudiced, mediocre writer." Clark devoted the entirety of his Wylie Avenue section to dismissing Parry and calling attention to the South's prejudiced criminal justice system. "Trial judges in most cases are jokes when Negroes are the defendants," he remarked bitterly, and despite class differences between jury members "they always remember that they are not bound by the customs of the South to respect the rights or life of a Negro." In response to the wave of criticism, the *Pittsburgh Press* published an editorial that disavowed Parry's opinions as not in keeping with its editorial policy.[44]

The *Courier*'s Yellow Journalism

Despite the noteworthy achievements of the *Courier* in stimulating black pride and promoting racial advancement, at times it offered contradictory messages and published stories that divided African Americans. For instance, the same February 1931 edition that featured a story encouraging readers to embrace their African heritage also included an advertisement for a hair-straightening gel that implicitly encouraged black women to reject their natural hair in order to "look more striking" and "be more beautiful and of course more popular."[45] Moreover, Vann occasionally adopted editorial positions that created public controversies and injured his reputation among other black leaders. One involved the NAACP. A wealthy white donor, Charles Garland, bequeathed the sum of $900,000 to the association for use in liberal causes, and in an October 9, 1926 article entitled "NAACP 'Slush Fund' Aired," the *Courier* accused James Weldon Johnson of misappropriating the money. The story suggested that the association's officers had spent far more than necessary on its various legal cases and programs, including its 1925 defense of Dr. Ossian Sweet in Detroit and its funding of research W. E. B. Du Bois undertook in South Carolina. The column may have voiced reasonable concerns about excessive spending, but the language through which it expressed them smacked of sensationalism. The author called the association's national officers— Johnson, Du Bois, and William Pickens—the "Fifth avenue barons" and insinuated that they conspired to use donations for their personal gain.[46]

In any case, the story caught the association off guard. After reading it, Walter White, a leading figure in the NAACP, dispatched a telegram to Vann and received a prompt reply.[47]

> WILL YOU ADVISE ME PERSONALLY BY WIRE IF ARTICLE ON FRONT PAGE OF COURIER OF OCTOBER NINTH RELATIVE TO N.A.A.C.P. APPEARED WITH YOUR KNOWLEDGE AND APPROVAL.
> WALTER WHITE
>
> YOUR WIRE CONCERNING FRONT PAGE ARTICLE RECEIVED. THE ANSWER IS YES
> VANN

Over the following weeks, black weeklies reprinted portions of the *Courier* article and expressed a range of opinions on the matter.[48] Vann himself received several letters criticizing him for publishing the piece. "I do not appreciate the pile of junk which is in your paper this week," wrote the head of the Urban League of Canton, Ohio. Another critic called the story's contributors "pygmy-brained marplots," stressed the "mental limitations" of the *Cou-*

rier's managing editor, Ira Lewis, and informed Vann that he had "relegate[d] the *Pittsburgh Courier* to the realm of muckrakers." Despite its personal attacks, the same letter posed a fair question: "Suppose you even meant to tell the truth. Knowing the purpose of the N.A.A.C.P., would it not be better to help such an organization rather than take joy in publishing damaging facts?"[49]

At the association's national office in New York, Johnson and other officials deliberated over whether they should publicly respond to the accusations. Personally, Johnson maintained that the charges were "mendacious and absolutely absurd," and he suggested that the Republican Party prompted Vann to publish the article "because of the Association's stand for political independence among Negroes. Vann . . . has for a long time been a Republican henchman and office seeker."[50] William Pickens speculated that the *Courier*'s editorial staff published the story to undermine the NAACP's effort to establish a permanent legal defense fund. "If ever a more slimy attack was made by a dirty newspaper," Pickens noted, "we have not heard of it."[51] Ultimately, by mid-October the association opted to defend itself in a press release from Johnson that addressed each of the *Courier*'s accusations and stressed its record of financial transparency.[52]

The controversy nevertheless persisted for almost three more years before Vann, Johnson, and Du Bois published statements indicating they had moved past the issue.[53] Still, although Vann evidently mended his relationship with Du Bois, he retained bitter feelings toward Johnson. When Walter White encouraged Vann to attend Johnson's funeral in 1938, the editor replied,

> You know, Walter, I must be frank about this. . . . Jim and I were not friends when he died, and had not been friends for some time. I have never forgiven him for the way he treated me over my difference with the N.A.A.C.P. . . . And so I say about his funeral the same thing I said about Huey Long's funeral—"I shall not be present, but I am glad it happened."[54]

Despite his occasional lapses into yellow journalism, for much of his career Vann ably used the *Courier* to contest racial injustice both in Pittsburgh and around the country, from housing inequality, health disparities, and employment discrimination to racist portrayals of African Americans in the white press and popular entertainment. Few of his crusades, though, were as ambitious as his 1932 campaign for FDR.

Mounting Frustration: Vann and the GOP

It is difficult to overemphasize the significance of Vann's campaign for Roosevelt. Democrats had earlier disfranchised almost all black voters in his hometown in North Carolina, and the party sanctioned far worse elsewhere in the South. By exploiting racial antipathies for their own political gain, southern Democrats supported a virulent and long-lived lynching epidemic that claimed the lives of several thousand black men and terrorized African Americans throughout the South. Moreover, in every southern state Democrats passed legislation that segregated and disfranchised African Americans. James Simmons, a Georgia migrant who moved to Pittsburgh in the early 1930s, did not even know what a voting poll looked like before he arrived north. "I thought a poll was something like a tree," he recalled.[55]

On the other hand, during the Civil War and Reconstruction the "Party of Lincoln" freed African Americans from bondage, created the Freedmen's Bureau to educate them and safeguard their legal rights, granted them full citizenship, and gave black men the right to vote. For these reasons, the roots of black loyalty to the GOP ran deep. An African American raised in Hackensack, New Jersey, recalled that in his community voting Democrat "was a form of heresy practically unknown and unpracticed." Similarly, Clarence Mitchell remembered that in black Baltimore supporting Democrats "was the equivalent of a traitorous act."[56]

African Americans in the late 1920s and early 1930s still had close ties to slavery. Most black voters had grandparents who were once slaves, and some former slaves were still alive. In 1928, a *Courier* reporter traveled south to interview a former slave named Martha Dorsey, who was then 101 years old. Dorsey was a slave on a Virginia plantation when she met her husband, Thomas Dorsey, who later fought and died for the Union while serving in a black regiment during the Civil War. The government pension Martha subsequently received served as a constant reminder of her husband's sacrifice and the importance of the GOP. "Because of the Republican party," she explained, "the government has taken good care of me." When the reporter asked if she planned on voting in the upcoming election, Dorsey sat upright in surprise. "Vote? Why child I've voted ever since that Republican Congress made it possible for me to vote."[57]

The presence of Vann and five thousand African Americans at a Democratic function in Forbes Field in October 1932 was thus unusual. Black leaders increasingly complained about the Republican Party during the early Depression, but most of them counseled loyalty to the GOP in the 1932 presidential election. The *Chicago Defender* reasoned that "four more years of [Hoover] as a Republican . . . will be better than a possible eight years of any Democrat."[58] To questions about what African Americans could expect from a Roosevelt presidency, the *Philadelphia Tribune* concluded that "the answer is certain . . . nothing."[59] The *New York Amsterdam News* warned that while "Governor Roosevelt would be a threat to the progress of the Negro," his conservative running mate from Texas, John Nance Garner, "would be a catastrophe."[60]

Vann himself supported the GOP most of his life. A party member since 1903, he campaigned for Republican presidential candidates from Warren G. Harding in 1920 to Herbert Hoover in 1928 as well as for the GOP candidate, Gifford Pinchot, in the 1930 state gubernatorial election. He devoted space in the *Courier* to their candidacies and traveled across the Northeast to galvanize black support for the Republican ticket.[61] Each time he expected prominent federal appointments and received almost nothing. The GOP also did not offer much support for racial justice, and it increasingly courted the votes of southern white segregationists.[62] These factors gradually eroded Vann's enthusiasm for the Republican Party.

Vann attended the 1920 Republican National Convention and felt confident that his party's presidential candidate, Warren G. Harding, would extend prominent cabinet level positions to African Americans. This hope faded soon after Harding's victory. Evidently fearing a backlash among his white constituents, Harding appointed only three African Americans to federal positions—all from the North. Moreover, the president withdrew his support from the Dyer antilynching bill when southern conservatives in the Senate threatened a filibuster. Although the bill passed the House, it never came to a vote in the Senate. Harding also hesitated to denounce the Ku Klux Klan, much to Vann's frustration. At 150,000 members, Pennsylvania had the nation's fourth largest Klan population, behind only Texas, Indiana, and Ohio.[63]

Nevertheless, in the 1924 presidential election Vann agreed to serve as the vice chairman of the GOP's Eastern Division of Colored Voters. In this role he coordinated publicity in the black press and delivered speeches across the eastern states in support of Calvin Coolidge and other Republican candidates. Vann expected a high government post for his efforts and significant patronage for his race, but once again GOP leaders reserved few positions for African Americans.[64] Only "two worth-while appointments have been the reward of the Negro population, thus far, for their efforts last year," the *Courier* complained in December 1925. "The political 'plums,' so freely promised during the heat of the campaign, have failed to fall."[65]

This pattern repeated in 1928 when Herbert Hoover ran for president.[66] In September and October Vann served as chairman of publicity for the black division of the GOP, and after Hoover won in a landslide rumors circulated that Vann would be appointed assistant attorney general.[67] This position ultimately failed to materialize for several reasons. Hoover won Pennsylvania by such a wide margin that Vann's services did not appear essential, and moreover, Hoover and the Republicans did not want to lose the support of the southern whites they had recently won over. Frustrated, Vann later complained to a Republican official that he "gave nine weeks of service to Mr. Hoover's campaign . . . [and] didn't even get a letter of thanks."[68] Over the next few years, the gravitational force of the Great Depression finally pulled Vann out of the Republic orbit.

The Onset of the Great Depression in Pittsburgh, 1929–1932

Following the stock market crash in October 1929, the already bleak economic fortunes of northern and southern blacks began a precipitous decline that did not level out until the late thirties. The depression hurt all Americans, but blacks especially. The social, political, and economic privation they endured during the twenties rendered them particularly vulnerable to a sudden and extensive economic downturn. Northern blacks greeted 1929 from the lowest and most expendable rungs of the employment ladder, from the poorest and most disease-ridden neighborhoods, and at a telescopic distance from the levers of power. "At no time in the history of the Negro since slavery," lamented T. Arnold Hill of the National Urban League, "has his economic and social outlook seemed so discouraging."[69]

When northern employers had to make cutbacks they often released black workers first, and whenever business recovered they put whites back to work before blacks. A 1930 NUL survey of twenty-five major cities revealed that blacks were two to four times more likely to be unemployed than whites.[70] Although foremen and managers often cited African Americans' relative inexperience when explaining this disparity, historian Dennis Dickerson finds that white workers of the same experience-level had much higher rates of employment.[71] Not coincidentally, the number of African Americans applying for work at Urban League offices in cities across the nation increased from 13 to 62 percent.[72] Most faced disappointing results. In 1930, Cleveland's Urban League reported a 60 percent decrease in its job placement rate, while Urban Leagues in Philadelphia, Louisville, Minneapolis, and St. Paul recorded placement declines ranging from 33 to 50 percent.[73]

As the economic landslide picked up speed and strength in the early 1930s, Americans of all colors scrambled to avoid getting buried, but in the mad dash for safety people of color got trampled underfoot. In the South, urban whites took any jobs they could find, including "Negro jobs" such as street cleaning, garbage collecting, and domestic work. The harder times got, the more they demanded African Americans vacate these occupations. "No jobs for Niggers until Every White Man Has a Job!" ran the slogan of the Black Shirts, a supremacist organization established in Atlanta in 1930. "Niggers, back to the cotton fields—city jobs are for white folks," chanted a similar group. By 1931 unemployment among African Americans in southern cities reached 33 percent, and the following year it climbed to 50 percent.[74]

Northern blacks confronted an equally grim employment situation. In 1932 black unemployment in Harlem and Philadelphia reached or exceeded 50 percent; in Chicago and Detroit 40 percent of black men and 55 percent of black women faced joblessness. By comparison, unemployment afflicted far fewer white men (23 percent) and women (14 percent) in these four cities.[75]

The depression hit Pittsburgh's steel industry like a sledge hammer. Already declining by the mid-twenties, several mills shut down completely in the months after the stock market crash. Others, like the Jones and Laughlin Company, reduced their operations by half.[76] By January 1931, barely one year into the depression, nearly seventy-nine thousand Pittsburghers had lost their jobs.[77] As elsewhere, this trend affected African Americans in disproportionate numbers. In 1930, Pittsburgh had only two wards where a thousand or more people were unemployed—the third and fifth, home to the city's largest concentration of African Americans.[78] The ULP's job placement reports from 1929 shed further light on the dim employment prospects for black Pittsburghers. That year, the league found work for only 110 of its 759 applicants.[79]

By 1931, unemployment among black Pittsburghers had climbed to well over 40 percent.[80] The ULP's industrial secretary glumly reported at the close of that year that "placement work for the year" had "reached an unprecedented low level."[81] Although some evidence suggests that steel executives did not expressly pursue race-based policies of work reduction, at the shop level foremen often did. Some even took advantage of African Americans' vulnerable positions in the mill and society to extort payments from them. One black worker complained to a ULP official about a foreman who "knows us colored folks has to put up with everything to keep a job so he asks for two-three dollars anytime an' if you don't pay, you get a poor payin' job or a lay-off." Another worker remembered a foreman who "charged me $20 one time for taking me back on, after he had laid me off; then asked me for $15 more after I had worked a while. I just got tired of that way of doin' and wouldn't pay him; now I'm out of a job."[82]

Because of their high unemployment rates, black Pittsburghers depended more on financial relief and charity than whites did. In the early 1930s over 40 percent of black Pittsburghers were on relief rolls, compared to about 16 percent of the white population. "Well, it looks like the niggers are going to get the most of the $100,000," a white official commented to a colleague in the elevator of Pittsburgh's city-county building—apparently unconcerned that an African American, Harold Lett, shared the elevator with them. By 1931, the city council had twice dispersed that amount to buttress the relief efforts of private charities. Lett, who served as industrial secretary of the ULP, observed the immense line of needy people gathering outside the city-county building, noting bitterly that over a third of them were African Americans, "sitting, standing, leaning, shuffling, in the narrow corridor—brown and black skins seemingly overwhelming the paler supplicants by sheer number." A middle-aged mother of six children stood among them. Because of overdue bills her gas had been turned off, in the middle of winter, and she was just days away from being evicted from her apartment. With tears in her eyes, she recalled her husband's disappearance.

> He worked in the steel mills for four-five years and was a good man. The mill closed and he was laid off. He went out early every morning and walked the streets until night, looking for work. Day after day he done this ever since last June. Once a man told him that he needn't trouble looking for a job as long as there is so many white men out of work. I guess us colored folks don't get "hongry" like white folks. He just got discouraged and one day he went out and didn't come back.[83]

The city council's relief efforts, and those of private organizations, provided only temporary comfort to the city's poor, especially its black poor.[84] Bartow Tipper, a black steelworker who migrated to Pittsburgh in the early twenties, remembered 1932 as a particularly bad year. He found multiple part-time jobs in the first two years of the depression and even managed to keep his car during that time. But work became almost impossible to find by 1932, and he had to sell his car and other possessions to help his family survive.[85] Merril Lynch, a native Pittsburgher who worked in the brick department at Jones and Laughlin, likewise recalled conditions reaching a nadir in 1932: "We were lucky if we made a day or two of pay" over a two-week period, he reported.[86] The Reverend Harold Tolliver helped organize an emergency feeding program in the black community, and he recalled how the poor "swarmed anywhere they heard that meals were being served during this terrible period of the depression."[87] One contemporary study found a third of black families in Pittsburgh living in poverty and another 41 percent facing utter destitution.[88]

Considering the magnitude of the depression for blacks, Hoover's initial reluctance to support federal intervention frustrated Vann.[89] Many African Americans shared this sentiment, including those who remained loyal to the GOP in the 1932 presidential election. Though the *Philadelphia Tribune* endorsed Hoover over Roosevelt, it noted that "every intelligent Negro understand[s] that the Republican party has not given the Negro a square deal."[90] On the other hand, Franklin Roosevelt's hints of massive federal intervention to address hunger and joblessness for all Americans, regardless of race, pulled Vann toward the Democrats. "It has been the theory of Republican leaders that relief is a local responsibility," Roosevelt explained in a speech juxtaposing his position from Hoover's. "The Democratic platform was framed with an eye to actual human needs. What could be finer than that bold and humanitarian statement pledging continuous responsibility of the Government . . . for human welfare."[91] Vann gradually came to believe that Roosevelt and the Democrats offered more for African Americans than the Republican Party, and by early summer 1932 he prepared to make a bold move.

The Campaign for Roosevelt

Vann formally switched parties sometime in July after attending both the Republican and Democratic national conventions and having several meetings with ranking Democrats. To him, the platform that the GOP produced at its convention provided further evidence that Republicans neglected their black constituents. "Eleven million Negroes occupied a space just about 1/136 of the platform," he complained. "Exactly ten times as much space was devoted to liquor."⁹² At the Democratic convention in Chicago, meanwhile, Roosevelt assured the black press that "the Negro is absolutely and impartially included in my reference of a 'New Deal' to the forgotten man."⁹³

Around this time Vann began speaking with Democratic National Committee chair James Farley as well as powerful Democrats in Pennsylvania about the possibility of his defection. Michael Benedum, a wealthy oil tycoon from Pennsylvania who donated large sums of money to the Roosevelt campaign, hoped that the editor might be persuaded to use his influence to sway black Pennsylvanians to the Democrats. Finding Vann receptive to the idea, Farley and Benedum introduced him to Joseph Guffey, the leader of the Democratic Party in Pennsylvania and a strategist for the Roosevelt campaign.⁹⁴

Guffey initially had reservations about investing campaign money into what seemed like a hopeless cause. Almost 276,000 African Americans of voting age resided in Pennsylvania in 1932, more than any other northern state, but converting them to the Democratic Party was no small feat. Black Philadelphia was heavily Republican, and a major black newspaper there, the *Philadelphia Tribune*, endorsed Hoover. On the other side of the state, Pittsburgh had fewer than ten thousand registered black Democrats.⁹⁵ In the Steel City's two wards with the heaviest concentration of African Americans, Republicans respectively constituted about 80 and 88 percent of the registered voters.⁹⁶ Despite these obstacles, Vann's enthusiasm encouraged Guffey. If the editor could deliver the black vote, Roosevelt might actually win the state. "Mr. Guffey's horizon, always wide, suddenly broadened," wrote Ruth Simmons in her 1944 study of black politics in Pittsburgh. "He saw millions of Negro voters, Republicans no longer, Democrats all." After their meetings, an inspired Guffey helped establish an African American division within the Democratic Campaign Committee and made Vann one of its heads.⁹⁷

Vann used these meetings to promote his political ambitions and gain patronage jobs for African Americans. While explaining to Guffey the failures of the GOP, he undoubtedly discussed the lack of political appointments extended to black Republicans. This was an important issue for Vann on both a personal level and from a broader social justice perspective. He felt he never got the recognition he deserved for his campaign services to the Republican Party, and he likewise believed that the Republican presidents he helped to elect had extended too few government positions to African Americans. Stressing his view that the GOP took the black vote for granted, Vann made clear to Guffey that the Democrats needed to deliver on this front if they expected to win and keep black support. Even after Roosevelt's victory in November, Vann warned that his allegiance would remain only so long as the Democrats addressed black concerns. "When this party gets to where they no longer offer my people any service I'll either go back to the Republican party or to some other party."[98]

Guffey probably assured Vann during their meeting that he would receive a high government post and that significant patronage would come to black Democrats, for afterward Vann formally began campaigning for Roosevelt. He commenced by establishing the Allied Roosevelt Clubs of Pennsylvania to drum up black support for the Democratic nominee, especially in Philadelphia and Pittsburgh. In this effort, he partnered with two of Philadelphia's leading African Americans, Samuel Brown and *Philadelphia Independent* publisher J. Max Barber. Vann directed the Allied Roosevelt Club in Pittsburgh, and Brown and Barber headed the Philadelphia branch.[99]

Later that year, on September 11, 1932, Vann delivered an important campaign speech for Roosevelt at the St. James Literary Forum in Cleveland. There, he traced the history of the Republican Party and laid out the reasons why black voters should switch to the Democrats. "The Republican Party, under Harding, absolutely deserted us," he declared. "The Republican party under Mr. Coolidge was a lifeless, voiceless thing. The Republican party under Mr. Hoover has been the saddest failure known to political history." Throughout the speech, Vann dichotomized patriots and partisans. A patriot placed the greater good above party loyalty while strict partisans remained faithful to a party or ideology even after it ceased to serve their interests. Revealing his pragmatic bent, Vann praised African Americans who "changed their political philosophy . . . [and] are selecting the party which they believe will guarantee them the privileges to which every patriot is entitled." Vann sympathized with African Americans who supported the Socialist and Communist parties, but he warned that "even sympathy must be practical. Neither one of these junior parties . . . is strong enough in its own right to overthrow the oligarchy now enthroned at Washington."[100]

The climactic moment of Vann's speech came at the end when he called on African Americans to turn their "pictures of Abraham Lincoln to the wall." Since the end of the Civil War, Lincoln's portrait had been a common feature in black households across the country. He was a revered figure who symbolized the freedom and hope embodied in the Republican Party. Lincoln's legacy assured Republicans of widespread black support for almost seven decades, which for Vann was payment enough.[101]

Vann subsequently published his speech both in the *Courier* and in a widely distributed pamphlet.[102] Black weeklies across the country reprinted his speech as well, catapulting him to national fame. Reporting on political alliances in Pittsburgh, a staff writer for the *Baltimore Afro-American* observed a "whirling new vortex of voters who are making up the new Democratic movement led by Robert Vann." More ominously for the Republican Party, nine out of every ten African Americans he interviewed in Pittsburgh said they planned to vote for Roosevelt in the upcoming election.[103] Vann became a national figure, and for the next two months he went on a lecture tour across the Northeast to persuade black Americans to join the Democratic Party.[104]

Vann also had the nation's preeminent black newspaper at his disposal. From its office building on the Hill District's Centre Avenue, each week the *Courier*'s staff churned out local, northern, eastern, and southern editions that could be found in every state.[105] Having used his paper throughout the 1920s to attack inadequate housing, Jim Crow segregation, and demeaning portrayals of African Americans in the press and popular culture, by the time he took on the Republican Party in 1932, he had considerable experience in shaping public opinion. Vann ordinarily gave his staff considerable leeway to express their political views, as long as their columns attracted readers. However, whenever he launched a major campaign, he marshaled his staff around it. This was especially true of his campaign for Roosevelt.

From June through August the *Courier* occasionally covered racial inequality in various Hoover programs, but after Vann's speech on September 11 the paper exploded with attacks on the GOP and its leader. Headlines like "Hoover and Slavery," "Hoover's Negrophobia Explained," and "Hoover Insults Labor" emblazoned its pages each week, along with biting columns and features on the failures of the Republican Party.[106] Floyd Calvin, who started his career writing for A. Phillip Randolph's *Messenger* before joining the *Courier* as a special-feature columnist, maintained that "there are any number of . . . instances of Mr. Hoover's double-dealing and double-crossing."[107] Another feature writer noted ironically that Hoover "means to save all of the real remedies for his dreamed of second term."[108] Vann also packed his editorial page with complaints about the GOP. One characteristic editorial suggested Hoover courted southern whites while he "avoided the colored brethren like the Devil dodges holy water."[109]

Vann's political cartoonist, Wilbert Holloway, participated in the campaign as well. Each week, from August 20 to November 4, he drew illustrations of Herbert Hoover ignoring black hardships and making false promises,

The political cartoons of Wilbert Holloway. "Sunnyboy Sam," *Pittsburgh Courier*, October 3, 1932 (above) and "Hoover Hooey," *Pittsburgh Courier*, November 5, 1932 (right).

of servile black Republicans begging for Hoover's picture, and of an elderly GOP elephant with bad hearing. For example, his cartoon from September 24 juxtaposed the decrepit elephant with a Roosevelt caricature sweeping out the old order and ushering in a new age. Holloway also produced a weekly comic strip called *Sunnyboy Sam* that he used to discredit Hoover. In one installment, Sunnyboy's friend Shorty explained to him that GOP had a new meaning: "Great on Promises."[110]

Although the *Courier* focused on discrediting the GOP, it also devoted space to establishing Roosevelt and the Democrats as champions of racial justice. For several months, the *Courier* covered Democratic senator Robert

Wagner's investigation of alleged mistreatment of black workers on a Hoover levee project in Mississippi—at once demonstrating the worth of the Democrats and the shortcomings of the Republicans.[111] The paper cast Roosevelt as the "dynamic and intelligent standard bearer" of the Democratic Party and praised "fearless" black leaders who supported his candidacy.[112] Through headlines like "Roosevelt Endorsed by Butlers," "Predicts Negro Roosevelt Vote," "Forum Sentiment Favors Roosevelt," and "Notable [Black] Democrats Outnumber G.O.P.'s by Three to One Count," the *Courier* gave the impression that most African Americans were turning Democrat and implicitly urged its readers to join the winning side.[113]

Vann's efforts intensified in the weeks leading up to the election. He participated in political forums in Pittsburgh, gave lectures in Philadelphia, and helped plan the ceremonies preceding Roosevelt's speech at Forbes Field on October 19.[114] That day, after the black female band finished playing the national anthem, Vann led a procession of five hundred African Americans across the baseball field carrying life-sized Roosevelt placards. The Democratic nominee joined them shortly afterward for the keynote event. "Let me make perfectly clear," Roosevelt thundered to the captive audience, "that if men or women or children are starving in the United States—anywhere—I regard it as a positive duty of the Government . . . to keep them from starvation."[115]

As historian William Leuchtenburg points out, Roosevelt's campaign speeches in 1932 often offered seemingly incongruous solutions to the depression. At the same Pittsburgh speech in which FDR promised emergency aid to the needy, he also pledged to reduce federal spending and balance the budget. It was the former message rather than the latter that caught the attention of Vann and other African Americans in attendance. Black Pittsburghers suffered from hunger and unemployment more than any other group in the city. If FDR's hints of massive federal intervention were moderated by competing promises of financial austerity, they still offered more hope than Hoover's platform. Ever the pragmatic utilitarian, Vann weighed these options and saw the scale tilt Democratic.[116]

A few weeks after Roosevelt's Pittsburgh speech, Vann and his political allies—including the Young Negro Progressives and Allied Roosevelt Clubs of Western Pennsylvania—organized a pro-Roosevelt parade through Pittsburgh's Hill District, the center of the black community, followed by a mass meeting at the Watt Street school auditorium.[117]

When the election finally took place on November 8, Vann felt pleased with the results. In Allegheny County, which includes Pittsburgh, FDR received 189,000 votes to Hoover's 152,000.[118] It was the first time the county went Democratic, and Roosevelt probably had black voters to thank for it. Considering FDR won the county by less than forty thousand votes, the approximately thirty-five thousand ballots cast for him by African Americans in the Pittsburgh area likely tipped the balance in his favor.[119] Lynch, the brick worker at Jones and Laughlin, was among them. Speaking for the black community as a whole, he recalled that "the way they was livin', they wanted improvement. And Hoover was no improvement, my God!"[120]

The election returns for Pittsburgh's third ward, which was almost half black, offer additional evidence of black voting behavior in the city. In 1928, Third Ward voters supported Hoover over Democratic challenger Alfred E. Smith by a total of 736 to 715. Four years later, FDR captured the ward by a tally of 1,369 to 973.[121] Hoover ultimately won Pennsylvania, but his loss in Pittsburgh was significant, considering that Democrats there constituted only 3 percent of the registered voters as of 1929.[122]

Outside western Pennsylvania, most African Americans remained loyal to the GOP. Although Roosevelt won forty-two of forty-eight states and defeated Hoover by over four hundred electoral points, only about a third of black voters cast their ballots for him. In Philadelphia and Detroit, for instance, Hoover received more than 66 percent of the black vote, and he carried eleven of the nation's fifteen largest black wards.[123] Roosevelt won black majorities in only three major cities: New York, Kansas City, and Pittsburgh.[124]

The diverging electoral results between Pennsylvania's two major cities merits some explanation. At over 220,000, black Philadelphia's considerable size encouraged state Republican leaders to concentrate support and patronage there instead of Pittsburgh's much smaller and politically less important black community of under 60,000. Historian Charles Pete T. Banner-Haley notes that for decades the GOP in Philadelphia dominated black and immigrant wards by providing favors and patronage to poor folk and by extending some government-level appointments to local black elites like Hobson Reynolds and E. Washington Rhodes. Through these means, Banner-Haley observes, "the Republican Party retained the image of the 'Emancipation' Party among the masses and made participation by the black middle class a symbol of high status."[125]

Consequently, in 1932 black Philadelphians probably had more to risk by supporting Roosevelt than their contemporaries across the state. But while black Pittsburghers may have been more receptive to calls for a switch to the Democratic Party, the *Pittsburgh Courier* transformed this receptivity into action. The vast majority of black newspaper patrons in the Pittsburgh area purchased the *Courier* over rival papers like the *Baltimore-Afro American*, *Chicago Defender*, or *Philadelphia Tribune*. Pride in the hometown paper and a desire to support a local business that provided about eighty jobs for black writers, technicians, typesetters, secretaries, and janitors, assured considerable support. Thus, while the *Courier's* months-long campaign for Roosevelt helped persuade African Americans across the nation to vote Democratic, its influence was strongest in the Pittsburgh area, where rival papers counseling support for the GOP reached a limited audience.

Despite his limited success at the national level, Vann maintained that the black vote tipped the balance for Roosevelt in fourteen states, and he thanked "my people all over the land who rose to a new sense of self-respect and voted a consolidated protest against abuses undeserved."[126] Vann probably overstated the black vote's role in securing Roosevelt's victory, but Democratic Party leaders nevertheless were encouraged enough that they established full-time black Democratic organizations in ten states.[127]

Shortly after the election, Guffey urged Roosevelt to appoint Vann as special assistant to the attorney general, and the president-elect complied.[128] Vann obtained the prominent post he long desired, and additionally he gained considerable influence over black patronage. From early 1933 to 1935, Vann received numerous letters from African Americans seeking political appointments ranging from minor clerkships in post offices to federal-level positions. NUL executive secretary Eugene K. Jones asked for Vann's help in getting appointed as an advisor on black affairs in the Department of Commerce, for example, and W. E. B. Du Bois wrote Vann on behalf of a friend who he wished to see reinstated in the Boston post office.[129] Theodora Jones, a prominent clubwoman in Los Angeles, explained to Vann that "I am seeking the post of Deputy Recorder of Deeds, District of Columbia . . . [and] I do hope you will recommend me for the appointment. I have the necessary legal and practical experience to fill the position."[130]

Vann had reason to feel pleased with the patronage extended to African Americans following FDR's election. Roosevelt appointed him, Jones, and at least forty other African Americans to high federal positions, more than any previous administration, and in the Pittsburgh area African Americans gained proportional representation in local work-relief projects along with a number of minor patronage appointments.[131] As one state Democratic official explained it, "Mr. Vann... has been most helpful not only to our state organization, but to the National Administration as well. We always try to carry out Vann's suggestions if possible."[132]

NOTES

1. Harrison Gant, interview with Peter Gottlieb, August 23, 1974, Pittsburgh Oral History Project, Heinz History Center, Pittsburgh.
2. Harrison Gant, interview with Peter Gottlieb, August 23, 1974, Pittsburgh Oral History Project. "Duquesne" refers to the power company, Duquesne Light.
3. "5,000 Negroes in Huge Crowd Which Greets Governor Here," *Pittsburgh Courier*, October 22, 1932.
4. Simon Topping, *Lincoln's Lost Legacy: The Republican Party and the African American Vote, 1928–1952* (Gainesville: University Press of Florida, 2008), 4.
5. Robert L. Vann, "The Patriot and the Partisan," September 11, 1932, box 31, folder 2, Robert L. Vann Papers, Percival Prattis Collection, Moorland-Spingarn Research Center, Howard University.
6. The index entry can be found on page 248 of Peter Gottleib's *Making Their Own Way: Southern Blacks' Migration to Pittsburgh, 1916–30* (Urbana: University of Illinois Press, 1987). See page 187 for one of the examples Gottleib cites.
7. John Bodnar, Richard Simon, and Michael P. Weber, *Lives of their Own: Blacks, Italians, and Poles in Pittsburgh, 1900–1960* (Urbana: University of Illinois Press, 1982), 9.
8. Lee Finkle, "The Conservative Aims of Militant Rhetoric: Black Protest during World War II," *Journal of American History* 60, no. 3 (1973), 692–713.
9. Andrew Buni, *Robert L. Vann of the* Pittsburgh Courier: *Politics and Black Journalism* (Pittsburgh: University of Pittsburgh Press, 1974), xiii, 61.
10. See Adam Lee Cilli, "The Pursuit of Happiness: Racial Utilitarianism and Black Reform Efforts in John T. Clark's Urban League," *Journal of Urban History* 45, no. 1 (2019): 6–22.
11. "All Voters Ought to Get Registered," *Pittsburgh Courier*, February 17, 1912, emphasis mine.
12. "The Political Muddle," *Pittsburgh Courier*, September 16, 1911; "All Voters Ought to Get Registered," *Pittsburgh Courier*, February 17, 1912.
13. Over 275,000 African Americans of voting age resided in Pennsylvania in 1932. See Buni, *Robert L. Vann of the* Pittsburgh Courier, 192.
14. Buni, *Robert L. Vann of the* Pittsburgh Courier, 271.
15. These negotiations illustrate a related point. The major monographs on this subject argue that African Americans moved to the Democratic Party because of the social justice concerns of New Deal liberals (Harvard Sitkoff, *A New Deal for Blacks: The Emergence of Civil Rights as a National Issue*, thirtieth anniv. ed. [New York: Oxford University Press, 2009], 45), the economic benefits of the New Deal (Nancy Weiss, *Farewell to the Party of Lincoln: Black Politics in the Age of FDR* [Princeton, NJ: Princeton University Press, 1983], 13–15), or the failures of the Republican Party to address racial issues (Topping, *Lincoln's Lost Legacy*, 26). While they rightly point to structural and institutional developments as the prime drivers of black realignment, they miss the spaces of agency,

the areas for maneuvering, in which race leaders like Vann used the black vote as a bargaining tool with which to wrest concessions from the Democratic Party.

These monographs simultaneously undervalue the role of the black press in communicating to black voters the merits of the New Deal, which likely accelerated (but was not the only factor in) their movement to the Democratic Party. Weiss and Topping, for example, discuss Vann's switch to the Democrats as an example of growing black frustration with the GOP, but they do not mention his negotiations with Democratic leaders or discuss how his campaign might have swayed thousands of black voters to join the Roosevelt camp. Moreover, recent works on the black press say nothing about Vann's campaign for Roosevelt. For example, see Ethan Michaeli, *The Defender: How the Legendary Black Newspaper Changed America* (Boston: Houton Mifflin Harcourt, 2016), and Todd Vogel, ed., *The Black Press: New Literary and Historical Essays* (New Brunswick, NJ: Rutgers University Press, 2001).

16. Robert L. Vann, "Robert Lee Vann," in *The Ahoskie Era of Hertford County*, ed. Roy Parker (Ahoskie, NC: Parker Brothers, 1939), 268–73.
17. Vann, "Robert Lee Vann," 272.
18. Vann, "Robert Lee Vann," 271, 273; James H. Brewer, "Robert Lee Vann and the *Pittsburgh Courier*" (master's thesis, University of Pittsburgh, 1941), 7–11; Henry G. La Brie III, "Robert Lee Vann and the Editorial Page of the *Pittsburgh Courier*" (master's thesis, West Virginia University, 1970), 12–13; Buni, *Robert L. Vann of the* Pittsburgh Courier, 13–15.
19. Buni, *Robert L. Vann of the* Pittsburgh Courier, 17–20. For more on the Red Shirt Revolution in North Carolina and the disfranchisement of the state's African Americans, see Glenda Elizabeth Gilmore, *Gender and Jim Crow: Women and the Politics of White Supremacy in North Carolina, 1896–1920* (Chapel Hill: University of North Carolina Press, 1996), 98–100.
20. See C. Vann Woodward, *The Strange Career of Jim Crow* (New York: Oxford University Press, 1955).
21. Vann, "Robert Lee Vann," 271, 273.
22. La Brie, "Robert Lee Vann and the Editorial Page of the *Pittsburgh Courier*," 12–13.
23. La Brie, "Robert Lee Vann and the Editorial Page of the *Pittsburgh Courier*," 13–14.
24. Brewer, "Robert Lee Vann and the *Pittsburgh Courier*," 12–27; Buni, *Robert L. Vann of the* Pittsburgh Courier, 19, 40.
25. "Hundreds Present at Big Dedication," *Pittsburgh Courier*, December 14, 1929; La Brie, "Robert Lee Vann and the Editorial Page of the *Pittsburgh Courier*," 15–23.
26. Later, the *Courier* also published exclusive features by national black leaders like W. E. B. Du Bois, Walter White, and Marcus Garvey. See Brewer, "Robert Lee Vann and the *Pittsburgh Courier*," 36–39, Buni, *Robert L. Vann of the* Pittsburgh Courier, 136–42, La Brie, "Robert Lee Vann and the Editorial Page of the *Pittsburgh Courier*," 21–28, and "Hundreds Present at Big Dedication," *Pittsburgh Courier*, December 14, 1929.
27. Buni, *Robert L. Vann of the* Pittsburgh Courier, 136–42.
28. Alice Walker, *The Color Purple* (New York: Harcourt, 1982), 129.
29. Percival Prattis, "Days of *Courier* Past," in *Perspectives of the Black Press: 1974*, ed. Henry G. La Brie III (Kennebunkport, ME: Mercer House Press, 1974), 70–71.
30. La Brie, "Robert Lee Vann and the Editorial Page of the *Pittsburgh Courier*," 28–29; Buni, *Robert L. Vann of the* Pittsburgh Courier, 226. Vishnu V. Oak notes that the

Courier's circulation of eighty thousand in 1932 made it the largest black weekly in the country (*The Negro Newspaper* [Westport, CT: Negro Universities Press, 1970], 126).

31. For more on the *Courier*'s national footprint, see Buni, *Robert L. Vann of the* Pittsburgh Courier, 257–58.
32. George Schuyler to Percival Prattis, October 19, 1936, box 12, folder 20, Percival Prattis Collection.
33. Prattis, "Days of *Courier* Past," 70–71.
34. Frank Bolden, interview in *Newspaper of Record: The Pittsburgh Courier, 1907–1965*, produced and directed by Kenneth Love (Pittsburgh: Kenneth A. Love International LLC, 2009), www.humanitydocs.com.
35. For example, see the petition and names of signers in *Pittsburgh Courier*, August 8, 1931, and "Engage Comic Pair at Picnic," *Pittsburgh Courier*, August 22, 1931. Also see Charles Pete T. Banner-Haley, *To Do Good and to Do Well: Middle-Class Blacks and the Depression, Philadelphia, 1929–1941* (New York: Garland, 1993), 87. Vann was not without his supporters, however. "I am fully in accord with the movement," the Reverend J. C. Austin, president of the Baptist National Convention, pronounced. "I will do all in my power to help you put it over." See J. C. Austin to Robert L. Vann, June 16, 1931, box 27, folder 15, Robert L. Vann Papers.
36. Florence Fisher Parry, "I Dare Say—Below the Mason and Dixon," *Pittsburgh Press*, April 12, 1933.
37. Even so, Walter White encouraged Brown to vigorously protest the Parry article. For Brown's response to the Parry article, see his correspondences with Walter White, April 18–19, 1933, NAACP Branch Records, pt. 1: G-191, NAACP Papers, Library of Congress.
38. R. L. Hill, "A View of the Hill: A Study of the Experiences and Attitudes of the Hill District of Pittsburgh, Pennsylvania" (master's thesis, University of Pittsburgh, 1974).
39. Homer Brown to Oliver J. Keller, editor of the *Pittsburgh Post-Gazette*, March 1, 1933, NAACP Branch Records, emphasis mine.
40. Program of lecture course for elevator operators, 1931, box 3, folder 124, Urban League Records, University of Pittsburgh Archives Service Center.
41. Ernest Rice McKinney, "The Psychology of Race," excerpts, January 14, 1931, box 3, folder 124, Urban League Records.
42. The Reverend J. C. Austin, president of the National Baptist Convention, praised the *Courier* as "a voice crying into the wilderness" for justice. See J. C. Austin to Robert L. Vann, August 27, 1930, box 27, folder 15, Robert L. Vann Papers.
43. Locally and nationally, black leaders also contended with pseudoscientific theories of racial intelligence. In the early twentieth century, many white Americans believed that Anglo-Saxon brains were more capable of higher-level functions than brains of other races, especially African Americans, and a number of scholars published papers and books that built off this idea. Between 1881 and 1930 scholars undertook at least 140 studies of racial intelligence. For many whites, the belief in the innate inferiority of African Americans served to justify their oppression and exploitation. But beginning in the 1930s a host of biologists, social scientists, and other scholars conducted studies that discredited the idea of innate racial inferiority. For instance, several psychologists challenged the validity of using intelligence tests to compare the neurological capabili-

ties of black and white students; instead, they conclusively demonstrated that environmental factors were a much stronger determinant of performance and that differences within races were far greater than differences between races. The increasing presence in the academy of gifted black intellectuals, including Ralph Bunche, Abram Harris, and W. E. B. Du Bois, cast additional doubt on theories of racial intelligence. See Sitkoff, *A New Deal for Blacks*, 143. Black journals and newspapers dedicated considerable space to discrediting racial theories of mental ability. For example, see Thomas R. Garth, "Eugenics, Euthenics, and Race," *Opportunity*, July 1930, Otto Klineberg, "The Question of Negro Intelligence," *Opportunity*, December 1931, and W. O. Brown, "Myths About Race," *Opportunity*, December 1931. Also see Charles H. Wesley, "Propaganda and Historical Writing: The Emancipation of the Historian," *Opportunity*, August 1935.

44. "Insulting Article in Defense of South Resented," *Pittsburgh Courier*, April 22, 1933; John L. Clark, "Wylie Avenue," *Pittsburgh Courier*, April 22, 1933.
45. See "Be Yourself, Advice of Robeson to Negroes," *Pittsburgh Courier*, February 7, 1931 (the same issue features the advertisement for hair-straightening gel). For other examples of *Courier* stories fostering race pride, see "America's Highest Paid and Most Glamorous Band, Led by the Inimitable 'Duke,' Coming Here for Monster Coronation," January 7, 1933, and "No Proof of Racial Superiority, Claim of White Professor," August 15, 1931. For accounts of Jim Crowism, see "'Let That Be a Warning to You,' Whites Cry as They Shoot at Southern Negroes Working on Highways," August 29, 1931, "12 People Victims of Mob Madness in 1929 against 25 This Year," January 3, 1931, and "Schuyler Jailed," January 14, 1933. An example of the *Courier* as a public forum for racial discussions can be found in "What Can Our Ministers Do Against Lynching?," January 31, 1931. For black internationalism, see "Haitians Strike to Protest Acts of U.S. Engineer," February 7, 1931, George Schuyler, "Views and Reviews," January 31, 1931, "Ethiopian King Puts Halt to Extortioning of Peasantry," January 14, 1933, "Says America Is a Real Friend of Liberia," January 21, 1933, and "Haitian Home Rule Still Idle Dream, Opinion," January 21, 1933. For a story about a young woman inducted into the prestigious Loendi club over a "tea engagement," see the women's activity section of the *Courier* from January 31, 1931. Such accounts likely had little resonance among working-class readers. Similarly, the Talk O' Town column in the women's activity section regularly featured accounts of exclusive meetings, galas, and other social events held by elite clubs such as Loendi and the Frogs. See, for example, August 11, 1934.
46. "NAACP Slush Fund Aired," *Pittsburgh Courier*, October 9, 1926.
47. See Walter White to Robert L. Vann and Robert L. Vann to Walter White, October 8, 1926, folder 9, box C201, pt. 1, NAACP Records, Library of Congress.
48. See examples from the *Fort Worth Light*, *New York News*, *Inter-State Tattler*, the *Arizona Times*, and the *New York Age* in folder 12, box C201, pt. 1, NAACP Papers.
49. Benjamin Tanner Johnson to Robert Vann, October 9, 1926, and H. D. Murphy to Robert L. Vann, October 14, 1926, folder 9, box C201, pt. 1, NAACP Papers.
50. James Weldon Johnson to Sherman S. Furr, and James Weldon Johnson to Moorfield Storey, October 14, 1926, folder 9, box C201, pt. 1, NAACP Papers.
51. See William Pickens, "The *Courier* Repeats Its Own Lies," October 8, 1926, folder 9, box C201, NAACP Papers.
52. NAACP press release, October 15, 1926, folder 9, box C201, NAACP Papers.

53. See "NAACP-Courier 'Bury The Hatchet,'" *Pittsburgh Courier*, September 14, 1929, and W. E. B. Du Bois to Robert L. Vann, August 27, 1929, folder 12, box C201, pt. 1, NAACP Papers.
54. Buni, *Robert L. Vann of the* Pittsburgh Courier, 161.
55. James Simmons, interview with Peter Gottlieb, June 13, 1974, Pittsburgh Oral History Project.
56. Weiss, *Farewell to the Party of Lincoln*, 4, 3. Elsewhere, membership in the Republican Party served as a mark of social distinction. See Charles Pete T. Banner-Haley, "The *Philadelphia Tribune* and the Persistence of Black Republicanism during the Great Depression," *Pennsylvania History: A Journal of Mid-Atlantic Studies* 65, no. 2 (1998): 190–202.
57. "West Virginia Centenarian for Hoover," *Pittsburgh Courier*, October 13, 1928.
58. Weiss, *Farewell to the Party of Lincoln*, 17. Also see Sitkoff, *A New Deal for Blacks*, 30.
59. Banner-Haley, "The *Philadelphia Tribune* and the Persistence of Black Republicanism during the Great Depression," 198.
60. *New York Amsterdam News*, October 19, 1932. A few black newspapers joined the *Courier* in supporting FDR in 1932. The *Baltimore Afro-American*, the *Washington Tribune*, the *Norfolk Journal and Guide*, and the *Indianapolis Recorder* all endorsed Roosevelt. See Buni, *Robert L. Vann of the* Pittsburgh Courier, 371.
61. Brewer, "Robert Lee Vann and the *Pittsburgh Courier*," 80–89.
62. See Ruth Louise Simmons, "The Negro in Recent Pittsburgh Politics" (MA thesis, University of Pittsburgh, 1944), 4–5.
63. Brewer, "Robert Lee Vann and the *Pittsburgh Courier*," 80–83; Buni, *Robert L. Vann of the* Pittsburgh Courier, 175–76.
64. Simmons, "The Negro in Recent Pittsburgh Politics," 7.
65. *Pittsburgh Courier*, December 12, 1925.
66. As Lawrence Hogan points out, the presidential election of 1928 offered some indication of growing black frustration with the GOP. That year, a few major black weeklies endorsed Democrat Al Smith over Herbert Hoover, including the *Chicago Defender*. The *Defender* resumed its traditional support of the Republican Party four years later, in 1932, when it tepidly supported Herbert Hoover over Franklin Roosevelt. (*A Black National News Service: The Associated Negro Press and Claude Barnett* [Haworth, NJ: St. Johann Press, 2002], 172).
67. Simmons, "The Negro in Recent Pittsburgh Politics," 7.
68. Buni, *Robert L. Vann of the* Pittsburgh Courier, 177–82, 187.
69. Quoted in Sitkoff, *A New Deal for Blacks*, 26–27.
70. "Unemployment on the Increase," *Pittsburgh Courier*, November 29, 1930.
71. Dennis C. Dickerson, *Out of the Crucible: Black Steelworkers in Western Pennsylvania, 1875–1980* (Albany: State University of New York Press, 1986), 119–22.
72. "Unemployment on the Increase," *Pittsburgh Courier*, November 29, 1930.
73. Kenneth L. Kusmer, *A Ghetto Takes Shape: Black Cleveland, 1870–1930* (Urbana: University of Illinois Press, 1976), 204–5; "Urban League Offers Hoover Unemployment Service Figures in U.S.," *Pittsburgh Courier*, November 1, 1930.
74. Sitkoff, *A New Deal for Blacks*, 27. Also see T. Arnold Hill, "What Price Black Jobs," *Opportunity*, October 1930. In their newspaper, the Black Shirts asked, "Why

shouldn't we protect ourselves and our families by replacing the Negro help with the white unemployed?"

75. Undeterred by the dreary employment data, about four hundred thousand southern blacks migrated to northern cities during the 1930s, far fewer than in the preceding decade but enough to increase the total northern black population by 25 percent. The influx of new migrants in the North placed additional strains on urban charity and relief associations, whose resources were already stretched thin. Nationwide, two million blacks were on relief roles in the early 1930s. See Sitkoff, *A New Deal for Blacks*, 28–29.
76. ULP, report of visits with companies, October 4, 1930, box 3, folder 119, Urban League Records.
77. Bruce M. Stave, "Pittsburgh and the New Deal," in *The New Deal*, vol. 2, *The State and Local Levels*, ed. John Braeman, Robert H. Bremner, and David Brody (Columbus: Ohio State University Press, 1975), 390.
78. ULP, 1930 annual report, box 6, folder 246, Urban League Records.
79. Arthur J. Edmunds, *Daybreakers: The Story of the Urban League of Pittsburgh, the First Sixty-Five Years* (Pittsburgh: Urban League of Pittsburgh, 1999), 78.
80. See Dickerson, *Out of the Crucible*, 120; Edmunds, *Daybreakers*, 86. Additionally, African Americans represented 22 percent of all employment seekers at Allegheny County's Emergency Association. See "Two Groups of the Unemployed in Pittsburgh," *Pittsburgh Business Review*, October 29, 1931, 12–16. By 1933, unemployment in Pittsburgh had reached 43.4 percent for African Americans and 15.7 percent for whites. See Stave, "Pittsburgh and the New Deal," 390–91.
81. ULP, 1932 annual report, box 6, folder 8, Urban League Records. The problems for blacks in Pittsburgh were made worse by new technological developments. As John Bodnar, Roger Simon, and Michael Weber point out, through increased mechanization the steel industry steadily eliminated unskilled positions. Between 1900 and 1930 unskilled positions decreased from 32 to 22 percent of the total workforce, which consequently increased competition at that level (*Lives of Their Own: Blacks, Italians, and Poles in Pittsburgh, 1900–1960* [Urbana: University of Illinois Press, 1982], 117). For an illuminating analysis of the depression and the shift from an industrial-based to a consumer-based economy, see Michael Bernstein, "Why the Great Depression Was Great: Toward a New Understanding of the Interwar Economic Crisis in the United States," in *The Rise and Fall of the New Deal Order: 1930–1980*, ed. Steve Fraser and Gary Gerstle (Princeton, NJ: Princeton University Press, 1989), 32–50.
82. Harold Lett, "Work," *Opportunity*, March 1931.
83. Harold Lett, "Work," *Opportunity*, March 1931.
84. Along with the city council, individuals and charitable organizations furnished some relief from the hardships of the Depression. The Mellon family and other wealthy Pittsburghers donated several hundred thousand dollars to the city's welfare fund, the Pittsburgh City Council voted to provide emergency relief aid, and several steel companies provided additional donations. Carnegie plants distributed food to needy employees and their families, and the Penn Iron and Steel Company provided free lodging to their black employees. See Buni, *Robert L. Vann of the* Pittsburgh Courier, 188, and Dickerson, *Out of the Crucible*, 119–22. The *Courier* also sponsored charity drives for the poor. In November and December 1930, for example, it led a campaign to provide relief for the hun-

dred neediest families in the Hill District. For a month, *Courier* employees went from store to store in the Hill to collect donations, offering as an incentive free advertising space in the newspaper. See "H-E-L-P!" *Pittsburgh Courier*, November 22, 1930.
85. Bartow Tipper, interview with Dennis Dickerson, March 4, 1980, Pittsburgh Oral History Project.
86. Merril Lynch, interview with Peter Gottlieb, August 22, 1974, Pittsburgh Oral History Project.
87. Reverend Harold Tolliver, interview with Dennis Dickerson, October 9, 1974, Pittsburgh Oral History Project.
88. Laurence Glasco, "Double Burden: The Black Experience in Pittsburgh," in *City at the Point: Essays on the Social History of Pittsburgh*, ed. Samuel P. Hays (Pittsburgh: University of Pittsburgh Press, 1989), 77.
89. Vann's concerns with Hoover's handling of the Depression contributed to his political defection. Rivalries among Pennsylvania Republicans, which delayed measures to address unemployment, likely played a role as well. Vann supported progressive Republican Gifford Pinchot in the 1930 state gubernatorial primary over the more conservative Francis Brown. Brown enjoyed the support of the old guard Republican machine under the control of William Vare of Philadelphia. Four years earlier Vare defeated Pinchot in a contest for a U.S. Senate seat, but in 1929 he lost his position when Pinchot brought corruption charges against him and a Senate investigative committee confirmed the allegations. Thus in the 1930 gubernatorial primary the humiliated Vare worked to defeat his rival. With Vann's help Pinchot subsequently won both the primary and general election, but the bitter contest divided state Republicans as the Depression entered its worst phase. For Vann, the fractured state of the Pennsylvania Republican Party, along with Hoover's tepid response to the Depression and his fast-declining popularity, incentivized a party change.
90. Banner-Haley, "The *Philadelphia Tribune* and the Persistence of Black Republicanism during the Great Depression," 198.
91. Franklin D. Roosevelt, "The Candidate Discusses the National Democratic Platform," in *The Public Papers and Addresses of Franklin D. Roosevelt*, vol. 1: *The Genesis of the New Deal, 1928–1932* (New York: Harper, 1969).
92. "Republican Confab 'Detours' on Negro Issue," *Pittsburgh Courier*, June 25, 1932.
93. Brewer, "Robert Lee Vann and the *Pittsburgh Courier*," 84.
94. See Brewer, "Robert Lee Vann and the *Pittsburgh Courier*," 84; Buni, *Robert L. Vann of the* Pittsburgh Courier, 190–93.
95. Simmons, "The Negro in Recent Pittsburgh Politics," 4.
96. Stave, "Pittsburgh and the New Deal," 380.
97. Simmons, "The Negro in Recent Pittsburgh Politics," 16.
98. Buni, *Robert L. Vann of the* Pittsburgh Courier, 202; Brewer, "Robert Lee Vann and the *Pittsburgh Courier*," 85.
99. For an example of Vann's leadership in these organizations, see "Roosevelt Clubs of PA Open Offices," *Pittsburgh Courier*, October 1, 1932.
100. Robert L. Vann, "The Patriot and the Partisan," September 11, 1932, box 31, folder 2, Robert L. Vann Papers.
101. Robert L. Vann, "The Patriot and the Partisan," September 11, 1932, box 31, folder 2, Robert L. Vann Papers.

The Ranks of this New Army   145

102. For the *Courier* version, see "This Year I See Millions of American Negroes Turning the Picture of Abraham Lincoln to the Wall," *Pittsburgh Courier*, September 17, 1932.
103. "Pittsburgh Voters Snarl at Hoover; Democrats and Communists Active," *Baltimore Afro-American*, October 8, 1932.
104. Brewer, "Robert Lee Vann and the *Pittsburgh Courier*," 88.
105. Glasco, "Double Burden," 85.
106. "Hoover and Slavery," *Pittsburgh Courier*, October 3, 1932; "Hoover's Negrophobia Explained," *Pittsburgh Courier*, October 15, 1932. Also see "And There Stood the One Hundred," *Pittsburgh Courier*, October 8, 1932, and "Two Local Hoover Meetings Flop," *Pittsburgh Courier*, October 15, 1932.
107. Floyd Calvin, "A Frantic Gesture," *Pittsburgh Courier*, October 15, 1932.
108. Muri Benson, "Just a Few of the Reasons Why Hoover Should Not Be Re-Elected," *Pittsburgh Courier*, October 22, 1932.
109. "Smoking Out Mr. Hoover," *Pittsburgh Courier*, October 8, 1932.
110. See *Pittsburgh Courier*, August 20 to November 5, 1932, for Holloway's political cartoons discrediting Hoover. Also see Sunnyboy Sam, *Pittsburgh Courier*, October 3, 1932.
111. See in the following articles in the *Courier*: "'Slave Labor' Charges to be Heard in Senate: Wagner to Seek Action," September 17, 1932, "Senator Wagner to Urge Probe of Delta Horror," September 17, 1932, "Senators Will Support Delta Probe Bill," October 22, 1932, "Wagner Measure Gaining Support," October 22, 1932, and "To Probe Levee Labor Jim-Crow Charges in Miss.," November 5, 1932.
112. "Our Political Importance," *Pittsburgh Courier*, October 3, 1932; "'I Am For Roosevelt,' Says Fearless Preacher From New Orleans," *Pittsburgh Courier*, October 15, 1932.
113. "Roosevelt Endorsed by Butlers," *Pittsburgh Courier*, October 1, 1932; "Predicts Negro Roosevelt Vote," *Pittsburgh Courier*, October 1, 1932; "Forum Sentiment Favors Roosevelt," *Pittsburgh Courier*, October 22, 1932; "Notable [Black] Democrats Outnumber G.O.P.'s by Three to One Count," *Pittsburgh Courier*, October 22, 1932. See also "Franklin Roosevelt Four-Square," *Pittsburgh Courier*, October 22, 1932, and "Life Begins," *Pittsburgh Courier*, November 5, 1932.
114. For accounts of Vann's participation in political events in Pittsburgh and Philadelphia, see respectively, "Forum Sentiment Favors Roosevelt," *Pittsburgh Courier*, October 1, 1932, and "Roosevelt," *Pittsburgh Courier*, October 1, 1932.
115. "5,000 Negroes in Huge Crowd Which Greets the New York Governor Here," *Pittsburgh Courier*, October 22, 1932. For the full transcript of Roosevelt's speech at Forbes Field, see "Campaign Address on the Federal Budget at Pittsburgh, PA," in *The Public Papers and Addresses of Franklin D. Roosevelt*, 795-811.
116. William Leuchtenburg, *Franklin D. Roosevelt and the New Deal, 1932-1940* (New York: Harper and Row, 1965), 11-12.
117. The *Courier*'s city edition advertised this event in a large caption at the top of the front page: "City Awaits Monster Roosevelt Mass Meeting." For details of the event, see on the same page, "Austin, Vann to Talk Here Friday," *Pittsburgh Courier*, November 5, 1932. The event took place on Friday, November 11, three days after the election.
118. Allegheny County election returns, cabinet 1, reels 8-10, University of Pittsburgh Archives Service Center.

119. See "Negroes Important Factor as Democrats Sweep into Power," "Negro Vote Not 'on Sale,'" and "Control in Fifth Ward Is Jolted," *Pittsburgh Courier*, November 12, 1932, Brewer, "Robert Lee Vann and the *Pittsburgh Courier*," 88, and Simmons, "The Negro in Pittsburgh Politics," 13.
120. Merril Lynch, interview with Peter Gottlieb, August 22, 1974, Pittsburgh Oral History Project.
121. Allegheny County election returns, cabinet 1, reels 8–10, University of Pittsburgh Archives Service Center.
122. Stave, "Pittsburgh and the New Deal," 376–77.
123. Sitkoff, *A New Deal for Blacks*, 31.
124. Sitkoff, *A New Deal for Blacks*, 31. Sitkoff's list includes only New York and Kansas City, but contemporary reports and the electoral records from Pittsburgh's Third Ward indicate that the majority of black Pittsburghers voted for FDR in 1932.
125. See Banner-Haley, *To Do Good and to Do Well*, 119.
126. For the Vann quote, see "Vann Says: 'Thank You,'" *Pittsburgh Courier*, November 12 1932. For assessments of black voting in Pennsylvania and nationally, see "Negroes Important Factor as Democrats Sweep into Power," *Pittsburgh Courier*, November 12, 1932; "Election Reveals Negro Democratic Swing," *Pittsburgh Courier*, November 26, 1932.
127. Buni, *Robert L. Vann of the* Pittsburgh Courier, 197–98.
128. Simmons, "The Negro in Recent Pittsburgh Politics," 16.
129. Buni, *Robert L. Vann of the* Pittsburgh Courier, 203–4.
130. Jones headed the Colored Women's Clubs of Southern California (Theodora Jones to Robert L. Vann, May 24, 1934, box 27, folder 14, Robert L. Vann Papers).
131. For instance, W. S. Fitts, Charles E. Jackson, and Jacob L. Phillips gained positions as real estate appraisers in the Home Loan Corporation, and Vann placed in the attorneys Theron Hamilton and P. J. Clyde Randall in the corporation's title searching department. Vann was particularly proud of securing a position for a young political organizer named Paul Jones as a workmen's compensation referee, which paid an annual salary of $5,000. See Buni, *Robert L. Vann of the* Pittsburgh Courier, 203–4, 217, Simmons, "The Negro in Recent Pittsburgh Politics," 17, and Stave, "Pittsburgh and the New Deal," 380.
132. Ralph M. Bashore, Pennsylvania secretary of forests and waters, to unknown recipient, March 20, 1935, box 27, folder 14, Robert L. Vann Papers.

CHAPTER FIVE

"The Taken-For-Granted Rights of American Citizenship"
REFORMERS AND THE QUEST FOR CIVIL EQUALITY
AND EDUCATIONAL JUSTICE, 1934–1937

Alice felt a pang of sadness when she handed her school books to the office secretary at Fifth Avenue High School in Pittsburgh and explained that she would not finish her senior year. It was October 1930. Her stepfather had recently died, and her mother, Ruby, had fallen ill. Alice had younger siblings to think about, and someone had to put food on the table and pay the rent. For a time, she held out hope that local social service agencies might provide assistance. Ruby had applied for aid from the mother's assistance fund after her second husband passed away, but it ultimately rejected her plea when it learned that she had never formally ended her first marriage.[1]

Alice's biological father still lived in Georgia. Ruby married him sometime in the 1910s, and the couple had three children together. They experienced considerable marital difficulties during this period, and eventually Ruby decided to leave him, take the children, and migrate to Pittsburgh. That she did not bother to file for divorce suggests she may have departed in haste and that the relationship did not end amicably. As Ruby boarded a northbound train, she hoped to leave her painful personal experiences behind her and start a new life across the Ohio River, where she could escape the crushing constraints of Jim Crow and set her children up for a better future.

But the ghosts of Ruby's past seemed to follow her to Pittsburgh. In the lower Hill District, African Americans lived in poor, isolated neighborhoods and attended under-resourced schools that were segregated in all but name. In public spaces, too, Ruby noticed traces of the racial caste system that she thought she left behind. Even moving on from her first marriage proved difficult, as she learned through her effort to obtain public assistance.

The historical record says little about Ruby's illness, but it proved serious enough that it prevented her from working and put her family in a desperate position. Upon learning of Alice's decision to drop out and enter the labor market, school officials notified the Urban League of Pittsburgh (ULP).[2] Along with its other programs, the ULP provided educational outreach services for struggling African American students in inner-city schools. It employed a home and school visitor to connect with them, identify problems, and support their success. Since the early 1920s, Georgine Pearce had filled this role for the league.

Like many black professional women, Pearce struggled to build a career in Pittsburgh. Born around 1900, she grew up in the city and came of age during the height of the Great Migration. Census records offer conflicting accounts of whether she finished high school, but around 1923 the league nevertheless hired her. It seems odd that the ULP would select a high-school dropout to work with students and represent the organization at local schools. However, surviving records by and about Pearce indicate that in appearance and comportment she presented herself as an educated, capable, professional woman prepared to perform valuable service for the league.

As the ULP's home and school visitor, Pearce acted as a liaison between struggling black students, their parents, and white school teachers and administrators. The rights and well-being of black children and teens represented her foremost concern, and she advocated for them throughout the twenties and early thirties. Pearce produced regular reports on this work—invariably well written, concise, and clear—that make plain her sincere commitment to the students she oversaw and her desire to promote cooperation between local teachers and parents. The setting in which she operated could vary considerably from one day to the next. She often sat in the office of a school principal to discuss one or more students, but she also spent considerable time traveling through the lower Hill District and other poor neighborhoods to visit students' homes and build relationships with their parents and guardians. In 1930 alone she made 278 visits to the schools, homes, and relatives of black students like Alice.[3] Pearce met with Alice late that year and spoke with her teacher at Fifth Avenue High School. Given the pressure on Alice to find a job, Pearce worked with the school and the children's service bureau to arrange for her to take evening classes during her senior year so that she could graduate with her classmates.

Given the circumstances, Pearce did the best she could for Alice. Life was not easy for black women in Pittsburgh, as she knew from personal experience. Three years earlier, Pearce enrolled at the newly established Henry Clay Frick Training School for Teachers, hoping one day to secure a more permanent and remunerative career as a public school teacher. If she indeed lacked a high school diploma, her record of service at the Urban League may have helped persuade administrators to register her anyway. Pearce graduated from Frick by the end of 1928, and additionally she spent a summer semester at Columbia University's Teachers College.[4] But like every black applicant before her, she failed to obtain a teaching job. In the teaching profession and in many other occupations in Pittsburgh, African Americans encountered stiff racial barriers that limited their economic and social mobility. Pearce knew well what migrants like Ruby and Alice learned gradually, that Jim Crow existed in northern cities under different guises.

In this difficult setting, staff in the Pittsburgh branch of the NAACP (PNAACP) labored to secure what local activist Homer Brown called "the full, taken-for-granted rights of American citizenship."[5] Like other reformers in the Steel City, Brown held a broad conception of citizenship that included access to economic opportunity and political empowerment along with the right to feel and be treated like a first-class citizen. Full citizens could swim in public pools alongside whites, they could use the pavilions at a local amusement park any day they wished, and they could stay at any hotel they could afford. Full citizens could order food from downtown restaurants in Pittsburgh, and they did not have to sit in the rearmost car of the B&O railroad, or in the balconies of local movie theaters, or in a segregated section of Forbes Field, where the Pirates played. Full citizens could work as salespersons in department stores, nurses in hospitals, and teachers in public schools.

While local Urban Leaguers worked primarily to improve the material prospects and physical well-being of black Pittsburghers, PNAACP staff strove to secure some of citizenship's less tangible but nevertheless important features. In the Steel City, blacks of all classes faced daily assaults on their sense of self-worth. They lived in a world full of coded social cues that indicated their subordinate status. African Americans read the code when the owner of a local coffee shop told them he did not serve "their kind," or when a writer for the *Pittsburgh Press* warned white women against the dangers of lustful black men, or when school administrators informed a group of black teens that they could not join their white classmates at the prom. Operating in the hostile racial climate of interwar Pittsburgh, PNAACP activists up-

Georgine Pearce, ca. 1932.
Arthur J. Edmunds, *Daybreakers: The Story of the Urban League of Pittsburgh* (Pittsburgh: Urban League of Pittsburgh, 1983), 62.

held the dignity of all African Americans and demanded that white America live up to the values embedded in the Declaration of Independence and U.S. Constitution.

Civil rights violations in Pittsburgh especially oppressed African American women. Georgine Pearce and young Alice embodied the experiences of many who felt the twin pressures of gender and race squeeze out the possibilities of their lives and smother their creative potential. By custom, the majority group closed off to black women a host of traditionally female occupations like teaching. PNAACP staff struggled for years to break down the barrier to public school employment, but they discovered that combatting northern-style Jim Crow came with special difficulties. Since no school policy or codified rule expressly prohibited African Americans from obtaining teaching jobs, the city's school board proved impervious to the association's repeated legal attacks in the twenties and early thirties.

Northern Jim Crow rebuffed the local association on other fronts as well. The PNAACP, as we have seen, waged a lengthy and unsuccessful legal battle to prosecute officials who unlawfully deported over forty black migrants to the West Virginia border in 1933. Ultimately, public officials' refusal to hold police accountable for their actions, coupled with the *Pittsburgh Courier*'s dramatic call to abandon the Republican Party, convinced PNAACP head Homer Brown and many other reformers to get more engaged in the electoral arena. As black Pittsburghers acquired greater political clout, they gained recognition from the major political parties and began electing African Americans to key government positions. By the mid-thirties, Pittsburgh's reform community could for the first time harness the power of the state to press for new civil rights legislation and break down the barrier to teaching jobs.

The Increasing Political Power of Black Pittsburgh, 1934–1935

In 1934 the citizens of Pittsburgh's First Legislative District, which comprised the Hill District as well as the adjacent first ward, elected Homer Brown to the Pennsylvania House of Representatives, making him the fifth black member of that body. Brown ran for office two years earlier and narrowly lost, but in 1934 black voters turned out in droves to elect him. Over 8,200 voters cast their ballots for Brown, and he consequently defeated his closest competitor by 3,466 votes.[6]

The election returns from Pittsburgh's third and fifth wards also suggest black voters had enough of Governor Gifford Pinchot and his attorney general, William Schnader. Still rankled over the way Republicans handled the Beaver County abduction case, they overwhelmingly voted for George Earle, Pinchot's challenger, and helped the Democrat win the governorship. Earle's election marked the culmination of black Pittsburghers' political realignment with the Democratic Party that had begun in 1932 when most of them voted for Franklin Roosevelt in the presidential election. The black electorate's transition coincided with the Democratic Party's political takeover of Pennsylvania, which just five years earlier seemed like an unassailable Republican stronghold. More than a few black reformers saw in these developments what Vann recognized in 1932—that acquiring political power through the ballot offered the best chance of reshaping their destinies. One journalist exclaimed that Brown's election heralded "a new political day for the Pittsburgh

Negro," and he put local political leaders on notice that "from now on race voters are more determined than ever . . . to vote for members of their own race and receive their just patronage through solid and concentrated political power."[7]

Yet black Pittsburghers faced natural challenges that made it difficult to marshal their full political and economic strength. Geologists describe western Pennsylvania as old topography—a region just beyond the reach of the last glacial advance where, over thousands of years, streams and rivers carved steep valleys and ravines into the landscape. The geomorphology of western Pennsylvania mattered for black Pittsburghers in the 1930s. Imposing hills and rivers divided their neighborhoods and made it difficult to hold mass gatherings or foster concerted action to the extent possible in other northern black communities. Even within the Hill District, which served as the political and cultural center of the black community, the walk from the lower Hill to the upper Hill required considerable physical effort.

Notions of class identity furthered the geographic separation of black Pittsburghers. In the Hill District, which housed about half the city's black population, poor and working-class African Americans often lived in the lower Hill while many middle-class blacks—including reformers like Homer Brown, Daisy Lampkin, and Grace Lowndes—preferred the more comfortable neighborhoods of the upper Hill, dubbed Sugartop. Elsewhere, black Pittsburghers concentrated in smaller communities south, west, and east of the Hill, like East Liberty, Beltzhoover, and the Northside. According to the February 1938 edition of the *Informer*, the ULP's monthly publication, these barriers consequently diluted black voting strength. Drawing from this source and mining the Allegheny County election returns, historian Laurence Glasco concludes that black Pittsburghers elected fewer black representatives than they could have, given their numbers.[8]

Even so, those they did manage to place in office during the interwar period made good use of their positions. Homer Brown's successful bid for the state legislature marked a major transition in his career as a civil rights activist. From 1925 to 1934 Brown helped transform the PNAACP into an effective organization while participating in a host of other institutions, including the Centre Avenue YMCA, the Working Girls' Home, and the Hill District Community Council.[9] Despite the PNAACP's achievements, Brown knew well the limits of litigation and protest. With his election in 1934, he was able to use the power of the state to combat discrimination and advance racial causes.

As a state legislator, Brown led an investigation of the Allegheny County Board of Education for discriminatory hiring practices, authored an amendment to the McGinnis labor relations bill to protect the right of black workers to join unions, petitioned for the impeachment of a Lancaster judge who openly condoned lynching, and helped establish Pittsburgh's Fair Employment Practices Commission, which ensured equitable employment of black workers in the city's defense industries.[10]

Nationally, African Americans elected Brown and sixteen other black candidates to state assemblies in 1934.[11] The New Deal period saw a sharp rise in black representation in state and federal positions. By 1935 Roosevelt had appointed over forty African American leaders to various New Deal agencies and high federal positions. They included young college graduates such as Ralph Bunche, Clark Foreman, and Robert Weaver as well as longtime civil rights activists like Eugene Kinckle Jones, William Pickens, and Robert L. Vann.[12]

While in Washington serving as special assistant to U.S. attorney general Homer Cummings, Vann joined an interdepartmental committee on black affairs that the press dubbed the "Black Cabinet." Its members met weekly at the home of Mary McLeod Bethune to discuss ways to link the president's New Deal agenda with civil rights. Among other actions, they pressed representatives of the Civilian Conservation Corps, Works Progress Administration, and other agencies to promote black rights. As historian Harvard Sitkoff has noted, "The Black Cabinet's very existence focused government attention on civil rights. It made the bureaucracy self-conscious of black matters, a necessary first step toward action by federal officials."[13]

The Black Cabinet and white advocates of racial justice, including Eleanor Roosevelt and U.S. Interior secretary Harold Ickes, applied pressure on Roosevelt and his administration to expand the scope of the New Deal to address racial issues. The increasing size of the black electorate added to the pressure. Black leaders believed the African American vote could tip the balance in national elections, and they sought to leverage that power to force Democrats and Republicans to make racial justice a greater priority. Eugene Kinckle Jones, executive secretary of the National Urban League (NUL) and member of the Black Cabinet, called on black voters to cast ballots for African American candidates at every opportunity; doing so, he maintained, represented an essential step toward wresting concessions from New Deal administrators.

Paul F. Jones, a black political organizer for the Democratic Party in Pittsburgh, shared Jones's sentiment. "A wave of race consciousness is sweeping the State of Pennsylvania," he exclaimed in 1934. With 220,000 African Americans in Philadelphia and another 100,000 in Allegheny County, he believed black Pennsylvanians could demand meaningful support from the Democratic Party.[14]

Vann had long coveted a federal post, but his experiences in Washington proved disappointing. "Not once while in the Justice Department did Vann handle any case of importance," his biographer noted. He could not even set up a meeting with the attorney general. Frustrated, Vann resigned his post in 1935 after only two years in office.[15] When he returned to Pittsburgh in 1935, Vann recommitted himself to building up the readership of the *Courier* and using the paper to promote black rights nationally and locally. In 1935 the *Courier* campaigned for national antilynching legislation, expressed support for the Scottsboro nine, and celebrated a landmark human-rights achievement in Pennsylvania: the state equal rights act.[16]

The Pennsylvania Equal Rights Act of 1935

In 1887 Pennsylvania legislators passed an equal rights bill that forbade discrimination based on race, but the law lacked meaningful enforcement measures and generally failed to safeguard civil rights for minority groups. Moreover, whatever class differences separated white employers and workers, they often shared a common expectation that the highest paying and most desirable jobs would go to whites. For these reasons, black leaders in Pennsylvania had lobbied for an amended law that would enforce the provisions in the original act, yet their efforts up to the mid-thirties proved unsuccessful. In 1913, 1915, and 1921 they forced the issue on the state legislature's agenda, but the Republican-led Senate voted against the measure each time.[17]

With the changed political landscape in the mid-thirties, however, black reformers believed they had an opportunity to force a robust civil rights act through the legislature. In the 1932, 1933, and 1934 elections they helped liberal Democrats sweep into local, state, and federal offices, and they had Homer Brown and four other black leaders positioned in Harrisburg. Whether inspired by a genuine interest in equality or an astute political assessment of black voting power, in the mid-thirties politicians from both parties began making racial progress a greater priority. With the fall elections looming, in May 1934 incumbent Republican senator David A. Reed called for the creation of a black national guard regiment, and a year later the Democrat-led

House and Republican-led Senate approved its formation.[18] A magistrate found the manager of Philadelphia's Earle Theatre guilty of denying first-floor seating to black patrons.[19] The mayor of Philadelphia ordered the appointment of black district detectives to counter the racial imbalance of the city's police force.[20] And George Earle, elected governor in 1934, condemned the history of racism in the state, argued that economic discrimination caused black poverty, and forced the University of Pittsburgh Medical School to admit black students.[21] Therefore, when Hobson Reynolds, a black Republican, introduced in the legislature a new civil rights bill, African American leaders vigorously campaigned for its passage.

The Reynolds bill—known officially as Public Law 297—provided stiff penalties for any hotel, restaurant, theater, hospital, school, or other institution found guilty of racial discrimination, including up to sixty days imprisonment and fines between $100 and $500.[22] In support of the act, the *Pittsburgh Courier* published stories calling attention to its historical significance, and the PNAACP, ULP, and Pittsburgh chapter of the National Negro Congress lobbied local and state officials for its passage.[23] Meanwhile, Homer Brown worked in Harrisburg to drum up support for the bill.

From the introduction of the Reynolds bill to its final passage into law, state Republicans and Democrats vied to gain strategic advantages from it. Hoping to regain the loyalty of black voters, Republican leaders encouraged Reynolds to sponsor the equal rights bill. The move came with political risks. A significant segment of state Republicans' constituency, including the powerful Pennsylvania Hotels Association, opposed any law that penalized racial discrimination. After the Reynolds bill passed the House, the Republican-led Senate voted to approve the bill. If Governor George Earle vetoed the bill, as they expected, Republicans could draw alienated black voters away from the Democrats without upsetting their white constituents. However, when the GOP learned that Earle intended to counter them by actually signing the act into law, Senate Republicans hurriedly introduced a resolution to recall the bill.[24]

Earle initially stated he would not sign the Reynolds bill until he had had time to study it and consider its implications, but the Senate's plan to recall the bill forced him to make a quick decision. If the bill returned to the Senate, Republicans likely would either scrap it or remove its most important provisions. Brown personally appealed to the governor and reassured him of its political merits. On June 11, just minutes before the Senate approved a resolution to recall the bill, Earle signed into law the Pennsylvania Equal Rights

Act. Standing next to him at the historic moment was David L. Lawrence, secretary of the commonwealth, Charles J. Margiotti, the attorney general, and Representative Brown.[25]

The event marked a major milestone in Pennsylvania's history of race relations, but some black leaders worried that the new law did not go far enough. Vann believed that since PL 297 did not name a court of jurisdiction to convict violators, it would prove difficult to enforce. For their part, many whites across the state expressed outrage over the new law and vowed to disobey it. "This bill is a terrible thing," proclaimed the manager of an amusement park. "We will positively not allow Negroes to enter our dance halls or our swimming pools except when there are Negro picnics." Franklin Moore, chairman of the Pennsylvania Hotels Association, likewise urged hotel managers across the state to ignore the new law.[26]

Over the next year, the PNAACP pursued test cases that defended the constitutionality of PL 297 and established legal precedents for the rest of the state. The first case concerned two city workers, a black man named Walter Wilson and his white friend, Terrence Mannus, who entered a restaurant in Pittsburgh's East Liberty neighborhood in February 1936 for a cup of coffee after shoveling snow from the street. The owner immediately ordered Wilson to leave but said Mannus could stay. When they reminded the owner of the new civil rights law, he insisted on his right to run his business how he saw fit. Soon after the incident, the PNAACP brought charges against him for violating the state civil rights act. The jury found him guilty, but his defense called for a retrial, claiming that the new law impinged on his constitutional rights. Finally, in October the court upheld the constitutionality of PL 297 and sustained the original ruling.[27]

Other cases followed shortly thereafter, one of which concerned Brentwood High School. The school's enrollment had declined over the years, and to sustain itself it began inviting student enrollment from nearby Baldwin Township, which had no high school. But when black students from Baldwin applied for admission to Brentwood, the school refused on the grounds that it made a verbal agreement that Baldwin would only send whites. The PNAACP took the case before a court of common pleas, and consequently it secured a mandamus that forced Brentwood to open its doors to black students.[28]

In a precedent-setting case, in October 1936 the PNAACP took action against the Borough of Avalon, which passed an ordinance that assigned certain days for African Americans to use its public pool. The association successfully demonstrated that the Borough had violated the civil rights act and had a court issue an injunction nullifying the borough's discriminatory ordinance.[29]

Although the 1935 Civil Rights Act made it more difficult to discriminate against African Americans in Pennsylvania, the law failed to eradicate some of the most obvious forms of discrimination. In 1941 Brown noted that blacks still could not dine in Pittsburgh's expensive restaurants, and hotels across the state continued to deny lodging to black customers.[30] Moreover, while the PNAACP did force Avalon to nullify its discriminatory policy for use of its public pool, it was not successful in desegregating the Highland Park public pool; through violence and intimidation, the pool remained closed to black swimmers until the early 1950s. On the economic front, black workers remained mired in the lowest positions industry had to offer and excluded from the protections labor unions might have provided.

"This Is Not a One-Man Job": Women in the PNAACP

By the time George Earle signed the Reynolds bill into law, Homer Brown had emerged as one of the preeminent civil rights leaders in Pennsylvania. Through surviving correspondence about him, along with accolades he received from national figures such as Walter White and Robert Bagnall, it seems evident that most of his colleagues thought highly of his litigation skills and credited him and Daisy Lampkin with transforming the PNAACP into an effective organization.

In February 1934, just before Brown turned his attention to his upcoming election campaign for the Pennsylvania state legislature, black leaders and white progressives in Pittsburgh held a banquet in his honor. The elite of Pittsburgh's reform community attended the event, including ULP head R. Maurice Moss, Ailene Briggs from the Association of Negro Social Workers, and prominent clergymen like the Reverend Harold Tolliver. The attendees dined on roast turkey, cranberries, and mashed potatoes as one speaker after another delivered talks showering praise on Brown.[31]

Beneath the surface of the accolades, however, the PNAACP had begun to show signs of internal fractures that would gradually break it apart. The local branch's decline after the mid-thirties owed much to Brown's departure to the state capital in Harrisburg and Daisy Lampkin's promotion to field secretary of the NAACP's national office in New York.[32] Yet Brown's authoritative leadership style seems to have played a role as well by alienating key members of the organization.

Determined to pursue justice and right wrongs in his adopted city, Brown demanded loyalty and support from both his staff and national leaders like Walter White. More than once, he complained to White that the national branch did not give the PNAACP its due credit for its achievements in Pittsburgh, and he felt insulted when Vann attempted to take over the "shanghai case." Brown cared deeply about racial inequality, but he also recognized the connection between the success of the PNAACP and his career ambitions. He had poured his talent and energy into the local association since taking it over in the mid-twenties, and by 1934 he had little patience with anyone in the organization who questioned his methods.

Like other branches, the PNAACP was supposed to hold regular elections for its officers. But by February 1934, Brown had postponed elections several times. Each time, he cited some more pressing issue that the association had to address. Jeanne Scott, who served multiple terms as the organization's secretary, gradually grew concerned about its increasingly hierarchical, male-driven leadership. "I whole heartedly approve of what Mr. Brown is trying to do here," she later confided, "but this is not a one-man job."[33] In early April 1934, Scott sent several letters to Walter White informing him about the elections. The information put the national leader in the awkward position of having to confront Brown on the issue. When he did, Brown offered an impatient dismissal.

> I don't know who brought this matter to your attention, but I have a suspicion that your office is being prodded by people here who would seek to tear down the work of the Association. If you have received letters concerning the operation of the branch, I should think it would be the proper thing for you to give me the information. . . . I personally do not feel that the time and money I have put into the work should also involve me into some dispute with a few disgruntles. Our [membership] campaign starts May 11th and our organization is whipping into shape nicely. At this particular moment I have no time to get involved in any dispute over any election.[34]

White could hardly be blamed if he bristled at the tone of the letter. In reply, he informed Brown that "the wisest way to avoid trouble from those who are critical, whatever their motives, is to give no just cause for criticism. . . . I should like to suggest personally that after the campaign is over a regular election be held."³⁵ PNAACP staff carried out the fundraising drive through May and early June with the hope of repeating their successes from 1929 and 1930, but they fell short of their goal by about $1,100—an enormous sum compared to previous campaigns.³⁶ Added to this, the campaign committee initially reported inaccurate figures to the PNAACP's executive board, prompting the board to ask Scott to prepare the organization's financial records for an audit.

While going through the files, Scott came across a copy of Brown's letter to White from two months earlier. Alarmed at its acerbic tone, she wrote a lengthy note to White to defend herself and clarify her position. "You know I am not one of the persons who would prode [sic] your office to seek to tear down the work of [the] association," she explained, "[but] I do believe now that we must save the Pittsburgh Branch from going down any further."³⁷

Though often excluded from leadership positions and left out of key decisions, women reformers performed much of the gritty grassroots work for Pittsburgh's racial-advancement organizations. Grace Lowndes went door-to-door in Pittsburgh's poorest neighborhoods to facilitate home economics programs, improve hygiene, and build connections with the black migrant community. Jeannette Washington helped lead health awareness campaigns to screen black infants, register them with local medical facilities, and educate their parents about preventative care. And Georgine Pearce monitored the education of local youth at their schools and homes. Sensitive to this disparity, Daisy Lampkin bemoaned the injustice of "men holding the leadership positions in the branches, [and women] having all of the work to do."³⁸

Along with Lampkin, Scott often served as one of the PNAACP's membership campaign officers who assumed the difficult task of persuading black and white Pittsburghers to become members and pledge money.³⁹ In both 1929 and 1930, the Pittsburgh branch was the first affiliate in the country to raise over $1,000 to support the NAACP's national projects, and this success owed much to the tact, persuasiveness, and persistence of Lampkin, Scott, and other women involved in the fundraising campaigns—a fact which sometimes escaped the notice of men in the organization.

In her letter to White, Scott suggested that Brown and other male officers alienated female fundraisers by ignoring their concerns and failing to recognize their contributions. In Scott's view, these actions caused the PNAACP's funding shortfall. "When women who raise ninety and one hundred dollars in each campaign are dissatisfied I believe it is best to try to determine what their grievance may be and get them to work," she maintained. But when

Scott raised this concern to a male officer, he replied, "Let them not work, the drive will go on just the same."[40]

Interwar-era black women faced seemingly insurmountable obstacles to their advancement both within mainstream social-justice organizations and in the greater society. In Pittsburgh, prevailing ideas about gender and race operated simultaneously to foreclose their chance for self-actualization. White women but not black women could find work as saleswomen in department stores. Positions for secretaries, typists, telephone operators, and nurses were almost always filled by white women. These barriers seemed unassailable at times, and black reformers often failed to break through them. But they almost never gave up on a cause once they deemed it important. They stayed organized, kept the issue on their radar, and tried new approaches. Reformers' collective efforts to open up careers in public education to African Americans illustrates their tough-minded resiliency.

The Struggle for Teaching Jobs in Pittsburgh

Black children and teens in the lower Hill District and other poor neighborhoods attended severely underfunded schools whose student bodies reflected the prevailing patterns of segregation in the larger community. Not coincidentally, their academic performance and graduation rates lagged far behind Protestant white students at better-resourced schools farther from the city center. The exclusion of black teachers compounded these inequities.

Since even predominantly black schools had at least some white students, the Allegheny County School Board never hired black applicants. School board members rejected on principle the idea of an African American instructing whites, and they understood that many white voters felt that way as well. "Colored teachers never will teach white children in the City of Pittsburgh," explained one board member in 1934. "Such a step would be suicidal and would bring upon the Board of Education the condemnation of the entire community."[41]

Reformers in other northern cities encountered and overcame this issue much earlier. In 1927, James Weldon Johnson of the NAACP wrote Brown that New York experienced the same problem until the association contested it and won. At the time he wrote the letter, several hundred black teachers worked in New York's public schools.[42] Pittsburgh trailed behind every major northern city on this issue. African Americans could graduate from local teacher-training schools, but their applications for employment invariably ended in failure. Black graduates in the Steel City found that they either had to move to another city or find some other occupation.

Unable to make use of her newly earned degree, Georgine Pearce returned to her post at the ULP as its home and school visitor. Likewise, Thelma Nelson earned her degree in 1930 but had to teach in a school outside Pittsburgh.[43] "Of the $6,000,000 pay roll to teachers of public schools in Pittsburgh, not a dollar goes to a Negro school teacher," one ULP worker reported bitterly.[44] Ernest Rice McKinney, a *Courier* contributor and member of the Socialist Party, noted the irony of this practice: "[The black domestic] may be nurse for the [white] children of the family, spend hours each day with them, directing their play, feeding them and finally tucking them away at night, but she cannot teach them in the public schools."[45]

The injustice stung black professionals. With teaching cut off from them, little else remained. Social researcher Jean Hamilton Walls, who in 1910 became the first black woman to graduate from the University of Pittsburgh, studied black alumni from that institution and found that half the men and 60 percent of the women lived outside Pennsylvania, principally because so few jobs were available to them in Pittsburgh.[46]

Since the Allegheny County School Board did not expressly prohibit hiring black teachers, pinning discrimination charges on it proved difficult. PNAACP workers tried various strategies over the years, but to no avail. In 1927, for instance, they attempted to coordinate black graduates to apply for teaching jobs en masse. If the board turned away all of them at once, Brown and his colleagues reasoned, they could prove that the school district discriminated against black applicants and have the county court issue a mandamus to force it to hire black teachers.[47] But in this instance and others to come they found the courts unwilling to cooperate.

In 1932 Homer Brown joined with other PNAACP staff, R. Maurice Moss of the ULP, and delegates from the *Pittsburgh Courier* to form a special steering committee tasked with breaking through the barrier to teaching jobs in Pittsburgh's schools.[48] The committee's ideological composition suggests the permeability of the boundary between reformers and radicals. Along with Brown and Moss, it featured black leaders from across the political spectrum, including McKinney, Reverend Tolliver, and middle-class professionals such as attorney Richard F. Jones.[49] It was not the first or last time mainstream reformers worked alongside radicals, as we have seen. The crushing racial pressure of interwar America disposed reformers to view the world through a racial lens, to pursue limited but achievable goals, and to develop alliances across the political spectrum.[50]

The minutes from the steering committee's meetings offer insights into how reformers negotiated the tricky terrain of race relations in the urban North, a place that abounded with cleverly camouflaged pitfalls. The members unanimously agreed that they needed to attract supporters from the majority group and that acquiring and distributing reliable information offered the most effective way to do so. "All of us here have had considerable contact with white people," one committee member pointed out. "It is largely a matter of converting them, but you must know what you are talking about.... [Y]ou must be prepared to say where you get your information, give authoritative sources, reference to page, volume, etc." With compelling evidence behind it, the committee believed it could win substantial white backing and bring a powerful case before the Allegheny County school board.[51]

These minutes also reveal much through what they *do not* say. At no point during the committee's meetings did any member mention its all-male composition. The records offer no explanation for why women professionals, whose lives were also affected by the school board's discriminatory practices, were excluded from the committee. The answer may have something to do with the committee's high prestige and perceived importance in the black reform community. Typically, women in the city's major racial-advancement organizations were relegated to middling roles that dealt with "women's issues," as indicated by their ranks and salaries, and they rarely held leadership positions. Perhaps equally troubling, the gendering of social justice work had the corollary effect of making it less likely that the records women produced would survive future office relocations or periodic file reductions, much less get passed on to local archives. In any case, the initiatives of the public education committee ended like those before it, with the barrier to teaching jobs remaining firmly in place.

In the mid-thirties, Pittsburgh's black leaders prepared for another attack against education discrimination. With Homer Brown in the state assembly, they could for the first time harness the power of the government to democratize the city's public schools. In April 1937, Brown introduced a resolution to create a special committee to investigate the hiring practices of the

Allegheny school board. The house approved the resolution, and it nominated Brown to serve as one of the five members of the investigatory committee. He also coordinated with a committee of race leaders in Pittsburgh tasked with assembling evidence against the school board. In the weeks leading up to the house committee's public hearings, which it held in Pittsburgh on April 24 and May 1, black leaders put together a compelling case.[52]

Acting as an expert witness, ULP executive secretary R. Maurice Moss testified that Pittsburgh's schools employed thirty-four hundred white teachers and no black teachers, despite having eleven thousand black students. As Moss pointed out, no other major northern city besides Pittsburgh had an all-white teaching staff.[53]

The racial composition of Pittsburgh's inner-city schools made the absence of black teachers all the more troubling. Of the eleven hundred students at Watt Street School, only twenty-five were white. Rose Street School, McKelvey School, Moorehead School, Franklin Street School, and Herron Hill Junior High had similarly disproportionate numbers. Despite having nearly all-black student populations, no black teacher could find work in these schools. Additionally, race leaders showed evidence that several of the black teachers denied jobs in Pittsburgh's schools actually had higher academic class rankings than white teachers who got hired.[54]

Such damning testimony ultimately convinced Brown's house colleagues that the Allegheny County school board consciously discriminated against nonwhite applicants, and as a result it compelled the board to begin hiring black teachers. Four months later, in early September 1937, Lawrence Peeler entered Watt Street School in the Hill District and became the first employed black teacher in Pittsburgh.[55]

With Homer Brown in Harrisburg and Daisy Lampkin working for the national branch of the NAACP in New York, the Pittsburgh NAACP declined steadily after the mid-thirties. By the close of World War II, activist Sophia B. Nelson observed that the PNAACP had gone from an "active" branch that hosted the NAACP conference in 1931 to an organization that rarely even held meetings. Edward Porter, who headed the organization's unsuccessful membership drive in 1944, echoed Jeanne Scott's observation from a decade earlier that lack of support from PNAACP officers doomed the effort.[56]

Still, even as the PNAACP declined through the late 1930s, Brown, Lampkin, and other PNAACP staff continued supporting the larger effort in the black reform community to pursue full citizenship. Few issues highlight how reformers across racial organizations cooperated with each other like the industrial labor movement, which is the subject of the next chapter.

NOTES

1. Georgine Pearce served as the home and school visitor for the Urban League of Pittsburgh through much of the 1920s and into the 1930s. In this role, she composed detailed reports that included statistical information on the number of schools and homes she visited, meetings she held, calls she made, students she contacted, and the like. She also wrote short descriptions of certain cases to illustrate common patterns. The anecdote at the beginning of this chapter comes from her October 1930 report. To protect students' anonymity, Pearce rarely mentioned their first names and never disclosed their last names. The experiences of the unnamed Fifth Avenue student in Pearce's October 1930 report bore close similarities to other young women that Pearce described throughout her time with the league (box 2, folder 81, Urban League Records, University of Pittsburgh Archives Service Center). In this chapter, I call the young woman Alice and her mother Ruby.
2. Georgine Pearce, home and school visitor report, October 1930, box 2, folder 81, Urban League Records.
3. ULP, 1930 annual report, box 6, folder 246, Urban League Records. Also see Pearce's reports from 1926 to 1930 (box 6, folder 81, Urban League Records).
4. Casework policy committee, minutes, February 5, 1929, box 2, folder 40, Urban League Records.
5. Quoted in Homer Brown, "Civil Rights," in *The WPA History of the Negro in Pittsburgh*, ed. Laurence Glasco (Pittsburgh: University of Pittsburgh Press, 2004), 215.
6. Officially, Brown ran as an independent. Although the state Republican and Democratic parties endorsed him, both parties sponsored candidates to run against him. Once in office Brown joined the Democratic Party. See newspaper clipping, "Aided Homer Brown," *Pittsburgh Criterion*, ca. November 10, 1934, box 2, folder 25, Homer Brown Collection, University of Pittsburgh Archives Service Center. Brown became the first black Pittsburgher to ever represent the city in Harrisburg. Nationally, he was one of seventeen blacks elected to state offices that year. See "Pennsylvania and Illinois Both Put Five in Assembly," November 10, 1934, *New York Amsterdam News*.
7. "Pennsylvania and Illinois Both Put Five in Assembly," *New York Amsterdam News*, November 10, 1934; "Brown Swept into Office," *Pittsburgh Courier*, November 10, 1934; "Homer Brown Sweeps Aside All Opposition to Land a Seat in State House of Representatives," *Pittsburgh Courier*, November 10, 1934. Brown received considerable campaign support from the Pittsburgh Colored Federation of Civic and Political Clubs, headed by W. T. Poole. Poole was an undertaker in the Hill District and was active in several political organizations and racial-justice institutions. See "Aided Homer Brown," *Pittsburgh Criterion*, ca. November 10, 1934, box 2, folder 25, Homer Brown Collection.

8. "Now It Can Be Told: Extracts from a Social Study of Pittsburgh," *Informer*, February 1938, box 10, folder 470, Urban League Records; Laurence Glasco, "Double Burden: The Black Experience in Pittsburgh," in *City at the Point: Essays on the Social History of Pittsburgh*, ed. Samuel P. Hays (Pittsburgh: University of Pittsburgh Press, 1989), 86.
9. "Brown Sweeps Aside All Competition to Land a Seat in State House of Representatives," *Pittsburgh Courier*, November 10, 1934; "Aided Homer Brown," *Pittsburgh Criterion*, ca. November 10, 1934, box 2, folder 25, Homer Brown Collection. Also see the biographical article of Brown entitled "Races: Ablest," *Time Magazine*, June 5, 1939, box 2, folder 24, Homer Brown Collection.
10. I explore Brown's amendment to the labor bill and other legislative actions in chapters 6 and 7.
11. "Pennsylvania and Illinois Both Put Five in Assembly," *New York Amsterdam News*, November 10, 1934.
12. "Vann Named to Important Post," *Pittsburgh Courier*, July 8, 1933; Harvard Sitkoff, *A New Deal for Blacks: The Emergence of Civil Rights as a National Issue*, thirtieth anniv. ed. (New York: Oxford University Press, 2009), 59.
13. Sitkoff, *A New Deal for Blacks*, 60.
14. Edward H. Larson, "Race Must Unite to Share in New Deal," *Pittsburgh Courier*, August 18, 1934; "'New Deal' Has Taught Race Power of Mass Action," *Pittsburgh Courier*, July 14, 1934.
15. Buni, *Robert L. Vann of the* Pittsburgh Courier, 205-7.
16. For example, see "Equal Rights Bill Is Signed," "History of State's Effort to Secure Equal Rights Bill," and "Mr. Vann Thanks the Governor," *Pittsburgh Courier*, June 15, 1935.
17. "History of State's Effort to Secure Equal Rights Bill," *Pittsburgh Courier*, June 15, 1935.
18. "Sen. Reed Wants Race in Pennsylvania to Have Nat'l Guards; Pinchot Vetoed It," *Chicago Defender*, May 5, 1934; "House Okays Negro National Guard," *Pittsburgh Courier*, March 30, 1935; "National Guard Is Approved by Senate," *Pittsburgh Courier*, April 13, 1935.
19. "Slaps at Jim Crow Policy of Earle Theatre: Magistrate Campbell Holds Manager for Racial Discrimination," *Philadelphia Tribune*, August 31, 1933.
20. "Mayor Wilson Orders New Deal for Negro Cops throughout the City," *Philadelphia Tribune*, August 27, 1936.
21. "Univ. of Pitt Ordered to Admit Medical Students," *Baltimore Afro-American*, June 22, 1935; "Earle Admits Unfairness to Negroes in U.S. Economic Setup," *Philadelphia Tribune*, August 20, 1936; "Earle Blasts Segregation in Pennsylvania by Advising State to Clean Own Back Yard," *Philadelphia Tribune*, September 27, 1934.
22. See "Equal Rights Bill Is Signed," *Pittsburgh Courier*, June 15, 1935.
23. For example, see "State Guard Bill Is Signed by Gov.," *Pittsburgh Courier*, June 8, 1935; "Equal Rights Bill Is Signed," "History of State's Effort to Secure Equal Rights Bill," and "Mr. Vann Thanks the Governor," *Pittsburgh Courier*, June 15, 1935.
24. "The Civil Rights Law," *Pittsburgh Courier*, August 31, 1935; "Equal Rights Bill Is Signed," *Pittsburgh Courier*, June 15, 1935.
25. "The Civil Rights Law," *Pittsburgh Courier*, August 31, 1935; "Equal Rights Bill Is Signed," *Pittsburgh Courier*, June 15, 1935.

26. Quoted in Brown, "Civil Rights," 212; "Equal Rights Law Too Weak, Vann's Opinion; White Hotel Owners Use State as Basis to Ignore Law," *Philadelphia Tribune*, September 12, 1935.
27. "Equal Rights Bill Faces First 'Test Suit' Here," *Pittsburgh Courier*, February 15, 1936; Brown, "Civil Rights," 213.
28. Brown, "Civil Rights," 213.
29. Brown, "Civil Rights," 213.
30. Brown, "Civil Rights," 214.
31. Homer Brown testimonial banquet program, February 12, 1934, NAACP Branch Records, pt. 1: G-191, Library of Congress.
32. At the time, Lampkin and Mary White Ovington were the only female officers in the national branch. Ovington served as treasurer.
33. Jeanne Scott to Walter White, June 14, 1934, NAACP Branch Records. In the same location also see Homer Brown to Walter White, April 27, 1934, and Walter White to Homer Brown, May 2, 1934.
34. Homer Brown to Walter White, April 27, 1934, NAACP Branch Records.
35. Walter White to Homer Brown, May 2, 1934, NAACP Branch Records.
36. For reasons that are not clear, in February 1934 Brown made the decision to exclude Scott from the campaign committee, despite her considerable experience organizing fundraising drives and building relationships with prospective donors in the community. Scott may still have felt insulted by this when she wrote her letters to Walter White in April and June.
37. Jeanne Scott to Walter White, June 14, 1934, NAACP Branch Records. In the same location also see Brown to White, April 27, 1934, and White to Brown, May 2, 1934.
38. Joe W. Trotter and Jared N. Day, *Race and Renaissance: African Americans in Pittsburgh since World War II* (Pittsburgh: University of Pittsburgh Press, 2010), 27.
39. Scott, who was born around 1899 and grew up about thirty miles south of Pittsburgh in Washington County, Pennsylvania, appears to have transitioned to social work around the time she got married, in 1926, at which time she served as social secretary for the Pittsburgh Association for the Improvement of the Poor. In around 1927, she became one of the PNAACP's officers, serving as its secretary until around 1935 or 1936, when the members of the organization gradually disbanded (1920 U.S. census, Monongahela Ward 3, marriage announcement; *Pittsburgh Courier*, January 3 1927; 1930 U.S. census, Ward 5; 1940 U.S. census, Ward 5).
40. Jeanne Scott to Walter White, June 14, 1934, NAACP Branch Records.
41. Trotter and Day, *Race and Renaissance*, 13.
42. James Weldon Johnson to Homer Brown, September 10, 1927, NAACP Branch Records.
43. Casework policy committee, minutes, February 5, 1929, box 2, folder 40, Urban League Records.
44. ULP, "Special Problems of Negro Workers in Pittsburgh," April 6, 1929, box 5, folder 235, Urban League Records.
45. Ernest Rice McKinney, "The Psychology of Race," excerpts, January 14, 1931, box 3, folder 124, Urban League Records.
46. Walls's sample included all blacks who graduated from the University of Pittsburgh between 1926 and 1936. See Glasco, "Double Burden," 84.

47. P.J. Clyde Randall to James Weldon Johnson, August 29, 1927, NAACP Branch Records.
48. The Ministerial Association sent delegates to the meeting as well.
49. Steering committee, minutes, March 14, 1932, box 2, folder 64, Urban League Records.
50. In May 1932, two months after the education committee formed in Pittsburgh, an editorial in *Opportunity*, the NUL's monthly publication, illustrated this race-first perspective as it took stock of political developments on the eve of the New Deal era: "That changes of vast import in the life of the American people are taking shape, no one can doubt. How will the Negro fare in the new dispensation? Will he be increasingly a participant in the life of the nation, or will he remain an industrial puppet dancing on the strings of opportunism alternately pulled by Capital and Labor?"
51. Steering committee, minutes, March 14, 1932, box 2, folder 64, Urban League Records.
52. "State Will Probe Negro Teacher Ban," *Pittsburgh Press*, April 8, 1937; report of the legislative committee appointed Pursuant to Resolution No. 27 of the House of Representatives of the General Assembly of the Commonwealth of Pennsylvania, session 1937–39, box 8, vol. 5, Homer Brown Collection.
53. "State Will Probe Negro Teacher Ban," *Pittsburgh Press*, April 8, 1937; report of the legislative committee appointed Pursuant to Resolution No. 27 of the House of Representatives of the General Assembly of the Commonwealth of Pennsylvania, session 1937–39, box 8, vol. 5, Homer Brown Collection.
54. Arthur J. Edmunds, *Daybreakers: The Story of the Urban League of Pittsburgh, the First Sixty-Five Years* (Pittsburgh: Urban League of Pittsburgh, 1983), 91.
55. Report of the legislative committee appointed pursuant to Resolution No. 27 of the House of Representatives of the General Assembly of the Commonwealth of Pennsylvania, session 1937–39, box 8, vol. 5, Homer Brown Collection; Edmunds, *Daybreakers*, 91.
56. Quoted in Trotter and Day, *Race and Renaissance*, 43.

CHAPTER SIX

"This Great Crusade"

REFORMERS AND THE INDUSTRIAL LABOR MOVEMENT, 1933–1939

> The Negro industrial worker came upon the Pittsburgh scene in the ignominious role of strikebreaker. The story of his break with such forces, his development into loyal, stalwart, and resourceful unionist is the honorable story of struggle against great odds, of escape from a position forced upon him into one for which he struggled consistently against misdirection and opposition.
>
> —William E. Hill, 1939

On February 6, 1937, over 350 people gathered at the Northside Elks lodge in Pittsburgh for the Western Pennsylvania Negro Labor Conference. Sitting at long tables in the lodge's warm convention hall, attendees from diverse ideological and class backgrounds dined together, discussed politics, and listened to a series of speeches on the labor movement. Phillip Murray, head of the Steel Workers Organizing Committee (SWOC), delivered the keynote address. "I ask you to pour ... your blood and your life into this great crusade to organize the colored workers employed in the great steel industry," Murray thundered to the audience, many of whom were black labor organizers.[1] As part of the Congress of Industrial Organization's (CIO) larger effort to unionize industrial workers across the country, SWOC established its headquarters in Pittsburgh. But persuading African Americans to join the labor movement proved challenging. Local unions had excluded them for decades, and they often faced open hostility from white workers, both native and foreign born. In this setting, black labor organizers and race reformers helped bridge the divide and facilitate the unionization of black workers.

As one of several hundred black labor organizers in Pittsburgh, Harrison Gant might have attended the conference at the Elks lodge and heard Murray's speech. The Georgia-born former cotton grower had migrated to Pittsburgh in 1916 and since then worked as a common laborer at the Jones and Laughlin steel plant. Over the ensuing twenty years, he witnessed and participated in several historic developments, including the Great Migration and the resulting transformation of the black community, the onset of the Great Depression, and the black electorate's embrace of the Democratic Party. Black Pittsburgh was in the vanguard of the national realignment of African Americans, and now, in 1937, it featured prominently in the industrial labor movement.

Organizers like Gant risked their livelihoods by helping the CIO. "During this period of organizing," he remembered, "J&L fired lots of men. My wife had a couple of brothers down in Aliquippa. They was fired for three years." At street corners, in bars, and on the shop floor, organizers urged workers to sign union cards. Like black reformers, their understanding of citizenship included economic opportunity. "It's a hard pull," Gant remarked about labor's struggle against capital, "but we got to keep fighting at it til one day we all can say 'we're free at last.'"[2]

The story of this fight played out across Pittsburgh: in mills, at church pulpits, over the radio, and at the labor convention held at the Elks lodge. There, amid the din of numerous conversations and clinking silverware, William E. Hill could look with satisfaction at a roomful of people gathered for a single purpose. As a representative of the Urban League of Pittsburgh (ULP) and National Negro Congress (NNC), Hill had spent the last several months helping to prepare the conference. Joining other reformers as well as local communists, he worked to bring together rank-and-file labor organizers and prominent civil rights leaders for the cause of the labor movement. The result was impressive. Alongside the labor organizers, a host of luminous African American dignitaries attended the gathering, including A. Phillip Randolph and John P. Davis from the NNC, Thyra J. Edwards of the International Ladies Garment Workers Union, *Pittsburgh Courier* editor Robert L. Vann, T. Arnold Hill of the National Urban League (NUL), Communist Party vice presidential candidate James Ford, and Carrie Horton and Nannie Reed from the National Association of Colored Women's Clubs.[3]

The event marked a promising moment for Hill, whose career trajectory typified the experience of many other reformers who passed through Pittsburgh during the interwar years. After graduating from a historically black university in his hometown of Charlotte, North Carolina, Hill moved to New York City, where he earned a master's degree in economics at Columbia University around 1924. He spent the remainder of the twenties as a struggling social worker at a small YMCA in Summit, New Jersey. These were lean years for Hill and his wife, Loretta. Unable to afford a place of their own, they lived as borders in someone else's house. Then, around 1934 Hill experienced a breakthrough in his career when the ULP hired him for a salaried position as its industrial secretary.[4]

Hill's arrival in Pittsburgh coincided with a period of strategic reorientation in the black reform community. Since the beginning of the Great Migration, the city's race leaders had fought on multiple fronts to advance the economic and civil rights of working-class blacks. Yet in the 1910s and 1920s few unions admitted black workers, and government officials gave businesses unchecked freedom to deal with their employees as they saw fit, balked at passing meaningful racial-justice legislation, and left social welfare to private charities. Facing an adversarial white working class and an ambivalent government, reformers often aligned themselves with industrialists and philanthropists. For instance, by tailoring their rhetoric and some of their programs to the interests of the white business class, officers in the ULP obtained jobs for black migrants and professionals as well as funding for their research, community development, and heath-campaign projects.

However, in the 1930s, structural changes related to the depression and New Deal created new openings for reformers to pursue their vision of citizenship. As white New Dealers and union leaders increasingly supported an interracial industrial labor movement, black reformers loosened their ties with company executives and joined the campaign to unionize black workers. This tactical reorientation, which began with Vann's campaign for Franklin Roosevelt in 1932, increasingly drew reformers into alliances with leftist and labor groups. The Aurora Reading Club attracted elite, conservative black women throughout the 1920s, but in 1934 it sponsored talks on the merits of the National Industrial Recovery Act and invited radical speakers like Ernest Rice McKinney.[5] Prominent black clergymen such as the Reverend T. J. King and Bishop William J. Walls provided rhetorical support for SWOC during their sermons. NAACP head and state representative Homer Brown pursued an amendment to Pennsylvania's labor relations act that helped ensure black workers' right to join unions.

Hill's activism both reflected and reinforced these developments. He organized the ULP's workers' council program in 1934 to foster dialogue between white and black workers and facilitate the movement of the latter into the labor movement. In 1937, he provided crucial support for Brown's nondiscrimination clause in the Pennsylvania labor relations bill, and that same year he joined with other reformers as well as black communists to form a Pittsburgh chapter of the NNC. Among its other functions, the local NNC worked to coordinate the efforts of labor organizers, union leaders, and civil rights activists. The Western Pennsylvania Negro Labor Conference was indicative of this. It created a setting in which reformers like Hill could meet with seasoned industrial workers like Gant and where members of both groups could see their work as part of a nation-wide crusade for economic justice.

A History of Exclusion

The industrial labor movement of the middle and late 1930s—which included a broad coalition of white liberals, leftists, and union leaders as well as black reformers, labor organizers, and communists—marked the culmination of a decades-long struggle over the right of black workers to join unions. The influx of southern migrants into northern industries precipitated by the First World War forced local white unions to contend with the question of whether to admit African Americans. American Federation of Labor (AFL) chapters had a long-standing record of excluding from membership unskilled and nonwhite workers. Although AFL policy forbade discriminatory clauses in the constitutions of its affiliates, through ritual practices locals found other ways of preventing African Americans from joining. For instance, part of the initiation ceremony for the International Brotherhood of Boilermakers, Iron Shipbuilders, and Helpers of America required new members to pledge never to recruit black workers.[6] By 1930 twenty-two national unions, including eleven AFL affiliates, excluded nonwhites from membership. African Americans that year constituted only 2 percent of all unionized workers.[7]

Northern black leaders offered a range of responses to this situation. Some adhered to a Booker T. Washington gospel of free enterprise and rejected unionism as a means of black advancement. But many saw in unions a way for black workers to improve their material conditions and gain greater parity with whites. As early as 1926, officers in the NUL called upon the AFL to recruit black labor organizers to facilitate the unionization of black workers.[8] The federation's refusal, coupled with its ineffectual response to the exclusionary practices of its affiliates, drew criticism from Urban Leaguers. In the league's national magazine, *Opportunity*, T. Arnold Hill urged AFL leaders to "work for the removal of constitutional and ritualistic clauses governing the conduct of labor bodies that limit membership to white workers." When whites and blacks fought against each other, Hill warned in 1930, it was "to the detriment of labor and the advantage of capital." Striking a Marxist note, he suggested the Urban League and AFL unite in an effort to help "the masses of workers realize the oneness of aim of all workingmen."[9]

The exclusionary practices of unions brought white and black workers into conflict with each other. In national strikes in 1919 and 1925, African Americans crossed picket lines and helped employers break strikes. African American leaders in Pittsburgh generally opposed scabbing. Throughout the 1920s ULP staff discouraged the practice and refused to refer black workers to mills under strike.[10] Though a successful businessman and proponent of black entrepreneurship, on several occasions Vann expressed support for striking workers and publicly recognized the merits of unions. But Vann was more pragmatic than idealistic. Personal experiences with prejudice taught him to think more in terms of race than class, and consequently, like many black leaders, he cultivated alliances across the political spectrum. "The *Pittsburgh Courier* offers no apology for any support it gives Negro movements in this country," he wrote in a 1928 editorial. "We believe it to be the policy of every well-regulated Negro journal to espouse the cause of the colored man of this country. The greatest good for the greatest number ought to be the program."[11]

During the interwar years black reformers in Pittsburgh adhered to a racial utilitarian outlook that made them flexible with respect to their ideological and strategic commitments. In the same editorial, Vann explained that since black workers could not join white unions, they should side with capital. Yet he left open the possibility of an abrupt defection. "When labor unions are ready to share the economic problems of the country with the colored worker it will be plenty of time for the colored man to make application for membership." That day, he predicted, was decades away.[12]

Race and Class during the Industrial Labor Movement

The five years that followed Vann's editorial witnessed an extraordinary outpouring of grassroots activism among urban industrial workers. As Lizabeth Cohen demonstrates in her classic study of interwar Chicago, the neighborhood social welfare institutions developed in Polish, Italian, and African American communities during the 1920s proved inadequate against the enormous economic challenges of the depression. Consequently, Cohen explains, industrial workers became increasingly class conscious, crossed racial and ethnic lines, joined labor unions, agitated for better wages and working conditions, and forged an alliance with the Democratic Party of Franklin Roosevelt.[13]

Partly in response to pressure from their working-class constituents, New Deal Democrats in Congress established workers' right to organize and bargain collectively through section 7a of the National Industrial Recovery Act, thus setting in motion a chain of events that culminated with thousands of African Americans joining unions.[14] Since the 1890s organized labor had been on the retreat in industries across the country, but 7a inspired grassroots labor activists to accelerate organization efforts.

It also raised afresh the issue of black workers' historic exclusion from unions. Jesse O. Thomas, a former Booker T. Washington devotee and founder of the Atlanta Urban League, believed that 7a presented an opportunity to organize an interracial labor movement at a critical juncture in American history. "Labor in the United States is facing the most firmly entrenched and ruthless capitalistic system of the world," he observed. "Any labor movement that is to survive the transition through which labor is now passing must be so constructed that it can lend itself to the highly integrated structure of American industry."[15] Yet with few exceptions AFL locals continued to exclude nonwhites.

In July 1935 a group of Urban League representatives traveled to Washington, DC, to speak at a hearing convened by the AFL's committee on racial integration. There, Reginald Johnson, who served as executive secretary of the Atlanta Urban League and later joined the ULP, read a statement that cataloged the federation's long history of racial exclusion and censured its leadership for failing to curtail the practice. Johnson reminded AFL representatives that "the National Urban League has stood squarely behind collective bargaining and organized action for Negro and white workers together," and he pointed out that almost all of the Urban League's affiliates "have followed this policy in spite of distressing experiences which many of [them] have had with the A.F. of L. locals in their territory."[16] Despite the league's longstanding support for interracial unions, the AFL refused its pleas to hire black labor organizers and expel discriminatory locals.

By the time AFL officers began taking racial discrimination more seriously in the mid-thirties, black leaders who had dealt with their ambivalence for more than a decade had lost interest in working with them. The "hypocritical attitude of the American Federation of Labor . . . has destroyed the last vestige of confidence which Negro workers ever had in the A.F. of L.," concluded the NAACP's executive secretary, Walter White, in 1935.[17] By then, reformers had new options to explore.

After the U.S. Supreme Court declared unconstitutional the National Industrial Recovery Act, including section 7a, Congress countered by passing the National Labor Relations Act—more commonly known as the Wagner Act. The Wagner Act reestablished workers' right to form unions, but unlike 7a it included a labor relations board to enforce the law and prosecute employers who violated it. Following the act's passage, a rift developed in the AFL that provided an opportunity for black leaders to part ways with it.[18]

Frustrated with the AFL's practice of organizing workers by craft or trade, in 1935 John L. Lewis of the United Mine Workers (UMW) and leaders in seven other international unions formed the Committee of Industrial Organizations (later renamed the Congress of Industrial Organizations) with the goal of uniting all industrial workers into "one big union." To accomplish this end in the steel industry, they created SWOC and appointed Philip Murray, former vice president of UMW, as its head. Like many labor leaders, Murray believed the failed steel strikes of 1892 and 1919 owed much to black strikebreakers who had been excluded from union membership. As leader of SWOC, which was headquartered in Pittsburgh, he made a special effort to win the support of black workers.[19] Activists from the ULP, PNAACP, and *Pittsburgh Courier* assisted him.

The task of convincing black workers to join unions came with special difficulties. The prejudicial treatment they had received from native and foreign-born white workers since the beginning of the Great Migration made many of them wary of participating in the labor movement. Seeming to forget black workers' long list of grievances against their white counterparts, Ernest Rice McKinney, Pittsburgh's leading black socialist, ridiculed them for not flocking to the CIO. "Despite all the columns of words that have been carried in the papers about the CIO . . . and the whole agitation around the steel organization campaign, Negroes remain uninformed and disinterested," he quipped. "Their ignorance is spacious and serene." A devoted Marxist, McKinney believed the CIO organizing drives foreshadowed proletarian democracy in America, and he became impatient with both reformers and workers who continued to advocate for racial solidarity. "The Negro worker must give up many foolish notions about race consciousness ... and begin to acquire a far more fundamental and basic class consciousness and class solidarity transcending the bounds of race," he advised.[20]

Even so, most black reformers in Pittsburgh joined the labor movement because it aligned with their racial goals. No matter what the McKinneys of the world said, history and their own experiences taught them that they lived in a racial caste system. "Negroes had never been allowed to catch the full spirit of Western civilization," Richard Wright observed in his 1945 autobiography, *Black Boy*. "They lived somehow in it but not of it."[21]

Certainly, as many historians have noted, employers recognized how race and ethnicity could be used to divide workers, and often they exploited this to inhibit union formation. But this argument can be overstated. White workers rarely needed prompting from employers to discriminate against African Americans, as David Roediger demonstrates in the *Wages of Whiteness*.[22] In Pittsburgh, this was true of both native and foreign-born workers. As we have seen, throughout the thirties local Italians repeatedly harassed would-be black swimmers at the Highland Park pool, and elsewhere, on the streets, fighting broke out between the two groups. On the shop floor, Polish workers used their numerical superiority over African Americans to gain control of certain departments and promote their own to skilled and supervisory positions. And in a few instances native white workers threatened to go on strike when they learned that some African Americans might be promoted to their respective departments.[23]

Whites of all classes enforced racial subordination in interwar America, and this system affected both black professionals and black workers. As W. E. B. Du Bois observed in 1934, "white people on the whole are just as much opposed to Negroes of education and culture, as to any other kind."[24] The intensity of white racism in the interwar years blunted the edges of black reformers' class identity, drew them closer to black workers, and imbued them with a race-first, pragmatic conception of activism. While keeping in sight the ideal of racial equality, they strove to capitalize on opportunities for achievable incremental progress.[25]

Tactical Realignment: The Urban League

Previous chapters have shown how a bleak racial reality imposed hard choices on reformers in the 1910s and 1920s. Bereft of resources and facing dire challenges, they were willing to make compromises and accept tradeoffs for modest gains. For Urban Leaguers, this meant rhetorically aligning their programs to employer interests in exchange for jobs and funding. Reformers often coupled this pragmatism with an ideology of racial uplift that, as historian Kevin Gaines has noted, placed special emphasis on "self-help, racial solidarity, temperance, thrift, chastity, social purity, patriarchal authority, and the accumulation of wealth."[26] In the absence of external support, reformers reasoned that solutions to racial problems had to be generated from within the black community through "adjustment programs" and education.

This outlook continued to influence Urban Leaguers in the early thirties even as their visions of progress evolved. For instance, in 1931 ULP industrial secretary Harold Lett delivered a speech on the centrality of vocational training for black economic advancement—a position guided by the belief that employers in a free market society would hire the most qualified applicants available, regardless of skin color.

> Every worker is a merchant in a sense. He has his time, his talent and his training or experience to sell. . . . He must display his fitness for the job to best advantage; attract employers to his services by offering the brand of service that is desired . . . [and] treat his patron (or employer) in a way that will command respect and good will. To do otherwise, as a business man or as a worker, is to invite bankruptcy in the one case, or persistent unemployment in the other.[27]

As Lett saw it, black economic progress hinged on the presence or absence of skill. Hence, upon joining the ULP Lett commenced an investigation to find out how many African Americans were enrolled in vocational courses. He discovered to his dismay that of the more than two thousand students in Pittsburgh's six vocational schools, only twenty were black. Worse still, these twenty enrollees only received training in the two skilled occupations then open to African Americans: molding and cement work. When he questioned the schools about this, they cited a survey of 100 local industries which found that over half of the 144 African Americans employed in skilled positions were molders and cement finishers. With such data before them, they explained, it made sense to train black enrollees accordingly. But Lett rejected their logic, maintaining that "the great task confronting the Race in the matter of breaking down the barrier of tradition . . . [requires] preparing the youth in specialized fields through every medium presented."[28]

In some ways, Lett typified the complexity of black reformers coming to grips with changing structural forces in the early thirties. Even while advancing the self-help gospel of uplift as a means for African Americans to obtain better jobs, he gradually embraced a more radical vision of racial justice that included a fairer relationship between labor and capital. In a 1931 article in *Opportunity*, he blamed economic inequality, or what he called an "unwise social order," for the high rates of poverty, crime, and disease among African Americans, and he bitterly refuted claims that the unemployed were lazy or indolent.[29] Two years later, Lett helped develop a ULP study that charted the growth of monopolies in the food industry and called for black workers and their allies to "make a frontal attack upon these big 'Trade Mark' organizations."[30]

A ULP informational brochure from 1933 further illustrates reformers' transition away from uplift tactics. It describes the journey of a skilled black mason in the South named "Hezekiah J." who moved to a northern city with his family for greater economic opportunity and political liberty. Yet like so many migrants before him, the pamphlet explained, he "experienced the futility of breasting impassible barriers." Hezekiah's skin color precluded him from joining a union, and consequently he was barred from positions in his trade. This forced him to settle for any job he could find, first as a janitor and later performing odd jobs for whoever could pay him. He eventually ended up on relief rolls, and the shame of it drove him to apathy and alcoholism. His wife, meanwhile, had to work fourteen-hour days as a domestic in white homes. Consequently, her two young children had to fend for themselves in the city's black ghetto. In the absence of a decent family life, sanitary housing, adequate schools, or even a playground, the malnourished youths became delinquents. Importantly, this pamphlet points to the centrality of structural racism, not the presence or absence of skill, as the fundamental driver of racial inequality. By the mid-thirties Urban Leaguers in Pittsburgh fully embraced the labor movement and worked diligently to open unions for the Hezekiahs of the community.[31]

The Workers' Councils

The NUL was one of the first organizations to commit significant resources to convincing black workers to join unions. In early 1934 John T. Clark traveled to NUL headquarters in New York to assist other league officers with developing the workers' council program. During his tenure at the ULP from 1918 until 1926 and then at the Urban League branch in St. Louis, Clark had worked against long odds to open unions to African Americans and promote their advancement to skilled positions.[32] But structural changes in American life brought about by the depression and the New Deal created new possibilities. Clark and other Urban Leaguers sensed changing political winds when Franklin Roosevelt promised government support for ordinary Americans, including industrial workers, and they trimmed the league's sails to catch its energy. They organized the workers' council program to promote interracial unions, enhance black bargaining power, and facilitate dialogue between black and white workers on the merits of cooperation. In an open letter dated April 19, 1934 addressed to "the five million negro workers in the United States," the league declared that it would create workers' councils across the country to "crystallize their activity and develop their bargaining power in the labor market." The letter cited the necessity of collective action:

> You must organize to compel the breakdown of discriminatory barriers that keep you out of unions, and, consequently, out of employment. You must organize to prevent the passing of legislation that will be a further aid to discrimination-practicing unions and employers. You must organize to demand, with other workers, a new deal for labor.[33]

Urban Leaguers also threatened to support company unions if the AFL did not abandon its exclusionary practices, and in the pages of *Opportunity* they repeatedly preached to black workers the virtues of collective action. Moreover, the NUL trained staff at local branches in protest techniques and helped them develop organizing strategies. As Harvard Sitkoff has noted, some affiliates remained dependent on financial contributions from local philanthropists and hesitated to embrace the tenets of the workers' councils.[34] However, most of the larger city branches created their own workers' councils and supported the union drive—including the ULP.[35]

William E. Hill set the ULP on a new course when he became its industrial secretary after the departure of Lett, who accepted a position as head of the Urban League branch in Newark, New Jersey. While Lett had focused on evening vocational courses, Hill directly addressed discrimination by employers and unions. Drawing inspiration from the NUL, he established a workers' council in Pittsburgh that brought together white and black workers to discuss the benefits of interracial unions. The International Ladies Garment Workers Union and the International League for Peace and Freedom provided the rooms where, between 1937 and 1938, more than five hundred workers attended open-forum meetings. There, local white and black leaders—including Dr. Francis Tyson from the University of Pittsburgh, Murray of SWOC, Brown of the Pittsburgh NAACP, Johnson of the ULP, and Percival Prattis from the *Courier*—led discussions on the merits of cooperation, labor problems, current events, and the "psychology of propaganda." Hill hoped these sessions would help smooth relations between white and black workers, clear barriers to union membership, and "train workers for intelligent participation in the processes of industrial and political democracy."[36]

Along with promoting worker solidarity, these meetings drew together African Americans of all classes in the common cause of the labor movement. "Labor brings to this work practical experience and an unbluffed mind," noted a ULP report. "The educators bring their academic training; together they make an excellent team for mutual learning, and a strong bulwark against reaction."[37]

Hill further advanced his mission through mass meetings. Attendees crowded into the Wesley Center Methodist Church for a conference sponsored by the workers' council on July 7, 1935, to hear speeches by white union representatives, New Deal liberals, and black leaders on the implications of the Wagner Act and the effects of AFL policy on black workers. Highlighting the racial character of the meeting, after the opening invocation delivered by the Reverend C. F. Jenkins, pastor of the Carron Baptist Church, the gathered assembly sang "Lift Every Voice and Sing," the African American national anthem.[38]

In addition to promoting interracial unions, the ULP supported existing black unions such as the Brotherhood of Sleeping Car Porters. Randolph, whose career as a labor leader and civil rights activist spanned over four decades, organized the brotherhood in 1925. During the mid-thirties the brotherhood repeatedly clashed with the Pennsylvania Railroad over its treatment of black porters. The company took the position that since porters worked only for tips they could not be classified as employees and therefore were not entitled to the protections under the Railway Labor Act. Its managers refused to negotiate with the brotherhood, and that compelled the union to seek help from outside allies.[39]

In November 1937, Ira B. Valentine, president of Brotherhood Local 4 in Pittsburgh, wrote a letter to Hill explaining the Pennsylvania Railroad's actions and entreating him "to use the influence of the Urban League and its resources to aid us in forcing the Pennsylvania Railroad to deal with us fairly and recognize our just claims and also our Organization.... I am positive that your help in this matter will go a long ways towards gaining for us the consideration we ask." Hill subsequently joined the chorus of voices urging the Pennsylvania Railroad to treat porters as employees and recognize their union. Ultimately, the lobbying efforts of the brotherhood and its allies forced the federal government to take action. In October 1938 the Interstate Commerce Commission ruled that porters were railway employees and therefore were entitled to the protections under the Railway Labor Act.[40]

Under Hill's leadership, the local workers' council also pursued affirmative action measures in the city. In the late thirties, the Pittsburgh Housing Authority proposed developing a housing project in the Hill District. Under pressure from the workers' council, it added a clause to its contracts that required construction firms to set aside for black workers 4.5 percent of the skilled positions and 29 percent of the unskilled positions.[41]

The workers' councils in Pittsburgh and other cities supported the unionization of black women as well. In 1937, the NUL called for the organization of nearly five million women employed in domestic work. Female domestics put in long days for little pay and no benefits, and their working conditions and terms of employment often were subject to the whim of their employers. This was especially true for black women, who comprised almost a third of the domestic labor force. In the mid-thirties a typical black domestic worked between twelve and fourteen hours a day and earned about a dollar less per week than her white counterparts. In its *Workers' Council Bulletin*, the NUL maintained that "the most effective means of combating undesirable conditions in household employment lie in organization of domestic workers themselves."[42] This proved a daunting task since the protections of the Wagner Act did not extend to agricultural and domestic workers. Still, although household employees remained unorganized, the league's pronouncements further indicate the increasing importance of unionization to its civil rights agenda.

In the fall of 1937, Hill of the ULP helped organize a housewives cooperative league to open a new front in the league's larger campaign against economic discrimination. Taking inspiration from earlier "Don't Buy Where You Can't Work" campaigns, the cooperative league's members worked to leverage black buying power by threatening to boycott businesses that did not employ African Americans while patronizing those that did.[43]

The meeting minutes of this organization reveal much about how reformers carried out their work in the interwar years. Its membership included seasoned women reformers like Daisy Lampkin, Frances Stewart, Alma Illery, and Cora Jones, who, drawing on years of committee experience, quickly drew up a plan of action and an organizational structure tailored to maximal impact with minimal resources. Following a utilitarian course of action, they agreed they lacked the strength to "scatter our blows" but rather had to "concentrate on a few staples" that black consumers purchased most, like milk, bread, gas, and coal. As one member explained,

> There are 83,000 Negroes in Allegheny County who spend $63,000,000 a year. . . . If wisely spent, this money would open up new avenues of employment in the way of clerks and white collar jobs, and some skilled jobs, break down 'jim crowism' in Pittsburgh, abolish discourteous discrimination. . . . There is no reason why we should not have something in return for the money we spend.[44]

As a matter of course, the members agreed that they needed to gather reliable information about the size and location of major employers in the Hill District, along with employment figures, in order to determine where to strike. Daisy Lampkin, who served as vice president of the *Pittsburgh Courier*, assured the others that the *Courier* would fund this portion of the cooperative league's efforts.[45] That fact-gathering featured so early in the group's minutes reflected reformers' longstanding belief in the power of research to identify society's ailments and offer achievable measures for curing them.

The trail of documents on the housewives cooperative league disappears after its third meeting, but the considerable support it garnered from key figures in the black reform community, coupled with its well-articulated program for future action, suggest that it probably carried out some of its plans to apply pressure on discriminatory employers. By the close of its first month in existence, it had established concrete steps for action and had begun to act on them. For instance, it contacted the Meadow Gold Milk Company with a threat to organize a boycott if it did not employ any African Americans. It followed this up by encouraging the black community to purchase milk from Rieck's Dairy instead, since it employed several African Americans.[46] For women reformers struggling to find a place in the industrial labor movement, participation in the housewives cooperative league provided a meaningful way to contribute to the economic justice initiatives sweeping through the black reform community.

Like the NUL and the ULP, the NAACP and many of its city branches strategically reoriented during the mid-thirties. The NAACP, once consid-

William E. Hill.
Arthur J. Edmunds, *Daybreakers: The Story of the Urban League of Pittsburgh* (Pittsburgh: Urban League of Pittsburgh, 1983), 89.

R. Maurice Moss, ca. 1932.
Historic Pittsburgh Image Collection, 811150802.UL, University of Pittsburgh Archives Service Center.

This Great Crusade 183

Pittsburgh Urban League Office, located at
806 Wylie Avenue in the lower Hill District, ca. 1930.
Historic Pittsburgh Image Collection, 81II50802.UL,
University of Pittsburgh Archives Service Center.

ered a radical organization, had come under considerable criticism in the early 1930s for focusing on civil and political equality while overlooking more salient pocketbook issues. Black intellectuals including Ralph Bunche, former ULP fellow Abram Harris, and W. E. B. Du Bois called on the NAACP to promote interracial unions and address the economic privation of the black masses. While not abandoning the quest for civil and political equality, Du Bois even suggested that African Americans should temporarily segregate themselves, build up their own businesses, and create an economic "nation within a nation." Du Bois's subsequent feuds with other NAACP officers led to his resignation in May 1934, but Bunche, Harris, and other leaders continued to call for black unionism. In response, in July 1934 the association commenced a reorientation of its tactics and policies. While it continued to press for antilynching legislation and an end to segregation, it also joined the effort to build a broad-based labor movement.[47]

The currents redirecting strategies at the national level also affected NAACP affiliates in cities across the country, including Pittsburgh. The approach of Brown, who had been president of the PNAACP since 1925, exemplified this shift. By the middle and late thirties, he had turned his attention mainly to expanding the economic rights of African Americans, and this included an effort to use the powers of the state to integrate unions.

Reformers and the Pennsylvania Labor Relations Act

For all its merit, the Wagner Act had at least one fundamental flaw: it did not penalize unions that continued to exclude black workers. Despite the protestations of the NUL, NAACP, and Brotherhood of Sleeping Car Porters, the bill's sponsors refused to include a nondiscrimination clause. But where national race leaders failed, Brown succeeded.[48]

On January 18, 1937, Senator Bernard B. McGinnis introduced to the Pennsylvania House of Representatives a labor relations bill modeled on the Wagner Act. Like its national counterpart, the Pennsylvania Labor Relations Act would establish the right of workers to organize and bargain collectively without fear of employer reprisal, and it would be enforced by a labor board. While the AFL fully endorsed the bill, Brown began gathering advice and material to author an amendment to it. He turned first and often to one of Pittsburgh's leading experts on black industrial conditions: Hill of the ULP. Hill provided Brown with valuable data on the unions that still excluded African Americans—including the International Union of Machinists, of which McGinnis himself was a member—and the means by which they did so. After reviewing the McGinnis bill, Hill suggested language to include in an amendment and offered strategic guidance for steering it through the legislature.[49]

With support and advice from local as well as national race leaders like T. Arnold Hill of the NUL, Brown drafted an amendment to the McGinnis bill that would prevent discriminatory unions from benefiting from its protections. Featured in section 3f, the amendment specified the law did not apply to "any labor organization which by ritualistic practice, constitutional or bylaw proscription, by tacit agreement among its members or otherwise, denies a person or persons membership in its organization on account of race, creed, or color."[50]

The AFL immediately voiced its opposition to the measure. Writing to the state assembly, John A. Phillips, president of the Pennsylvania Labor Federation, which represented the AFL, advised that the amendment "should by all mean [sic] be stricken out because it virtually nullifies the whole act." Citing the voluntary nature of labor unions and the right of members to run them as they saw fit, Phillips explained that Brown's amendment would "destroy the whole character of such organization by allowing any individual who is antagonistic to the purpose of such organization connivingly to claim such discriminations and thereby cause turmoil and disorganization, thus defeating the purpose of the act."[51]

Phillips urged legislators to focus on the economic dimensions of the act and leave race out of it, but he omitted from his public comments the AFL's underlying motive for opposing Brown's amendment. The federation had recently expelled the CIO, and thereafter the two organizations vied for the loyalty of Pennsylvania's industrial workers. Brown's amendment threatened to undermine the AFL in this struggle, since many of its locals continued to exclude African Americans. Sensing opportunity to gain supporters, Hill informed Brown that the CIO likely would take any chance to "drop one more tack in the sock of the A.F. of L." Therefore, he explained, "the time is most opportune for the support of such an amendment."[52] His prediction proved accurate. While the AFL opposed the amendment, CIO leaders openly supported it.[53]

Even with the CIO's endorsement, Brown faced considerable opposition. The amendment first had to clear a joint committee of the house and senate, on which he was the sole African American. The *Philadelphia Tribune* reported that the committee members argued bitterly over the amendment before agreeing to send it to the house for a vote.[54] And while it passed easily in that chamber by a count of 198 to 0, it encountered delays in the senate, which divided along party lines over how to handle the measure. According to the *Courier*, Republicans supported an up or down vote on the amendment, but the Democrats, who had a majority, preferred to delegate the issue to Democratic governor George Earle.[55] Internal divisions among Pennsylvania Democrats might account for this procedural maneuvering. While a bloc led by U.S. senator Joseph Guffey aligned with the CIO, a rival faction headed by David L. Lawrence from the state legislature supported the AFL and may have felt political pressure to oppose Brown's measure.[56]

Even so, on May 26, 1937, the Pennsylvania General Assembly adopted

Brown's amendment to the McGinnis bill, and soon after Governor Earle signed it into law. "Finally we have the enemy and the enemy is ours," a triumphant Brown wrote to Walter White. "After much debate, violent protest from the American Federation of Labor, and other dilatory tactics, we finally managed to stand our ground and the bill passed with the amendments as inserted." Brown's correspondences attest to the stiff resistance he encountered from opponents in and outside the general assembly, but he felt the victory merited the struggle: "I do believe we have made the first step in an attack upon a vicious system." Subsequently, Brown received praise from around the country. Pennsylvania was the first state to adopt a nondiscrimination clause in its labor bill, and T. Arnold Hill, Reginald Johnson, and Walter White hoped it would set a precedent that others would soon follow.[57]

Like many black leaders in Pittsburgh and across the country, Brown developed his civil rights agenda around a principle of racial utility. As external barriers to unions began crumbling in the mid-thirties, he joined his fellow reformers in the effort to facilitate their integration. But they had racially motivated reasons for supporting the labor movement that trumped its class implications. Widespread prejudice directed toward African Americans in Pittsburgh and across the country, which came from whites of all ranks, compelled black leaders to think and act in terms of racial advancement. For this reason, since the 1910s many of them had regarded union involvement as a tool for black economic advancement rather than as part of a historic battle between labor and capital. Black activists on the political left, however, tended to view the matter differently.

African Americans and the Political Left

In the early 1930s the American Communist Party (CPUSA) emerged as an outspoken champion of social justice, but while doing so it repeatedly dismissed black reformers and mainstream racial organizations as puppets of white capitalists. The nationally famous Scottsboro case provides an example. In 1931, two white prostitutes accused nine black teenagers of raping them on a train car near Scottsboro, Alabama. Local authorities detained the youths, and an all-white jury quickly convicted and sentenced to death all of them except twelve-year-old Roy Wright. The CPUSA's legal advocacy branch, the International Labor Defense (ILD), quickly appealed the decision and took up the defense of the black teenagers. A series of retrials and additional appeals followed, and the case persisted for the remainder of the 1930s.

During this period, the ILD aimed searing attacks at the NAACP, which it denounced as "an active agent of the ruling imperialist bourgeoisie in helping to prepare the way for fascism."[58]

Leaders in the NAACP recognized their moral imperative to contribute to the Scottsboro defense, but joining ranks with the ILD put them in an awkward position. The ILD's attacks against the association undermined its place as the legal champion of black rights.[59] Therefore it was with some hesitation that the NAACP joined the ILD in 1933 to help defend the Scottsboro Nine. "Unquestionably, this is not going to end our difficulties with the I.L.D. and the communists," Walter White confided to Daisy Lampkin, "but we did not see how, in the name of humanity, we could do otherwise." Lampkin, who served as vice president of the PNAACP and helped raise funds for the Scottsboro defense, supported White's opinion but remained concerned about the ILD's stance against the association. "I am naturally anxious to know as soon as possible the reaction of the ILD," she wrote. "Will they agree to our help, or will they continue to misrepresent us and our motives?"[60]

With the rising threat of Nazi Germany in 1935, the CPUSA abruptly changed policy and began courting liberals, socialists, trade unions, New Deal Democrats, and civil rights groups to form so-called popular fronts. In a kind of Orwellian rewrite, officers in the NAACP and Urban League went from being capitalist stooges to comrades in the fight against fascism.[61]

By contrast, leaders in mainstream civil rights organizations tended to hold fairly consistent views of communists. Since the early 1930s a number of them praised the CPUSA's positive racial record, but they argued against joining it for fear of provoking a white backlash. As Asbury Smith, a black pastor and executive member of the Baltimore Urban League explained, "the white people of America have an intense hatred of Communism . . . , [and they] also have a prejudice against the Negro. To join the hatred of Communism with the prejudice against the Negro will release the forces of fury among the masses of the whites."[62] W. E. B. Du Bois echoed this concern in a 1931 editorial in the *Crisis*. "American Negroes do not propose to be the shock troops of the Communist Revolution," he wrote. "Negroes know perfectly well that whenever they try to lead revolution in America, the nation will unite as one fist to crush them and them alone."[63] Vann of the *Pittsburgh Courier* expressed similar sentiments in his campaign speech for Franklin Roosevelt in 1932, and that same year P. B. Young, editor of the *Norfolk Journal and Guide*, argued that "because the Negro is marked racially, he becomes a ready target for anti-Communist venom."[64]

Angelo Herndon learned this lesson the hard way. Herndon joined the CPUSA's Unemployed Council in 1932 and shortly afterward traveled to Georgia to organize black and white workers into a labor union. There, officials arrested him on charges of insurrection, and an all-white jury quickly found him guilty. The judge sentenced Herndon to eighteen to twenty years in prison. After a series of appeals and two years in prison, Herndon regained his freedom in 1937, but the case nevertheless reinforced the belief among many black leaders that linking their fortunes with another persecuted group made little sense.[65]

Even so, as the New Deal accelerated and the CPUSA's membership increased, by the mid-1930s a number of prominent African Americans—including Du Bois, Mary McLeod Bethune, Ralph Bunche, Richard Wright, Paul Robeson, and Langston Hughes—formed close associations with communists. Other black leaders, such as Lester Granger and T. Arnold Hill, though not radicals themselves, worked alongside communists to promote racial causes.[66]

Pittsburgh hosted active left-wing communities. In January 1930 the ILD held its fourth annual convention in the Steel City, and the occasion provided an opportunity to demonstrate its commitment to racial equality. When the Monongahela Hotel refused to provide lodging for its black members, 328 ILD delegates and several hundred workers converged on the hotel lobby for a protest demonstration. Hotel officials called local police to the scene, but they did not interfere. Inside the hotel lobby a host of speakers—including ILD national secretary J. Louis Engdahl, *Daily Worker* editor Robert Minor, and black delegates such as Frank and Harold Williams—delivered talks on racial equality. An hour later, the protesters, numbering about five hundred, left the hotel and marched to the convention while displaying banners that read "Struggle against Race Prejudice" and singing "The Internationale." At the convention, the delegates adopted a resolution boycotting all hotels and restaurants that discriminated against nonwhites.[67]

Two years later, the ILD won additional support from black Pittsburghers when several of its members rushed to the aid of a jobless tenant in the Hill District. As a sheriff and his deputies evicted the man from his home, several white ILD members confronted the police and moved the tenant's belongings back into the house. An altercation ensued between the police, ILD, and local blacks that led to the arrest of the white communists. The ILD eventually won the acquittal of its members, but more importantly, according to a columnist for the *Baltimore Afro-American*, the incident "created such a sentiment against evictions of jobless tenants that there have been few since."[68]

The CPUSA's outspoken advocacy of black rights won the respect and loyalty of a number of working-class African Americans in the lower Hill District as well as several black professionals, including Alonzo D. Brewer, a student at the University of Pittsburgh.[69] Indeed, historian Kenneth Heineman has noted that until the mid-thirties Pittsburgh hosted more black communists than Harlem. Ben Careathers was one of them.[70]

Careathers was born near Chattanooga, Tennessee, sometime in the 1890s. His father had been a slave before the Civil War and became a sharecropper afterward. In 1903, Careathers received his first lesson in racial violence when word spread that a black man had been lynched on the nearby Tennessee River Bridge. The event imprinted itself on Careathers's psyche. Several years later, the looming threat of racial violence coupled with his family's poverty to convince him to join thousands of southern blacks migrating north. "[But] everyplace I had gone, including Pittsburgh, I found that Mr. Jim Crow dominated the scene," he later remembered. He had learned the upholstering trade, but racial barriers to skilled positions forced him to settle for a job as a common laborer in a steel mill. Frustrated, Careathers joined the local Communist Party in the early thirties and served as one of its most outspoken advocates for the next twenty-five years.[71]

He also provided critical support to SWOC's organizing drives. At the behest of Phillip Murray, in 1937 Careathers, Ernest Rice McKinney, and several other organizers traveled to the Jones and Laughlin plant in Aliquippa. Company management had crushed earlier attempts to unionize the plant, as Harrison Gant recalled. Two of his brothers-in-law had lost their jobs for participating in labor drives.[72] To avoid the company police patrolling the grounds, Careathers dressed as an employee and entered the mill during a shift change. Over the next few days, the SWOC organizers gathered thousands of signatures. Careathers alone may have recruited over two thousand workers.[73]

Additionally, Careathers participated in the larger struggle to promote class consciousness among workers from diverse racial and ethnic backgrounds. In 1935, he joined with James Alexander, Lee Hill, and other local communists to establish the Pittsburgh Workers School.[74] For a small registration fee, workers of all races could attend weekly classes on the labor movement, class struggle, political economy, American history, world events, racial inequality, and New Deal politics. Like the ULP workers' council, the party's school helped build connections between white and black workers and promote racial justice. In the late thirties Careathers taught courses such as "Problems of the Negro Liberation Movement," "National Minorities," "The Negro Question in the United States," "The Struggle for Negro Rights in Pittsburgh," and "Negroes and the Democratic Front."

More than a few Pittsburghers opposed the principles and aims of the workers school. In 1938, the *Pittsburgh Post-Gazette* published a series of articles portraying it as a secretive and subversive sect that merited investigation by local authorities. The newspaper pointed to the school's close ties to the CPUSA and noted that its classes were centered around the principles of what its members called scientific socialism. In countering the *Gazette*'s attacks, the workers school committee published a statement of its principles, which included support for American democracy, opposition to antidemocratic activity, and solidarity against fascism at home and abroad. The members of the committee held up their school as the embodiment of American freedom and democracy while branding their opponents at the *Gazette* as "officious, little-minded, tin-hat would-be-Hitlers."[75]

Moreover, while most reformers readily worked with activists on the political left, more than a few middle-class black Pittsburghers remained skeptical of leftists throughout the New Deal period. Some, especially "Old Pittsburghers" (OPs), disdained any talk of aligning with socialists or communists, whose motives they mistrusted. When activists challenged hotels and restaurants that continued to deny service to African Americans even after the Pennsylvania Civil Rights Act of 1935, several middle-class blacks suggested the Communist Party put them up to it simply to promote its own agenda. Frustrated, Homer Brown criticized these OPs for their "laxness" in defending racial justice.[76] At the national level, a few prominent civil rights leaders likewise discouraged collaboration with communists. In 1933, for instance, Howard University professor Kelly Miller accused the party of luring "gullible" African Americans into their ranks with false promises of a racial panacea.[77]

Anticommunist fervor caught up with Ben Careathers in 1953. Though suffering from tuberculosis, he and fellow communist Ben Nelson were put on trial for allegedly advocating violent overthrow of the government. The court eventually dropped the charges against Careathers, but it sentenced Nelson to two years in prison. They represented two of the hundreds of victims of the Red Scare that had gripped the nation.[78]

Ben Careathers, August or September 1960.
Teenie Harris Archive, Carnegie Museum of Art, Pittsburgh.

While the Communist Party's black membership increased during the 1930s, the Socialist Party remained relatively small. With his party stuck between liberal Democrats and radical Communists, Ernest Rice McKinney, a *Courier* contributor, SWOC organizer, and one of the most famous black socialists in the country, could do little to attract converts.

McKinney had been an outspoken labor activist since the 1920s, when he helped A. Philip Randolph organize Pullman car porters and served briefly as a contributing editor for Randolph's magazine, the *Messenger*. In the early depression McKinney joined a Socialist Party splinter group, the Conference for Progressive Labor Action (CPLA), which later became the American Workers Party. McKinney rose to a high post in CPLA, and along with other local members he helped establish the Unemployed Citizens League of Allegheny County in 1932.[79]

As a journalist, activist, and, later, a professor of labor history at Rutgers University, McKinney committed himself to the cause of interracial unionism, which, as the title of one of his articles suggests, he believed represented the "Negroes' Road to Freedom." In this *Labor Age* article published in 1932,

McKinney blamed racial strife on the machinations of employers who sought to keep workers divided. But he predicted the shared hardships of the depression would soon open the way for class solidarity.

> The tragedy is that white workers ... helped the ruling class to segregate us, proscribe us and discriminate against us. And it is the white worker who lynches the Negro worker. It never dawned on the white toilers in the capitalist vineyard that the black wage slaves were part and parcel of them. I believe though that three years of unemployment will create a new outlook. When a black and white ex-worker approach a garbage can together for breakfast their actual equality in the eyes of the ruling class is thereby proclaimed.[80]

While most reformers did not share McKinney's commitment to class solidarity, they agreed that unifying black and white workers ultimately would help African Americans gain greater economic security. To that end, in the mid-thirties reformers in Pittsburgh and across the country increasingly forged alliances with leftists.

The NNC and the Western Pennsylvania Labor Conference

The formation of the NNC in 1936 reflected this development. The NNC included communists, labor leaders, and former Garveyites as well as leaders in mainstream racial organizations. Randolph served as its first president, and its membership featured some of the nation's leading civil rights advocates, including Granger and Hill of the NUL, Wilkins of the NAACP, and prominent intellectuals like Bunche and Harris. NNC leaders established a political platform that stressed the connections between racial and economic exploitation. Without access to good jobs, they argued, racial inequality would persist.[81]

Out of deference to the diverse institutional commitments of its members, the NNC issued a pledge that "it will not usurp the work of any organization" and that "it seeks to accomplish unity of action of already existing [racial] organizations."[82] Yet by 1937 it was informally competing with the Urban League for a partnership with the CIO. In a letter to a CIO officer, John P. Davis of the NNC claimed that the NNC was the only racial-advancement institution concerned with organizing black workers, even though the Urban League's workers councils predated its existence by several years. His appeals proved successful later that year when the CIO granted $1,000 to the NNC to hire black labor organizers and print prolabor pamphlets.[83]

Black reformers in Pittsburgh wasted little time in establishing a local NNC branch. Its leadership included communists like Ben Careathers as well as officers in established racial organizations, most notably William E. Hill, who organized the ULP workers' council in 1935. Hill served as chairman of the Pittsburgh NNC and used the position to promote the unionization of black workers.[84]

From the outset, Hill and his fellow NNC officers cultivated a close relationship with CIO leaders, especially Golden Clinton and Phillip Murray, and in October 1936 they began organizing the Western Pennsylvania Negro Labor Conference. Pittsburgh NNC officers fanned out across western Pennsylvania to generate enthusiasm for the conference. Careathers covered the industrial towns of Beaver County, including Aliquippa, which housed a massive Jones and Laughlin steel plant, and Hill managed the Johnstown area as well as several other communities. They also secured the support of prominent black clergy including Bishop William J. Walls of the AME Zion Church, the Reverend T. J. King of Ebenezer Baptist Church, and the Reverend J. C. Austin, who had pastored in Pittsburgh throughout the 1920s before moving to Chicago.[85]

Ultimately, representatives from almost every major racial-advancement organization attended the conference on February 6, 1937, along with several hundred labor organizers. Careathers opened the meeting in the morning, and a series of prominent leaders delivered talks leading up to Murray's keynote address.[86] Vann was among them. During his speech, he pledged the *Courier*'s full support for the union drive and promised to expose any African Americans who sided with employers. Like Murray, Vann warned black organizers that gaining advantages over area employers required sacrifice and militancy.

> You men might as well make up your minds that if you're to win anything worthwhile that you can call your own, you must be prepared to spill your own blood.... In your way, this time as always, you'll find stool pigeons and Uncle Toms of your own race, employed by the companies. You've got to fight them, blast them out.[87]

Vann made good on his promise to support the labor movement. In 1936 and 1937, the *Courier* featured dozens of stories trumpeting the benefit of the CIO to African Americans. George Schuyler helped drive this effort. A bril-

Phillip Murray, then president of the CIO, at a union rally near Braddock, Pennsylvania (just outside Pittsburgh), on April 26, 1950.
Historic Pittsburgh Image Collection, 601022.UE, University of Pittsburgh Archives Service Center.

liant novelist and satirist, Schuyler's regular column, Views and Reviews, offered biting commentary on racial issues in America. Schuyler hewed to a Marxist understanding of politics during the twenties and thirties, and like McKinney he saw racial solidarity as an obstacle to class unity.[88] In 1937 he investigated organizational efforts in Harlem, Akron, Cleveland, Memphis, Gary, St. Louis, and Chicago, and he reported on employers in those communities who fostered race hatred to break up unions.[89] The titles of other *Courier* articles, including "Porters, Waiters Praise Lewis, CIO Leader" (March 27, 1937), "Negro Workers Lead in Great Lakes Steel Drive" (July 31, 1937), "Negro Men on Board of Texas CIO Unions" (August 14, 1937), "Klan Rides Again in Dixie; Defies C.I.O." (December 10, 1938), and "CIO Demands Negro Managers in Kroger Stores in Detroit" (August 13, 1938), further demonstrate the paper's prolabor stance.

The CIO enjoyed widespread support from black organizations, and it reciprocated by promoting equal rights and opposing Jim Crow segregation. While this partnership continued well into the 1940s, the NNC's role in it did not. In the wake of the Nazi-Soviet nonaggression pact in late 1939, communists in the NNC abruptly reversed their antifascist position, resumed their attacks on mainstream racial advancement institutions, and alienated less radical members of the organization. The Communist Party sent an overwhelming number of communist delegates to the NNC's third convention in 1940, where they booed and jeered speakers who disagreed with party-driven resolutions. Consequently, Randolph, Bunche, and other prominent leaders resigned from the organization in protest, along with droves of their supporters, leaving it in the hands of a small group of hardcore communists. The NNC never again held the power and influence it once had, and it dissolved in 1947.[90]

Historians considering the legacy of the NNC have noted with good justification that it helped move labor unionism to the front of the civil rights agenda, but its role has been overstated at times. While Thomas Sugrue maintains that the NNC "opened a space in black politics that pulled the entire movement leftward," this chapter suggests that space had already been opened by earlier activists responding to structural changes in society.[91] Urban Leaguers in Pittsburgh and other major cities actively supported the labor movement before the NNC formed, and they continued to do so after it fragmented in 1940.

Civil Rights Unionism

The interracial industrial labor movement held out the possibility that significant numbers of black industrial workers might for the first time enjoy the benefits of union membership, including greater job security, better wages, and safer working conditions. "When the CIO come in . . . . it was a mass improvement," Merril Lynch recalled. Lynch was born in Pittsburgh in 1904. After his parents died during his early childhood, he and his younger sister moved in with his aunt in the lower Hill. Lynch attended Watt Street School until 1917, when his aunt had a stroke. Thereafter, Lynch felt compelled to contribute to the family's earnings. He dropped out of school at age thirteen and began working at the Black Diamond coal mine in nearby Lawrenceville, where he opened shaft doors and performed other simple tasks. Several years later, he left the mine to help his aunt perform janitorial work in a local office.[92]

Black and white steelworkers outside the United Steelworkers of America office in Pittsburgh, July or August 1946.
Teenie Harris Archive, Carnegie Museum of Art, Pittsburgh.

During this period, around 1922, Lynch met Murray—then a high-ranking official in the United Mine Workers. A massive coal strike took place in the winter of 1921–22, and the strikers needed a place to collect community donations. Local plumbers loaned their pool room to the striking miners, but it was very dirty. Lynch volunteered to clean the room free of charge, and Murray personally thanked him when he finished. Years later, Lynch recalled meeting Murray again at a CIO rally and noted with satisfaction that the labor leader remembered his earlier services. Lynch felt proud to be among the first twenty-five thousand men to join the CIO. "My own number was 21,389," he recalled. In its first year, SWOC recruited over three hundred thousand steelworkers.[93]

Lynch was among thousands of black workers who, for the first time, could take part in a collective bargaining process that improved their economic prospects. In 1937, for instance, U.S. Steel forged an agreement with SWOC that ensured for all workers a minimum wage of $5.00 a day and a forty-

"Second Helper" Ernest Moses (left) testing the quality of the metal drawn from the open-hearth furnace at the Carnegie Steel Plant in Homestead, Pennsylvania, ca. 1943.
Urban League Collection, box 10, folder 509, University of Pittsburgh Archives Service Center.

hour work week. Although few African Americans gained leadership positions in local unions, their involvement as rank-and-file members placed them in a stronger economic position than most of their predecessors. Lynch never became an officer, but he remained committed to the union for his entire working life. "When my time come to pick a duty, I was there," he proudly remembered. "When they had meetings in the hall, I was there. Whenever there was a vote, I was there."[94]

The CIO depended on the participation of black workers, and to that end it received crucial support from the NNC, the Urban League, the NAACP, and the black press. In return, the union emerged as a powerful advocate for racial justice.[95] It elected African Americans to its national offices, adopted resolutions condemning Jim Crow segregation, and spread the gospel of racial equality to millions of white Americans through its comic books, pamphlets, and news magazines. "There has been born in America a new, modern labor movement dedicated to the proposition that all who labor are entitled to equality of opportunity," CIO president Lewis declared. "Our Declaration of Independence says that we hold all men to be created equal. That means, regardless of his creed, his color, his race or his nationality."[96]

By 1940, the efforts of black labor organizers, communists, and reformers, along with that of a host of white New Dealers, CIO leaders, and radicals, had culminated in the unionization of thousands of black workers in steel mills, coal mines, meatpacking facilities, shipyards, and automobile plants across the country. Between 1935 and 1940, black union membership increased by 400 percent. For the first time, large numbers of working-class blacks joined their white counterparts against the business elite, and consequently many of them gained better wages, working conditions, and job security than they or their parents had ever known. LeRoy McChester, a migrant from Arkansas who worked at the Jones and Laughlin plant in Pittsburgh's South Side during the 1930s, remembered that once the CIO came in "they pinned the company down. It takes a whole lot of red tape to fire ya now." Additionally, Lynch believed the CIO improved safety in the region's mills. "Since the union's come in here, conditions in the mill have improved 100 percent," he observed. "When I come in here a lot of people were scared to work in the mill because of safety reasons. Too many men getting hurt; too many men getting killed."[97]

NOTES

1. "Phil Murray Urges Negro Workers to Join Great Steel Industry Union," *Pittsburgh Courier*, February 13, 1937. For more on the conference, and for the source of this chapter's epigraph, see William Hill, "The Negro Wage Worker," in *The WPA History of the Negro in Pittsburgh*, ed. Laurence Glasco (Pittsburgh: University of Pittsburgh Press, 2004), 225–26.
2. Harrison Gant, interview with Peter Gottlieb, August 23, 1974, Pittsburgh Oral History Project, Heinz History Center, Pittsburgh.
3. "Phil Murray Urges Negro Workers to Join Great Steel Industry Union," *Pittsburgh Courier*, February 13, 1937.
4. Because Hill moved so frequently, piecing together his biography proved challenging. The U.S. census records for Charlotte, North Carolina (1910 and 1920) and Summit, New Jersey (1930) offer some information. Also see the following *Courier* articles: "Hill Named Bedford Manager," December 9, 1939; "Hill Joins Race Relations Group," February 10, 1945 and "Toki Types," June 22, 1963.
5. Program of activities, February 7, 1934, box 1, folder 4, Aurora Reading Club Collection, Heinz History Center.
6. Abraham Epstein, "The Negro Migrant in Pittsburgh" (senior thesis, University of Pittsburgh, 1917), 37, 39.

7. Ira Reid, "Lily-White Labor," *Opportunity*, June 1930, 170–71. Also see Harvard Sitkoff, *A New Deal for Blacks: The Emergence of Civil Rights as a National Issue*, thirtieth anniv. ed. (New York: Oxford University Press, 2009), 19, and August Meier and Elliot Rudwick, *From Plantation to Ghetto* (New York: Hill and Wang, 1966), 242.
8. Reid, "Lily-White Labor," 172.
9. T. Arnold Hill, "Open Letter to Mr. William Green, President, American Federation of Labor," *Opportunity*, February 1930, 56–57.
10. Peter Gottlieb, *Making Their Own Way: Southern Blacks' Migration to Pittsburgh, 1916–30* (Urbana: University of Illinois Press, 1987), 172–73.
11. Robert L. Vann, "The Camera," *Pittsburgh Courier*, May 12, 1928. For an example of the *Courier*'s prounion stance, see "Courier Opposed in Mining Camp; Its Fight for the Negro Too Strong," *Pittsburgh Courier*, December 4, 1926.
12. Robert L. Vann, "The Camera," *Pittsburgh Courier*, May 12, 1928.
13. Lizabeth Cohen, *Making a New Deal: Industrial Workers in Chicago, 1919–1939* (New York: Cambridge University Press, 1990).
14. Cohen, *Making a New Deal*.
15. Jesse O. Thomas, "Negro Workers and Organized Labor," *Opportunity*, September 1934, 278.
16. Reginald Johnson, "The Urban League and the A.F. of L.," *Opportunity*, August 1935, 247.
17. Walter White to John L. Lewis, November 27, 1935, box 105, folders 1–7, American Catholic History Research Center and Archives, Catholic University of America.
18. Steve Fraser, "The 'Labor Question,'" in *The Rise and Fall of the New Deal Order: 1930–1980*, ed. Steve Fraser and Gary Gerstle (Princeton, NJ: Princeton University Press, 1989), 68.
19. Dennis Dickerson, *Out of the Crucible: Black Steelworkers in Western Pennsylvania, 1875–1980* (Albany: State University of New York Press), 131; Sitkoff, *A New Deal for Blacks*, 137–38.
20. Ernest Rice McKinney, "Difficulties Face Task of Organizing the Negro Worker," *Pittsburgh Courier*, September 19, 1936. Also see Ernest Rice McKinney, "The Negroes' Road to Freedom," *Labor Age* 21, no. 9 (1932), box 1, folder 9, Ernest Rice McKinney Papers, University of Pittsburgh Archives Service Center, and Ernest Rice McKinney, "Race Solidarity: An Ideal of No Importance," *The World Tomorrow*, January 1929.
21. Richard Wright, *Black Boy (American Hunger): A Record of Childhood and Youth* (New York: Harper Collins, 1945), 43.
22. David R. Roediger, *The Wages of Whiteness: Race and the Making of the American Working Class* (New York: Verso, 2007).
23. See chapters 4 and 2 in this book.
24. W. E. B. Du Bois, *Crisis*, June 1934.
25. W. E. B. Du Bois gave voice to the racial utilitarian perspective in 1903 when distinguishing his agenda from Booker T. Washington's. In pursuing full civil and political equality he maintained that race leaders must take "advantage of the opportunities at hand ... [while] remembering that only a firm adherence to their higher ideals and aspirations will ever keep those ideals within the realm of possibility." See *The Souls of Black Folk* (New York: Fawcett, 1903), 50–51.

26. Kevin Gaines, *Uplifting the Race: Black Leadership, Politics, and Culture in the Twentieth Century* (Chapel Hill, NC: University of North Carolina Press, 1996), 1–2. Reverend Harold Tolliver believed the presence of robust black businesses in the Hill District provided an important psychological boost to the black community. In his view, these examples of African Americans "lifting themselves up by their own bootstraps" stood as proof that the race could succeed in American society (Harold Tolliver, interview with Dennis Dickerson, October 9, 1974, Pittsburgh Oral History Project).
27. ULP, "Lecture Course for Elevator Operators, Bellmen, and Attendants," 1931, box 3, folder 124, Urban League Records. Harold Lett is the most likely author of the introductory passage in the piece describing the program, since as industrial secretary he planned and organized the events listed therein.
28. Quoted in Arthur J. Edmunds, *Daybreakers: The Story of the Urban League of Pittsburgh, the First Sixty-Five Years* (Pittsburgh: Urban League of Pittsburgh, 1999), 80. While insisting on equal employment opportunities, Lett nevertheless organized vocational training classes for traditionally "black jobs": janitors, elevator operators, chauffeurs, waiters, and domestics. At the ULP's training program for elevator operators in 1931, speakers delivered lectures intended to make the audience more competitive in the labor market. See program of lecture course for elevator operators, 1931, box 3, folder 124, Urban League Records.
29. Harold Lett, "Work: Negro Unemployed in Pittsburgh," *Opportunity*, March 1931, 81.
30. As industrial secretary of the ULP, it seems likely that Lett helped facilitate this project. See ULP, "The Relation of the Negro to Unemployment in Food Products," 1933, box 10, folder 448, Urban League Records. Around the same time, Lett condemned the "vicious cycle . . . that grasps the Negro boy and girl upon their leaving school, and retains its relentless and inhuman hold until the individual is cast upon the human scrap heap as unfit to meet the rigid requirements imposed by industry even in the limited sphere of their activities" (Edmunds, *Daybreakers*, 79).
31. ULP, "Racial Barriers," 1933, box 6, folder 242, Urban League Records.
32. See Parris and Brooks, *Blacks in the City*, 248–51.
33. T. Arnold Hill, "Workers to Lead the Way Out," *Opportunity*, June 1934, 183.
34. Sitkoff, *A New Deal for Blacks*, 187.
35. The ULP maintained its ties to Edwin May of the May Drug Company and Edgar Kauffman Jr., whose father owned a major department store. Both men had shown far greater interest in racial equality than most of the city's employers, who sought to exploit African Americans as a source of cheap labor and a wedge against unions. For years May and Kauffman provided critical financial support for the league's programs, including the workers' council. Still, May was among several white executive members of the ULP who helped limit access to the organization's highest position: only two black men ever served as president of the ULP between 1918 and 1983. And Kauffman's father only hired white women to work at the sales desks of his department stores. See Edmunds, *Daybreakers*, 91, 96.
36. Edmunds, *Daybreakers*, 89–91.
37. Edmunds, *Daybreakers*, 90.
38. Workers' Council of Pittsburgh, conference program, July 7, 1935, box 3, folder 155, Urban League Records; "The Urban League in Action," *Opportunity*, August 1935, 319.

39. "ICC Renders Decision Favorable to Red Caps," *Workers' Council Bulletin* no. 22, October 15, 1938, box 3, folder 151, Urban League Records.
40. Ira B. Valentine to William E. Hill, November 4, 1937, box 3, folder 151, Urban League Records. Just a week earlier A. J. McGhee, system president of the Brotherhood of Sleeping Car Porters, wrote R. Maurice Moss asking for his assistance dealing with a grievance filed by a porter in Pittsburgh (October 27, 1937, box 3, folder 151, Urban League Records; see also William Hill to C. I. Leiper, district manager of the Pennsylvania Railroad, December 4, 1937, box 3, folder 151, Urban League Records). According to historian Beth Tompkins Bates, the *Pittsburgh Courier* was the first major black weekly to lend its support to the Brotherhood of Sleeping Car Porters (*Pullman Porters and the Rise of Protest Politics in Black America, 1925–1945* [Chapel Hill: University of North Carolina Press, 2001], 54, 75).
41. William Hill, "The Negro Wage Worker," 226.
42. "The Need of Organization Among Household Employees," *Workers' Council Bulletin* no. 16, May 28, 1937, box 3, folder 155, Urban League Records.
43. See the minutes of the Housewives Cooperative League, September 7, September 15, and October 22, 1937, box 7, folder 321, Urban League Records. Also see Joe W. Trotter and Jared N. Day, *Race and Renaissance: African Americans in Pittsburgh since World War II* (Pittsburgh: University of Pittsburgh Press, 2010), 33–34.
44. Activist Roy Garvin, who authored this quote, served alongside Hill as one of two male members of the housewives cooperative league. The organization appears to have had about fifty members, including about six to eight officers. Women like Daisy Lampkin, Alma Illery, Laura Parr, Cora Jones, Frances Stewart, and Christina Jeffries appear to have held all the major posts. Additionally, to further advance its program, the organization made plans to establish contacts with the larger network of women reformers in the city's other major racial organizations. For instance, it identified Grace Lowndes as its contact person in the Urban League of Pittsburgh (minutes of the Housewives Cooperative League, September 7, September 15, and October 22, 1937, box 7, folder 321, Urban League Records; Trotter and Day, *Race and Renaissance*, 33–34).
45. Minutes of the Housewives Cooperative League, September 7, September 15, and October 22, 1937, box 7, folder 321, Urban League Records; Trotter and Day, *Race and Renaissance*, 33–34.
46. Minutes of the Housewives Cooperative League, September 7, September 15, and October 22, 1937, box 7, folder 321, Urban League Records; Trotter and Day, *Race and Renaissance*, 33–34.
47. Sitkoff, *A New Deal for Blacks*, 188–91; Thomas Sugrue, *Sweet Land of Liberty: The Forgotten Struggle for Civil Rights in the North* (New York: Random House, 2008), 18–21.
48. Reginald Johnson, "Not A Bad Year," *Opportunity*, March 1938, 71–74; Sugrue, *Sweet Land of Liberty*, 54. The AFL's opposition to Brown's nondiscrimination clause prompted an editorialist from the *Philadelphia Tribune* to quip that "labor wants liberal laws, but only for white workers." See "The Right to Work," *Philadelphia Tribune*, May 27, 1937.
49. William Hill to Homer Brown, memo, February 23, 1937, box 1, folder 3, Homer Brown Collection.

50. Congressional committee on Senate bill 639, report, box 5, folder 59, Homer Brown Collection.
51. John A. Phillips to the members of the Pennsylvania General Assembly, ca. April 1937, box 5, folder 59, Homer Brown Collection. In the same box and folder, see Homer Brown to Walter White, May 27, 1937.
52. William Hill to Homer Brown, memo, February 23, 1937, box 1, folder 3, Homer Brown Collection.
53. "Color Bar Ties Up PA. Assembly," *Pittsburgh Courier*, May 22, 1937.
54. "The Right to Work," *Philadelphia Tribune*, May 27, 1937.
55. "Color Bar Ties Up PA. Assembly," *Pittsburgh Courier*, May 22, 1937.
56. James H. Brewer and Andrew Buni discussed the emergence of these factions in the context of the 1938 gubernatorial primary campaign in Pennsylvania, but it seems plausible that these divisions began developing a year or more earlier when the CIO first split from the AFL. See James H. Brewer, "Robert Lee Vann and the *Pittsburgh Courier*" (master's thesis, University of Pittsburgh, 1941), 93–95, and Andrew Buni, *Robert L. Vann of the Pittsburgh Courier: Politics and Black Journalism* (Pittsburgh: University of Pittsburgh Press, 1974), 280–91.
57. Homer Brown to Walter White, May 27, 1937, box 5, folder 59, and T. Arnold Hill to Homer Brown, June 5, 1937, box 1, folder 3, Homer Brown Collection; Reginald Johnson, "Notes on Negro Life," ca. 1937, 9, box 10, folder 453, Urban League Records.
58. Glenda Elizabeth Gilmore, *Defying Dixie: The Radical Roots of Civil Rights* (New York: Norton, 2008), 124. I cover the Scottsboro case in chapter 3 as well.
59. See Mark Naison, *Communists in Harlem during the Depression* (New York: Grove Press, 1983), 20.
60. Walter White and Daisy Lampkin, correspondence, April 16–18, 1933, NAACP Branch Records.
61. Sugrue, *Sweet Land of Liberty*, 24–26; Meier and Rudwick, *From Plantation to Ghetto*, 265.
62. Asbury Smith, "What Can the Negro Expect from Communism?," *Opportunity*, July 1933, 211–12, 219; also see T. Arnold Hill, "Communism," *Opportunity*, September 1930, 278.
63. In Charles T. Pete Banner-Haley, *From Du Bois to Obama: African American Intellectuals in the Public Forum* (Carbondale: Southern Illinois University Press, 2010), 21.
64. While Young lauded the CPUSA for opposing segregation in Pittsburgh and other cities, he expressed concern that widespread conversion to the party could exacerbate racial problems for African Americans ("Negro Editors on Communism: A Symposium of the American Negro Press," *Crisis*, April 1932).
65. For photographs and newspapers clippings on the Herndon case, see box 1, folder 4, American Left Ephemera Collection, University of Pittsburgh Archives Service Center.
66. Sugrue, *Sweet Land of Liberty*, 23.
67. "Race Delegates Were Refused Accommodation," *Baltimore Afro-American*, January 4, 1930.
68. "Pittsburgh Voters Snarl at Hoover; Democrats and Communists Active," *Baltimore Afro-American*, October 8, 1932.
69. "Pittsburgh Voters Snarl at Hoover; Democrats and Communists Active," *Baltimore Afro-American*, October 8, 1932.

70. Kenneth Heineman, *A Catholic New Deal: Religion and Reform in Depression Pittsburgh* (University Park: Pennsylvania State University Press, 1999), 145. Heineman notes that Careathers was Pittsburgh's leading black communist and that throughout the Depression Careathers held secret meetings at a candy shop where he and other radicals discussed politics.
71. "The Frame-Up of Benjamin Lowell Careathers," May 1953, box 1, folder 7, Leon Swimmer Collection, University of Pittsburgh Archives Service Center.
72. Harrison Gant, interview with Peter Gottlieb, August 23, 1974, Pittsburgh Oral History Project.
73. Dickerson, *Out of the Crucible*, 140; Careathers's account of infiltrating the Jones and Laughlin mill and gathering signatures can be found in Art Shields, *On the Battle Lines, 1919–1936* (Mishawaka, IN: Better World Books, 1986).
74. The school was located on Stevenson Street, between 1300 and 1400 Fifth Avenue. See Pittsburgh Workers School brochure, winter 1939, box 1, folder 15, A. E. Forbes Communist Collection, University of Pittsburgh Archives Service Center; also see the brochures from 1938 to 1939.
75. Pittsburgh Workers School, statement, December 1938, box 3, folder 156, Urban League Records. The rise of fascism in Europe provided American leftists with rhetorical leverage to use against their political opponents. Ned Sparks, the western Pennsylvania district organizer of the Communist Party, was among many leftists who painted with the brush of fascism Republicans and antiunionists. In a 1936 radio address he castigated Republicans for "removing all remnants of popular influence upon the government ... [and] creating fascist storm troops, such as the ... Ku Klux Klan." The speaker explained that Pennsylvania's upcoming gubernatorial election pitted democracy against fascism ("The Election Campaign and the Relief Crisis," July 14, 1936, box 6, folder 275, Urban League Records).
76. See Brown, "Civil Rights," in *The WPA History of the Negro in Pittsburgh*, 214.
77. See Kelly Miller, "Should Black Turn Red," *Opportunity*, November 1933, 328–32, 350.
78. "The Frame-Up of Benjamin Lowell Careathers," May 1953, box 1, folder 7, Leon Swimmer Collection; Phillip Jenkins, *The Cold War at Home: The Red Scare in Pennsylvania, 1945–1960* (Chapel Hill: University of North Carolina Press, 1999), 87–88.
79. Ernest Rice McKinney, "The Tactics of the Socialist Party in Pittsburgh: A Rejoinder," box 1, folder 4, Ernest Rice McKinney Papers; Ernest Rice McKinney, "The Negroes' Road to Freedom," *Labor Age*, 21, no. 9 (1932), box 1, folder 9, Ernest Rice McKinney Papers.
80. Ernest Rice McKinney, "The Negroes' Road to Freedom," *Labor Age* 21, no. 9 (1932), box 1, folder 9, Ernest Rice McKinney Papers. Also see Pamela Twiss, "Ernest Rice McKinney: African American Appalachian, Social Worker, Radical Labor Organizer and Educator," *Journal of Appalachian Studies* 10, nos. 1–2 (2004): 95–110.
81. Sugrue, *Sweet Land of Liberty*, 40.
82. National Negro Congress, promotional pamphlet, 1935, 30, box 7, folder 329, Urban League Records.
83. John P. Davis to John Brophy, April 28, 1937, box 106, folders 2–14, American Catholic History Research Center and Archives. For information on the NNC's request for funding, see John P. Davis to John L. Lewis, August 13, 1937, and Ralph Hetzel to John P. Davis, August 27, 1937, American Catholic History Research Center and Archives.

84. Roger Laws, secretary of the Pittsburgh NNC, to John Davis, October 19, 1936, box 7, folder 329, Urban League Records. In the same box and folder see Roger Laws to W. W. Mendenhall, June 22, 1936, and William Hill to James Washington, October 12, 1936. William Hill was the leading figure in the Pittsburgh NNC. In early 1936 he visited the Soviet Union to learn more about the country's social and economic organization, and in 1937 he represented Pittsburgh at the NNC's national conference in Philadelphia.
85. Joe W. Trotter, *River Jordan: African American Urban Life in the Ohio Valley* (Lexington: University of Kentucky Press, 1998), 134–35; Dennis Dickerson, "The Black Church in Industrializing Western Pennsylvania, 1870–1950," *Western Pennsylvania Historical Magazine* 64, no. 4 (1981): 329–44; "Phil Murray Urges Negro Workers to Join Great Steel Industry Union," *Pittsburgh Courier*, February 13, 1937.
86. "Phil Murray Urges Negro Workers to Join Great Steel Industry Union," *Pittsburgh Courier*, February 13, 1937. For more on the conference, see Hill, "The Negro Wage Worker," 225–26.
87. "Phil Murray Urges Negro Workers to Join Great Steel Industry Union," *Pittsburgh Courier*, February 13, 1937; Hill, "The Negro Wage Worker," 225–26.
88. Later in his career, Schuyler moved to the political right and published conservative pieces with titles like *The Communist Conspiracy against Negroes*.
89. For more on Schuyler's background, see Charles Pete T. Banner-Haley, *To Do Good and to Do Well: Middle-Class Blacks and the Depression, Philadelphia, 1929–1941* (New York: Garland, 1993), 19–21. For more information on Schuyler's 1937 investigations see the following stories in the *Pittsburgh Courier*: "Union Drive Slows in Border Cities," September 11, 1937, "Harlem Boasts 42,000 Negro Labor Unionists," August 21, 1937, "Industrial South Shaky as Unions Woo Negro Labor," September 18, 1937, and "Negro Workers Lead in Great Lakes Steel Drive," July 31, 1937.
90. Meier and Rudwick, *From Plantation to Ghetto*, 266.
91. Sugrue, *Sweet Land of Liberty*, 40.
92. Merril Lynch, interview with Peter Gottlieb, August 22, 1974, Pittsburgh Oral History Project.
93. Merril Lynch, interview with Peter Gottlieb, August 22, 1974, Pittsburgh Oral History Project.
94. Merril Lynch, interview with Peter Gottlieb, August 22, 1974, Pittsburgh Oral History Project. The information on SWOC membership and the agreement with U.S. Steel comes from Bruce M. Stave, "Pittsburgh and the New Deal," in *The New Deal*, vol. 2, *The State and Local Levels*, ed. John Braeman, Robert H. Bremner, and David Brody (Columbus: Ohio State University Press, 1975), 399.
95. For more on the racial activism of the CIO, see Robert Rodgers Korstad, *Civil Rights Unionism: Tobacco Workers and the Struggle for Democracy in the Mid-Twentieth-Century South* (Chapel Hill: University of North Carolina Press, 2003).
96. Sitkoff, *A New Deal for Blacks*, 140; John L. Lewis, quoted in "CIO Bans Race, Creed or Color in Labor's Fight," *Pittsburgh Courier*, November 26, 1938.
97. Sitkoff, *A New Deal for Blacks*, 140; LeRoy McChester, interview with Peter Gottlieb, July 9, 1974, Pittsburgh Oral History Project; Merril Lynch interview with Peter Gottlieb, August 22, 1974. Also see Hill, "The Negro Wage Worker," 226.

CHAPTER SEVEN

"The Freedoms We Cherish"

REFORMERS AND THE STATE, 1933-1945

> It is necessary that some agency see to it that Negroes get a square deal in employment; that they get a square deal from the labor unions; that they get a square deal from the relief agencies; that they get their proper share of education funds; that their legislative representatives work energetically in their interests to remove all disabilities imposed because of race and color.
>
> —Robert L. Vann, *Pittsburgh Courier*, August 11, 1934

> A truly democratic government has an obligation to see that the right to work, and all other fundamental rights, are guaranteed to every citizen without regard to race, creed, color, or national origin.
>
> —Grace Lowndes, *Informer*, May 1945

John Adams had grown accustomed to sweltering tropical heat and monsoon rains by 1945. Like many black soldiers deployed in the Pacific theater, he served with a racially segregated unit tasked with shipping supplies to the front lines along a windy, mud-ridden jungle road in Burma.[1] The country served as an important land bridge between Allied forces in India and China, and since 1942 Japan had used it to launch campaigns against both. As a staff sergeant in a Negro Quartermaster Trucking outfit, Adams recorded the contents, destinations, and locations of all the vehicles in his unit. They had more than once come under fire from Japanese snipers as well as an occasional fighter plane running a strafing attack.[2]

Like many GIs, Adams also battled homesickness. He thought often about the family he left behind in Pittsburgh. James Adams, his father, grew up in Lexington, North Carolina, and worked at the Coca-Cola bottling plant there. His mother, Lucy Wade, came from nearby Yancyville, North Carolina, and she married his father in 1917. The couple began having children soon after the wedding. John was their third child, born in 1922, and he spent at least part of his early childhood in Lexington. But later in the decade his parents migrated to Pittsburgh—driven, like so many, by the hope of gaining greater economic opportunity and personal liberty.[3]

Spring 1945 found young John busy managing Allied supply trucks in a Burmese jungle, but he occasionally had time to reflect on how his life had changed over the last few years. He received his draft orders in 1942 and left home soon after to go to basic training. When the army gave him some leave time before his deployment to the Pacific theater, Adams returned to Pittsburgh and married Pearl Parrot—whose family lived across the Ohio river from his.[4] John had a life waiting for him back in Pittsburgh, a life put on hold by a war that seemed like it might continue for another year or more. Standing in deep mud on a remote jungle road in southeast Asia, a low-ranking soldier like Adams had no way of knowing how long the war might drag on, and this uncertainty could take an emotional toll.

It was in this setting that an old friend from Pittsburgh unexpectedly stepped into Adams's field of vision: Frank Bolden. As a journalist for the *Pittsburgh Courier* and one of two African Americans accredited as a war correspondent, Bolden had traveled up and down Burma covering the contributions of black service members to the war effort. One of his earlier stories celebrated the achievements of the Engineer Construction Battalion, a black unit headed by white officers that earned recognition for building key airstrips in "a remote corner of . . . heat-ridden and pestilential jungle" that made possible bombing raids on Japanese forces in Burma.[5] Although the army generally confined African Americans to labor duties and rarely used them for combat on the front lines, the *Courier* worked to highlight their service to the nation.

This effort reflected the black weekly's decades-long initiative to celebrate the achievements of African Americans while debunking the logic that justified their subordination. Operating against white-owned newspapers and other products of popular culture that focused on black criminality and perpetuated derogatory racial stereotypes, the *Courier* bolstered black pride through its positive coverage of the everyday lives of people of color, its accounts of the contributions of ancient African kingdoms to world history, its stories chronicling the achievements of jazz luminaries like Duke Ellington and Lena Horne, and its columns detailing the contributions of African Americans to the war against the Axis powers.

Bolden grew up in Washington, Pennsylvania, a few hours south of Pittsburgh, where his father, Frank Bolden Sr., worked as a mail carrier. After graduating from Washington High School, he left home to attend college at the University of Pittsburgh. There, he studied biology, became the first African American to play in Pitt's marching band, and helped pay for his tuition by occasionally contributing stories to the *Pittsburgh Courier*. When he graduated, he tried to enroll in medical school but discovered, like so many black applicants before him, that racial barriers existed across the professions in the Steel City. His application for a public teaching job likewise ended in failure, so Bolden cobbled together a living in the mid-thirties by working at the Centre Avenue YMCA in the Hill District and writing pieces for the *Courier*. His colorful prose, knack for beat reporting, and timely delivery of materials apparently caught the attention of the paper's editorial staff, which gradually increased his salary and gave him more stories to cover. During World War II, the *Courier* submitted Bolden's name to the War Department's Bureau of Public Relations, and after a thorough vetting it selected him as a war correspondent.[6]

During the war, Bolden spent time embedded with the Ninety-Second Infantry Division in Italy, one of the few black units that directly participated in combat, and he conducted interviews with Franklin Roosevelt, Winston Churchill, Joseph Stalin, Chiang Kai-shek, and Mahatma Gandhi.[7] Bolden encountered John Adams sometime in spring 1945 while starting a new report on African Americans transporting supplies along a route in Burma called the Stillwell road.

Adams eagerly asked about friends and family in Pittsburgh during their conversation, and like many black service members he wanted to know what his employment prospects would be like when he returned to civilian life. Remembering the discriminatory treatment African Americans received from employers in the Steel City, Adams wondered if the Pennsylvania state legislature passed a key bill introduced in March 1945 by Pittsburgh NAACP (PNAACP) head and state representative Homer Brown.[8] Brown had proposed creating a permanent fair employment practices agency in Pennsylvania that would have power to investigate and penalize discriminatory hiring practices by public and private employers, and his bill had obvious importance for black workers across the state.

Soon after the two men parted ways, Bolden wrote a story that described their happy meeting and recounted how Adams's commanding officer praised his work ethic, punctuality, and discipline. This account appeared in the June 30 issue of the *Courier*, and a few weeks later Adams began receiving letters from loved ones who, after reading it, wanted to express how proud they were of his achievements. In an interview many years later, Adams recalled how this made him feel:

> The article that Frank wrote about me was one of the greatest morale builders that I had ever received. We used to sit around and wait for mail to come from home. And it was just so nice to receive a letter that said "We read about you. Keep up the good work. We're praying for you. We're looking forward to you coming home."[9]

The encounter between Bolden and Adams offers an example of how the lives of reformers and working-class African Americans intersected in the decades preceding the civil rights movement. Since the beginning of the Great Migration, black social workers, civil rights activists, and journalists had worked to mitigate the physical manifestations of racial inequality, expose discriminatory practices, and politically mobilize black voters in pursuit of full citizenship for all African Americans.

This effort included making sure that African Americans received their fair share of jobs in government-funded programs during the New Deal years and harnessing the power of the state to enforce racial equality during World War II. In Pittsburgh, reformers in the *Courier* and Urban League of Pittsburgh (ULP) used the newfound political clout of black Pennsylvanians to open pathways to public sector employment for African Americans. Robert L. Vann's campaign for Franklin Roosevelt in 1932 alerted Pennsylvania Democrats to the possibility of winning the black vote in the state and capturing a major Republican stronghold. Attuned to this, reformers secured for African Americans in the Pittsburgh area a significant number of patronage appointments as well as proportional employment in work-relief projects.

As the United States prepared for and entered the Second World War, racial activists across the country experimented with more militant tactics as they pressed the Roosevelt administration to expand employment oppor-

Frank Bolden, war correspondent, ca. 1940s.
Percival Prattis Collection, box 1, folder 49,
University of Pittsburgh Archives Service Center.

tunities for African Americans in defense plants and end segregation in the armed services. Homer Brown's effort to establish a Pennsylvania fair employment practices agency took inspiration from this. Meanwhile, staff at the *Pittsburgh Courier* launched a national Double V campaign in 1942 that rhetorically equated fascism in Europe with Jim Crow segregation in the United States. Through hundreds of articles, photographs, and drawings, the campaign reached black homes and street corners from California to Massachusetts, and the political pressure it applied during a time of war likely hastened federal-level decisions to end the exclusion of African Americans from the marines, army air corps, and coast guard, open the women's auxiliary corps to black women, and expand the role of black service members in the army and navy.

As a member of a segregated military unit relegated to support services, John Adams understood that the state could and did perpetuate racial injustice. But the government could also serve as a powerful weapon against it, if it was forced to do so. In the 1940s, reformers in Pittsburgh increasingly blended the pragmatic tactics of the interwar years with the more militant, direct-action methods that later characterized activism in the fifties and sixties. In doing so, they helped compel the Roosevelt administration to make meaningful concessions. These victories provided important lessons for a younger generation of activists. During WWII, social and political battle lines began forming on the home front that remained in place through the midcentury civil rights revolution.

African Americans and the New Deal, 1933-1940

Nearly thirteen million Americans had lost their jobs by the time Franklin Roosevelt entered the White House in March 1933, and the gross national product, which stood at $104 billion four years earlier, had fallen to $56 billion. One in four Americans were out of work, and every day thousands of hungry men and women stood in bread lines in cities across the country. Roosevelt had promised a new deal for "forgotten" Americans during his campaign, and in his first year in office he persuaded Congress to pass a series of measures to stabilize the banking system, provide emergency financial relief, and create jobs. New agencies, including the Public Works Administration (PWA), Civilian Conservation Corps (CCC), and Civil Works Administration (CWA), launched thousands of projects to get the unemployed back to work through constructing schools, hospitals, bridges, roads, public buildings, and parks.[10]

The New Deal provided much-needed financial assistance, temporary employment, and hope to millions of Americans, but not all groups shared equally in its benefits. When the Agricultural Adjustment Administration called for reduced crop production in the South and West to increase farmers' profits, landowners evicted thousands of tenant farmers, many of whom were African Americans.[11] Under pressure from southern whites and the American Federation of Labor, Democrats removed an antidiscrimination clause from the National Labor Relations Act. And since local authorities controlled the dispensation of jobs in New Deal work-relief projects, African Americans received disproportionately fewer positions and rarely obtained supervisory positions.[12] Indeed, many work-relief projects in the South excluded blacks entirely. Under such a system, T. Arnold Hill of the National Urban League (NUL) warned, "a Negro engineer, architect, stenographer, brick-mason, or structural iron worker will often not be provided with work in his field and will, therefore, be judged 'unemployable' and subject ... to direct relief from state or city funds." Nationally, government relief rolls included twice as many African Americans as whites during Roosevelt's first term in office. In Pennsylvania, 35.2 percent of African Americans and 13.3 percent of whites received government relief.[13]

Moreover, the CCC, which put young men to work constructing parks, placed African Americans in segregated camps. In 1935, blacks constituted forty-nine thousand of the half million men working in CCC camps. At 3,485, Pennsylvania had more black enrollees than any other state besides Texas. African American army officers headed some of the black camps in Pennsylvania, such as camp Robert L. Vann.[14] But in most cases white officers were put in charge, and this was especially true at camps that featured both black and white enrollees. Major-General Robert Callan, commander of the Third Corps Area, which included Pennsylvania, ordered the replacement of six black officers with white ones to ensure that white enrollees would not "be placed under colored leaders or assistant leaders." When questioned, Callan explained that white men could only take orders from white officers because that was the "natural condition."[15]

Black Reformers Confront the New Deal

Black leaders recognized the limits of Roosevelt's domestic programs. At a conference at Howard University in 1935, delegates from across the country gathered to discuss the New Deal and consider ways to pressure the Roosevelt administration to address its racial shortcomings. The same year, speakers at the NAACP's annual convention offered scathing critiques of the president's "lily-white rehabilitation" of the economy.[16] Moreover, beginning in 1933 and continuing into Roosevelt's second term, black journals and newspapers attacked discriminatory practices in the New Deal. *Opportunity*, the NUL's monthly publication, expressed bitter frustration over the administration of CWA and PWA projects, while an editorial in the *Chicago Defender* concluded that the National Recovery Act and its many codes "have been a detriment." Even the *Pittsburgh Courier*, which staunchly supported FDR's 1932 presidential campaign, complained about discriminatory management of work-relief projects and called for "determined pressure on the Administration by aroused Negroes everywhere."[17]

Established racial-justice organizations campaigned to extend the benefits of the New Deal to all Americans. The NAACP organized the Joint Committee on National Recovery in 1933 to call attention to the unequal wage rates written into the codes of the National Industrial Recovery Act. Meanwhile, officers in the NUL pressured the Roosevelt administration to include African Americans proportionally in federally funded projects. Eugene Kinckle Jones, Ira Reid, Lester Granger, and T. Arnold Hill made so many trips from their New York City headquarters to Washington, DC, where they lobbied government officials and testified before Congress, that they earned the nickname "the brief-case boys."[18]

Leaders in the ULP likewise insisted on just administration of New Deal programs. By 1933, unemployment in Pittsburgh had reached 43.4 percent among African Americans and 15.7 percent among whites.[19] Therefore, whenever local work-relief projects began, ULP staff worked to ensure African Americans got their fair share of jobs.[20] Executive secretary R. Maurice Moss made contact with local CWA officials and managed to secure placement for two black examiners in the state employment office and five black staff members. This feat, he proudly remarked, "tended to immediately counteract the charges of discrimination against Negro workmen, both of the laboring and of the white-collar group, and our latest report shows 2,146 Negroes . . . have been placed . . . on CWA projects." Moss also noted that "contact was maintained with those in charge of recruiting and placing in the Civilian Conservation Corps," with the result that "15 per cent of all the Pittsburgh boys sent to the reforestration camps were Negroes."[21]

Statistics from a February 1934 ULP report suggest that African Americans in Allegheny County, which includes Pittsburgh, received a considerable share of jobs in local work-relief projects. Although they constituted just 6 percent of the county's total population, African Americans held 10 percent of the white collar positions and 12 percent of the manual labor jobs.[22] These data seem incongruous with figures showing 43 percent of black Alleghenians on relief rolls, which is almost tripled the rate for whites.[23] The discrepancy may be accounted for by the proclivity of foremen and supervisors in local industries to fire or lay off African Americans at much higher rates than whites.[24] Despite noteworthy gains in the public sector, the discriminatory practices of employers in the private sector created a disproportionately large population of jobless African Americans dependent on government relief.

Robert L. Vann, Percival Prattis, and an unknown government official, ca. 1936.
Robert L. Vann Papers, box 34, Percival Prattis Collection,
Moorland-Spingarn Research Center, Howard University, Washington, DC.

Eleanor Roosevelt, an outspoken advocate for racial equality, seated left, with black reformers Percival Prattis, editor of the *Courier's* city edition, standing to the far right and perhaps R. Maurice Moss, executive secretary of the Urban League of Pittsburgh, seated to the right of Roosevelt.
Percival Prattis Collection, box 33, folder 31, Moorland-Spingarn Research Center,
Howard University, Washington, DC.

The lobbying efforts of the ULP, combined with Vann's influence over state Democrats, may help explain why black Alleghenians received such a large share of work-relief jobs. As a prominent African American editor in a crucial electoral state, Vann leveraged his position to wring significant concessions from the Democratic Party. "Mr. Vann is one of our very good friends," explained a state Democratic official. "We always try to carry out Vann's suggestions if possible." In addition to placing African Americans in the federally run Home Loan Corporation, Vann also had considerable success in finding jobs for African Americans at the local level. The ULP reported that "there are now sixty Negro workers on the payroll of the County Emergency Relief Board, ranging from an assistant executive, and supervisors, to emergency aids."[25]

The ULP also found work for African American professionals through the research projects it developed, which had the additional benefit of producing valuable information about the city's black community. After three years of service as the ULP's industrial secretary, Harold Lett departed the city to head the Urban League branch in Newark, New Jersey, but he left for Moss a plan for a survey of black employment in Pittsburgh's major industries. In a short time, Moss, University of Pittsburgh professor Francis Tyson, and several other league officials submitted to the Federal Emergency Relief Administration (FERA) a research grant proposal that if approved would employ thirty black professionals to carry out a four-week study. FERA officials ultimately approved almost $1,000 in funding, half of what the grant requested but enough for the league's researchers to survey more than seven hundred of the largest employers in Allegheny County and collect data that provided a snapshot of black job prospects in the region.[26]

Moss summarized the findings in the February 1935 issue of *Opportunity*. The survey sample size included a third of all African Americans employed in Allegheny County, which amounted to 10,821 people across 731 firms. Of these, 56 percent held jobs in manufacturing, 18 percent in mining, and 12 percent in janitorial services. Regardless of the field, almost all African Americans worked as common laborers and consequently received the lowest pay rates allowed under the codes established by the National Industrial Recovery Act. Most disturbing of all, 282 (or 38 percent) of the firms surveyed employed only whites. The reasons they gave for not hiring African Americans included "the mill next door hires Negroes," "in white locality," "white help better," "no work that can be segregated," and, perhaps most insulting, "the nature of our work makes it necessary to go into the intimate recesses of homes."[27]

The Pittsburgh Housing Authority

The discriminatory hiring practices of so many private sector employers made it all the more imperative that black reformers open economic pathways in the public sector. In addition to their other efforts, ULP staff helped secure proportional employment in the construction of federally funded housing projects. After passage of the U.S. Housing Act in 1937, the Pittsburgh Housing Authority (PHA) proposed building several low-rent apartment complexes in the Hill District and other low-income communities in the city. The first was the Bedford Dwellings project, which it planned to build by the Allegheny River on a spot next to Greenlee Field, home of the Pittsburgh Crawfords, one of the most successful teams in the Negro Leagues. Hill, who served as industrial secretary of the ULP and headed its Workers' Council program, led efforts to persuade PHA officials to include an affirmative action clause in their contracts that required construction firms to reserve for African Americans 29 percent of the unskilled positions and 4.5 percent of the skilled positions.

The ULP followed this up by creating a contact committee to meet with building contractors and ensure they complied with the measure. Construction began on the Bedford Dwellings project in March 1939, and a few months later the PHA began building a second, larger development in the Hill called Terrace Village. By November, PHA contractors had paid out nearly $70,000 in wages to black construction workers on these projects, which represented more than one-fifth of the total payroll.[28]

Government-subsidized housing programs had a mixed record during the New Deal. In the Hill District, the Bedford Dwellings and Terrace Village projects provided improved living conditions for over nine thousand low-income Pittsburghers, the vast majority of whom were African American.[29] Two decades earlier, black newcomers arriving in the lower Hill District encountered a dire housing situation. City officials had previously deemed many of the units there unfit for human habitation, and few developers invested in renovating old houses or building new ones. In the midst of the Great Migration, demand far exceeded supply, which empowered landlords to charge high rents for exceptionally poor-quality housing.[30] Social researchers investigating black living conditions in the lower Hill observed units with low ceilings, poor ventilation, peeling plaster, broken windows, and inadequate sanitation. Undoubtedly, these conditions contributed to the health crisis in the black community that claimed hundreds of lives.[31]

While the housing projects in the Hill improved life for several thousand black Pittsburghers, they also reinforced preexisting patterns of segregation in the city. By 1937, discriminatory hiring practices, racially exclusive unions, and neighborhood covenants had helped to create several impoverished black enclaves in the city, including the lower Hill District, which held the greatest concentration of African Americans. While the *Courier* boasted that the Bedford Dwellings project was "one of the first in the country to feature mixed occupancy," in practice tenancy in it and Terrace Village followed prevailing residential patterns.[32] Citywide, the percentage of African Americans in housing projects far exceeded their proportion of the population. In 1941, they represented 56 percent of the 10,669 occupants of government-subsidized housing.[33]

While government housing projects in the Hill perpetuated segregation, their location had some practical benefits for poor African Americans. Both physically and emotionally, many found it easier to move to a nearby housing project within the black community, close to familiar places like Greenlee Field, than to one in a more integrated neighborhood across the city.

Even more problematic were the government-backed loans provided through the Federal Housing Act of 1934. The act underwrote home mortgages to boost homeownership, but frequently local administrators deemed black communities uncreditworthy. Cut off from federally backed loans, African Americans benefited little from the Federal Housing Act. Moreover, the FHA frequently insured mortgages containing clauses that restricted future sales to whites only.[34]

Lacking access to credit and decent jobs, African Americans depended disproportionately on government-subsidized housing and public relief. Roosevelt's promise of a New Deal for all Americans, regardless of race, remained unfulfilled in the estimation of a number of black leaders, including Vann.

Robert L. Vann and New Deal Disillusionment

In the four years that had elapsed since Vann's campaign for Roosevelt in 1932, Democrats in Pennsylvania had gained the governorship and both U.S.

Senate seats. Vann campaigned again for Roosevelt in the 1936 presidential election despite a brief and forgettable experience as special assistant to U.S. attorney general Homer Cummings. The office secretaries refused to take dictation from him because he was an African American, and Cummings ignored him. Tucked away in a tiny office, Vann performed menial, insignificant tasks. He also served intermittently in the informal Black Cabinet headed by Mary McLeod Bethune, but after two years he resigned from his position in the capital and turned his full attention to the *Courier*.[35]

Despite the pressures of the depression, the paper's circulation grew during this period because of Vann's knack for identifying issues that African Americans cared about and covering them more extensively than the other black newspapers.[36] From 1934 to 1938 the *Courier* reported on the rise of boxing star Joe Lewis and was the only black newspaper to send a correspondent to cover the Italian invasion of Ethiopia. Joel Rogers's lurid and somewhat sensationalized accounts of the heroism of the Ethiopians defending their homeland against overwhelming fascist forces instilled pride among African American readers and proved a circulation boon to the *Courier*.[37] In 1937, the *Courier*'s circulation spiked to 250,000 before settling to a steady 149,000 for the remainder of the decade. Even then, it far exceeded its closest competitors, the *Baltimore Afro-American* and the *Chicago Defender*, which respectively had circulations of about seventy thousand and fifty thousand.[38]

Meanwhile, Vann aided the industrial labor movement in the late 1930s. He had advocated for black inclusion in organized labor since the 1920s, and like other reformers he recognized the importance of assisting the Congress of Industrial Organizations (CIO) in its effort to organize workers across racial and ethnic lines. He spoke at labor rallies, and the *Courier* expressed support for the CIO in dozens of stories.[39]

Despite supporting progressive causes throughout the 1930s, Vann became disillusioned with the Roosevelt administration, both owing to the serious racial limitations of certain New Deal programs and to the fact that the president, under pressure from southern Democrats, refused to recommend the antilynching bill.[40] Moreover, during the state Democratic primaries in 1938 Vann got caught up in an intraparty feud. At stake that year was the governorship and a seat in the U.S. Senate. The election provided an opportunity for the Democrats to retain their control over Pennsylvania, but early on in the primaries two rival factions emerged. Joseph Guffey (Vann's political patron) and John L. Lewis of the CIO endorsed Thomas Kennedy for governor and backed Davis Wilson for the senate. On the other side, Democratic state committee head David L. Lawrence partnered with William Green of the American Federation of Labor (AFL) in supporting Alvin Jones for the governorship and George Earl for the senate seat. The AFL had recently expelled the CIO, and in the state Democratic primaries the two organizations vied for influence over organized labor in Pennsylvania.[41]

The Lawrence faction ultimately won the primaries and dethroned Guffey as the head of Pennsylvania Democrats, leaving Vann on the outside. His stature among Democrats may already have been on the wane. In the 1936 presidential election Roosevelt won Pennsylvania by a wide enough margin that the black vote did not seem crucial to success.[42] Lawrence evidently recognized this, and he made it clear to Vann that he would not be as receptive as his predecessors to demands for patronage jobs.[43]

Disappointed with the Roosevelt administration and sensing that Pennsylvania Democrats under Lawrence would neglect the black electorate, Vann decided once again to use his influence in support of the Republican Party. A few months after the Lawrence faction's victory in the primaries, Vann endorsed the Republican gubernatorial candidate Arthur James and used the *Courier* to campaign for him. As he explained to his former political patron Joseph Guffey,

> When you were undisputed leader, your promises to me were kept. ... [But] your Party opponents developed the idea that they could destroy your leadership. The Guffey policy towards my race began to wane, and at this writing, we are practically ignored and forgotten.... I do not know what your convictions are with respect to Party harmony, but I am quite certain of my convictions with respect to my race.... Our fight in this particular State campaign is to restore your leadership. If it requires the defeat of the Democratic organization and its ticket, then defeat must be made certain and very definite.[44]

The move was consistent with Vann's theory of the liquid vote, but this time he misread the political situation. He hoped that his actions would reassert his political influence, restore Guffey's prominence, and alarm Democrats into expanding patronage for black Pennsylvanians. Instead, it ruined his standing in the party. Guffey had little choice but to denounce Vann, and a rift developed between the two men that would not be repaired. Meanwhile the Lawrence forces further distanced themselves from the black editor, especially after their candidate lost the gubernatorial election. Worse still, when Republican Arthur James took office he rolled back work-relief programs that benefited African Americans, stopped enforcing the state equal rights bill, and offered no patronage to Vann.[45]

Vann nominally remained a Democrat up to 1940. That year, though fighting a losing battle with stomach cancer, he endorsed Republican Wendell Willkie over Roosevelt. Vann joined other Democrats in opposing on principle a three-term presidential candidate, and he remained disappointed with Roosevelt's inaction on segregation in the armed services and the persistence of discrimination in New Deal programs like the Tennessee Valley Authority and the FHA.[46] By then, African Americans were not receptive to calls for a return to the GOP. Despite the New Deal's racial shortcomings, they had gained jobs and relief through it that alleviated their material hardships. Vann died in October, shortly before Roosevelt was elected to a third term with overwhelming black support.

Race and the Home Front During World War II

On October 10, 1943, as bombs fell over Germany and Allied Forces pushed into Italy, prominent black reformers and white progressives gathered in Portland, Maine, for a ship dedication ceremony in honor of Vann. With a brisk New England breeze whipping the air and a 10,500-ton Liberty Ship hulking behind him, Ira F. Lewis, the longtime managerial editor of the *Pittsburgh Courier*, delivered a speech to commemorate the occasion and celebrate Vann's accomplishments. In describing Vann's early life in the small community of Ahoskie, North Carolina, and tracing his rise to editorship of the nation's largest black newspaper, Lewis cast him in the rags-to-riches mold and held up his life as proof that anybody, "irrespective of race, creed or color," could succeed in America "if he but works hard and makes the most of his opportunities." Lewis mixed with this thick patriotic brew dashes of subtle yet poignant critiques of American race relations. In celebrating Vann's life, Lewis dwelled on the ways Vann combated Jim Crowism in the military, and he extolled as a virtue Vann's belief "that the Negro vote should at all times remain organized and liquid; liquid that it might move from party to party where the political and economic interests of the Negro were factors." Lewis's remarks captured the essence of racial utilitarianism. Operating during and immediately after a period that historian Rayford Logan famously labeled the nadir of American race relations, black reformers courted white allies from across the political spectrum and seized upon opportunities

Daisy Lampkin (center), Ira Lewis, and Jesse Vann (holding the flowers) in Portland, Maine, with Percival Prattis and George Schuyler standing in the back left, at the christening ceremony of the SS *Robert L. Vann* on October 10, 1943.
Teenie Harris Archive, Carnegie Museum of Art, Pittsburgh.

Homer Brown (far left), Ira Lewis (next to Brown) and other dignitaries at the Lafayette Hotel in Portland, Maine.
Teenie Harris Archive, Carnegie Museum of Art, Pittsburgh.

for incremental progress wherever they could be found. Hence Lewis's speech was both conservative and radical, patriotic and critical; he took into account the audience members and, in terms they appreciated and understood, linked "Americanism" and racial equality.[47]

Most African Americans at the ceremony had traveled to Maine from other parts of the country to honor Vann. Among them were several of the old guard reformers who fought alongside Vann to advance the cause of human freedom: Daisy Lampkin, who helped elevate the PNAACP before gaining a position with the association's national office; George Schuyler, the gifted *Courier* columnist; Hobson Reynolds, who sponsored the 1935 Pennsylvania civil rights bill; and Homer Brown, the PNAACP president-turned-state legislator. Two relative newcomers to the *Courier* staff, Percival Prattis and Charles "Teenie" Harris, also attended the ceremony, and in the following years they helped usher the paper into a new era.[48]

The event symbolized a transition under way in Pittsburgh's black activist community. Vann, the archetypical reformer who tailored his pragmatic and measured activism to the difficult racial realities of early twentieth-century America, had died. During the Second World War, antiracism moved noticeably closer to the mainstream of white middle-class respectability in the North. In the 1940s CIO leaders forcefully called for an end to segregation, and liberals from Eleanor Roosevelt in Washington to David L. Lawrence in Pittsburgh openly condemned racial discrimination. Meanwhile a host of new interracial civil rights organizations—such as the Pittsburgh Interracial Action Council and the Citizens Coordinating Committee of the National Defense Program—emerged in Pittsburgh and in cities across the North.[49] If moving forward on the perilous racial landscape of interwar America required a careful, plodding approach, during the Second World War the terrain smoothed enough to permit a faster gate. Many reformers, once so cautious and calculating, increasingly adopted bolder tactics and broader aims.

Activists in Pittsburgh continued to chip away at inequality through letters, pamphlets, board meetings, community development programs, and vocational courses, but simultaneously they embraced the March on Washington Movement (MOWM) and launched a national Double V campaign. During the postwar period, they picketed discriminatory department stores in Pittsburgh. While younger activists, including Prattis and Harris of the *Courier* and K. LeRoy Irvis of the ULP, often assumed leading roles in the direct-action initiatives of the 1940s, a number of older reformers like Lampkin, Brown, and Tom Barton embraced their methods and objectives. The increasing militancy of the black activist community may partly be attributed to an infusion of youth, but changes in external conditions, which old guard reformers helped to bring about, represent the most important factor.

The MOWM

Despite the advances of the interwar period, the World War II years plainly revealed the persistence of racial inequality in America. African Americans discovered they could not enlist in the marines, coast guard, or air corps, and the navy and army forced them to serve in segregated units; meanwhile industries with government defense contracts hired disproportionately few black workers and confined them to the lowest-paying positions. Black activists in Pittsburgh and across the country responded swiftly to the situation. In April 1940 the *Pittsburgh Courier* initiated the Committee on Participation of Negroes in the National Defense to challenge the exclusionary policies of the military. The NAACP and NUL put additional pressure on the administration by demanding that Roosevelt issue an executive order to block discriminatory hiring at defense plants.[50]

Later that year, in September 1940, longtime civil rights leader and labor advocate A. Philip Randolph, NAACP head Walter White, and T. Arnold Hill of the NUL met with Franklin Roosevelt to discuss segregation in the armed forces. During the meeting Roosevelt agreed to consider the matter, but shortly afterward he issued a statement that segregation would continue in the military. The black press pounced upon the story and placed much of the blame on Randolph, White, and Hill. George Schuyler of the *Courier* denounced the meeting as a "fraud."[51]

Realizing that Roosevelt would not act unless compelled to do so, in spring 1941 Randolph, White, and Bayard Rustin launched the MOWM, which called for one hundred thousand African Americans to descend on Washington, DC, on July 1 to protest discrimination in the military and defense industries. In the months following its formation, the MOWM established affiliates in Harlem, St. Louis, Chicago, San Francisco, and a host of other cities, including Pittsburgh. There, several hundred members of the Brotherhood of Sleeping Car Porters joined activists in the PNAACP and ULP in support of the movement. The brotherhood's newspaper, the *Black Worker*, became the official voice of the MOWM. In articulating the movement's aims in May 1941, it captured the changed tone of civil rights activism. The paper called on all African Americans "to fight for jobs in National Defense[,] . . . struggle for the integration of Negroes in the armed forces . . . [and] demonstrate for the abolition of Jim Crowism in all Government departments and defense employment."[52]

The MOWM also enjoyed widespread support from the black press, which in the early 1940s reached nearly four million readers.[53] As the date for the proposed march neared, Roosevelt grew increasingly concerned that it might undermine his effort to build support for aiding the Allies against Nazi Germany. On June 24, 1941, he issued Executive Order 8802, which banned discrimination in industries with defense contracts. To enforce the order, he instituted the Fair Employment Practices Commission (FEPC), which had power to investigate firms accused of noncompliance.[54] Not since Reconstruction had the federal government enacted so sweeping a measure on behalf of African Americans, and it represented a major victory for Randolph, who kept his end of the bargain by calling off the march. Nevertheless, the MOWM continued pressing for an end to segregation in the military for the remainder of the war. "Who can fight for democracy in a Jim-Crow outfit?" asked E. Pauline Myers, the national executive secretary of MOWM. "The very existence of caste is anti-Democratic—and anti-American. . . . The whole institution of segregation must be destroyed and uprooted as a pattern for American life."[55]

"Plain, Just Americanism": Black Reformers and the Pennsylvania FEPC Act

African American industrial workers in Pittsburgh gradually obtained greater job security and higher wages after their entry into CIO unions in the late 1930s. The production demands of the Second World War and the presence of the FEPC, which established an office in the city in 1943, accelerated this trend. With the FEPC pressuring local industries, black workers began moving into skilled and semiskilled positions that previously had been the exclusive domain of white workers. In 1943, for instance, none of the motormen for the Pittsburgh Railway Company were black. A year later, five African Americans occupied this position and several others were "in training" for it. In several departments at the Carnegie-Illinois Steel Plant, black workers obtained "jobs never before held by Negroes," reported one FEPC examiner in March 1944.[56]

As an end to WWII came gradually into view, black activists began lobbying federal authorities to establish a permanent place for the FEPC in labor-employer relations. Writing in the *Courier*, Percival Prattis urged Roosevelt and other northern liberals to ignore the protestations of southern Democrats and press for the enactment of a fair employment measure. He identified four key groups involved in the struggle over the FEPC: African Americans who supported the measure, southern Democrats who opposed it, a Democratic president whose political loyalties extended to both camps, and the voting white public outside the South who had not yet decided on the matter. Even before WWII had ended, Prattis recognized social battle lines forming on the home front that came to define the civil rights movement.[57]

Indeed, Prattis's column straddled the pragmatic reformism of the interwar years and the more militant activism of the civil rights movement. Like civil rights leaders of the fifties and sixties, Prattis believed that African Americans had to hit the streets and agitate for justice in order to rouse the conscience of the American people and force federal officials to act against racial discrimination. Yet he also showed elements of the pragmatic utilitarianism that characterized reform work in the interwar years. Echoing the liquid-vote tactic espoused so often by his former boss, Robert L. Vann, Prattis argued that black voters should consider returning to the Republican Party if Democratic leaders failed to create a permanent fair employment practices agency. More than simply a matter of jobs, this issue connected with reformers' long-held view that full citizenship included economic as well as political rights. Prattis called it "plain, just Americanism."[58]

In 1945, with Franklin Roosevelt dead and Harry Truman overseeing the final stages of the war, federal legislators introduced in the U.S. House of Representatives several bills to establish such an agency. When none of them passed, officials in several states proposed similar measures at a local level. In Pennsylvania, Homer Brown submitted a sweeping bill in March 1945 calling for an act outlawing discriminatory hiring practices and creating a permanent committee with powers to investigate allegations of discrimination. House Bill 354, otherwise known as the Brown Bill, met with considerable opposition from state Republicans. One of them, Representative Adam Bower of Northumberland County, claimed the anti-Semitic and antiblack views of his constituents required him to oppose HB 354. When House legislators cast their votes in April, 102 out of 107 Republicans voted against it while all 92 Democrats supported it. Frustrated, Brown remarked that "the battle was lost but not the war."[59]

Just a month later, a delegation of black reformers from Pittsburgh, including R. Maurice Moss of the ULP, traveled to Harrisburg to continue lobbying for a state bill.[60] Brown supported their efforts, but in the wake of his defeat some activists in Pittsburgh began considering other ways to ensure the fair treatment of black workers in the city. The Pittsburgh chapter of the American Civil Liberties Union urged local legislators to create a Pittsburgh fair employment practices arm, and they received support from prominent reformers like Alma Illery, president of the Housewives Guild, and the Reverend J. O. Williams, pastor of the Warren Methodist Church. Fearing this would undermine ongoing efforts to secure a statewide commission, Brown and Moss opposed such localized initiatives.[61]

Over the next year, as political pressure mounted on the state Republican Party, it gradually began expressing support for a fair employment practices measure, and its 1946 party platform included a plank advocating for it.[62] But internal divisions within the GOP over the stipulations of the measure, coupled with continued opposition from Republicans like Bower, repeatedly stymied its passage. Finally, in 1955 the state legislature passed the Pennsylvania FEPC Act, which drew heavily from Brown's original bill.[63]

Although long-delayed, social justice activists in Pennsylvania saw the realization of a goal formed when Roosevelt first created the FEPC in 1941. Executive Order 8802 offered a stunning indication of how the federal government could be made to support racial justice if enough people demanded it. Early in 1942, *Courier* staff drew from this lesson for their Double V campaign.

The Double V Campaign

Sometime in January 1942, James Thompson, a young cafeteria worker in Wichita, Kansas, sat down to write a letter to the editors at the *Pittsburgh Courier*, not knowing that it would inspire a national program. The letter, which the *Courier* published on January 31, urged the black weekly to launch a simultaneous campaign against fascism abroad and racial injustice at home.

> The V for victory sign is being displayed prominently in all so-called democratic countries which are fighting for victory over aggression, slavery and tyranny. If this V sign means that to those now engaged in this great conflict, then let we colored Americans adopt the double VV for a double victory. The first V for victory over our enemies from without, the second V for victory over our enemies from within. For surely those who perpetrate

The *Courier*'s Double V emblem.
First printed in the *Courier* on February 7, 1942.

these ugly prejudices here are seeking to destroy our democratic form of government just as surely as the Axis forces.[64]

Thompson's letter prompted the *Courier*'s editors to join with the paper's longtime political cartoonist, Wilbert Holloway, in designing the Double V emblem that ultimately inspired African Americans and their allies across the country to speak out against discrimination.[65]

Like the MOWM, the Double V campaign led by the *Pittsburgh Courier* provides another indication that the long struggle for racial equality underwent a transition in the 1940s. The Double V slogan served as a platform from which *Courier* staff launched a frontal attack against Jim Crowism in America. Beginning on February 7, 1942, exactly two months after the attack on Pearl Harbor, every issue of the *Courier* featured the Double V emblem emblazoned on the front page along with several columns expressly linking racist practices in the United States with fascism in Europe. "We, as colored Americans, are determined to protect our country, our form of government and the freedoms which we cherish for ourselves and for the rest of the world," the *Courier* declared in justifying its campaign. "Thus in our fight for freedom we wage a two-pronged attack against our enslavers at home and those abroad who would enslave us."[66] By the end of 1942, the *Courier* had published 469 articles, 380 photographs, and 121 drawings related to the Double V campaign.[67]

The campaign reached black homes and street corners from Philadelphia to Los Angeles. Through most of 1942, over two hundred thousand black subscribers across the country opened the *Courier* on Saturdays and read stories that equated patriotism with racial equality and that cast segregationists as anti-American obstacles in the struggle against Germany and Japan. "Advocates of the theory of 'white supremacy' are a definite handicap to those nations engaged in the war against the Axis Powers," Frank Bolden explained. "Nations that want to win democratic victories must exercise democracy at home. The morale of fighting nations must be predicated on a sincere feeling of national unity and sacrifice."[68]

The *Courier* adeptly promoted the Double V campaign by distributing Double V stickers, buttons, and banners and by publishing photographs of prominent African Americans making V signs with their fingers, including singer Marian Anderson, New York councilman Adam Clayton Powell, Roy Wilkins of the NAACP, and the members of the Ink Spots.[69] *Courier* reporter Phyl Garland remembered that "there were cartoons that were presented with the two Vs. And then there was a Double V song, and slogans, and there was a hairstyle."[70] The Double V song, "A Yankee Doodle Tan," was performed by jazz musician Lionel Hampton and broadcast to two million listeners on an NBC national radio program in May 1942. Additionally, African Americans sponsored Double V days at Negro League baseball games, created Double V gardens, and held Double V flag-raising ceremonies. If they sent in a nickel, *Courier* subscribers across the country received a Double V pin as well as a card notifying them that they had become Double V members. Subscribers also formed Double V clubs that engaged in community activism and wrote congressmen letters protesting poll taxes and other forms of discrimination. By August 1942, as many as 206 Double V clubs operated across the country.[71]

The Ink Spots holding Double V literature (top) and
making a V sign in support of the Double V Campaign (bottom), 1942.
Teenie Harris Archive, Carnegie Museum of Art, Pittsburgh.

For thousands of African Americans, the Double V campaign infused new meaning into the war. "This Double V means more to us than the 'Buy a Stamp' or 'Buy a Bond' drive," Willa Smith wrote from her home in Portland, Oregon.[72] A Baptist minister in Ohio hoped the campaign would "teach Mr. Charlie of the South a new lesson and . . . shake the foundations of the hypocritical North," while a Texas woman noted how it highlighted the reality that "many Americans are more dangerous to [blacks] than some of our enemies abroad."[73] The Double V emblem could be found in towns and cities across the country, including Detroit, St. Louis, Omaha, Fayetteville, Canton, and Los Angeles.[74] Eventually, other black weeklies began promoting the slogan as well, and the MOWM adopted a similar message: "Winning Democracy for the Negro Is Winning the War for Democracy."[75]

As historian Lee Finkle has pointed out, the Double V campaign had conservative elements. While the scope and forcefulness of the Double V campaign set it apart from the more cautious reformism of the interwar period, Finkle argues that *Courier* staff tailored their message to appeal to and gain support from white Americans. *Courier* writers framed their attacks in terms of patriotism and promoting the war effort. Like the racial utilitarians of the twenties and thirties, they straddled a line between radicalism and conservatism. For their own sakes, and for the sake of maintaining the support of the black masses, their demands had to be forceful; yet they could not be so radical as to alienate white allies, whom they felt they needed in their struggle for justice. Hence, like their predecessors, *Courier* staff harnessed the value system of middle-class society to advance their racial agenda. While the Double V campaign may have tempered working-class black radicalism as Finkle maintains, it also unified thousands of black Americans around a common slogan and pushed antiracism closer to the mainstream of American political discourse.[76]

Not everyone supported the *Courier*'s efforts, however. While Finkle characterizes the Double V campaign as essentially conservative, J. Edgar Hoover saw it as dangerous and subversive. In early 1942, FBI staff began collecting information on the black press as part of its larger effort to investigate "enemy" communities in the United States, such as Japanese Americans, German Americans, Italian Americans, and Communists.[77] Later in the year, Hoover urged Franklin Roosevelt to have several black editors indicted for "sedition" and "interference with the war effort."[78] FBI agents also met with staff at the *Pittsburgh Courier* and other major black weeklies in an effort to censure them.[79] Undaunted, Schuyler noted that "the old days of scared, timid, ignorant Negroes are gone forever."⁸⁰ Bolden bitterly recalled a meeting he had with Hoover and other officials.

> J. Edgar Hoover ... wanted [*Courier* staff] charged with sedition. He said they were disrupting the country. At a time of war, they were out here worrying about something they couldn't do anything about. I remember staring him in the face across the table. I called him a Neanderthal psycho-ceramic. A natural crackpot.⁸¹

Outside the FBI, government officials debated whether to censure the black press. By spring 1942 there were widespread reports of low morale among black civilians and service members. While many African Americans expected the federal government to embrace racial justice in a spirit of national unity, they discovered instead that several branches of the military did not want them and that the Red Cross refused to accept blood donations from people of color. Nevertheless, several high-ranking officials in Roosevelt's administration blamed the black press for lowering African American morale during a time of war, and they pressed the Justice Department to silence it. A top aid in the Office of Facts and Figures warned that "as long as the Negro press is permitted to continue its present practices with impunity, we can expect very little improvement in morale of the Negro population."⁸²

Despite these pressures, by 1943 a number of prominent white celebrities, politicians, and labor leaders had endorsed the Double V program and helped spread antisegregationist sentiment. Movie stars Humphrey Bogart and Gary Cooper, comedian Eddie Cantor, and novelist Sinclair Lewis posed for photos either wearing a Double V lapel pin or reading the *Courier*.⁸³ Wendell Willkie, who won the GOP's presidential nomination a few years earlier, warned that fascism "within our own borders is as serious a threat to freedom as is the attack without." Thomas Dewey, the Republican governor who became his party's presidential candidate in 1944, declared "our enemies abroad are well known to us. Our enemies at home are intolerance, injustice and the tyranny of ignorance." On the other side of the aisle, Speaker of the House John McCormack wore a Double V button on his jacket, Vice President Henry Wallace made clear that those who condone racist practices in the United States "are taking the first step towards Nazism," and New York governor Herbert Lehman noted that every American should support "the cause of democracy here and abroad."⁸⁴ Phillip Murray of the CIO and William Green of the AFL also wore Double V badges, and at the annual United Auto Workers convention in 1942 delegates adopted a resolution endorsing the Double V campaign and condemning racist practices. The union called on Congress to give the FEPC more enforcement powers, to launch an investigation of the KKK, and to end segregation in the military.[85]

Like the MOWM, the *Courier*'s Double V campaign seized on wartime urgency to compel the federal government to support racial justice. In 1942 the army air corps, marines, and coast guard began enlisting African Americans; blacks in the army and navy, who had earlier been confined to menial tasks like digging latrines, gained opportunities to fight in North Africa and the South Pacific; the Red Cross reversed its former position and started taking blood donations from African Americans; and black women gained entry into the women's army corps. In light of these developments and the ever-increasing presence of blacks in defense plants, the *Courier* gradually ended the Double V campaign in late 1942 and early 1943. As Bolden explained it, "These gains showed good faith intentions by the government and other people, and we felt we should follow suit. . . . [T]he Double V was like a Roman candle. It flared up, it did its work and then it died down."[86]

While historian Patrick S. Washburn notes that "some of the[se] accomplishments would have occurred eventually without the Double V, simply because of the urgency of the war," he maintains that "the campaign unquestionably hastened their implementation and magnitude."[87] Moreover, it served as yet another example of the power of unflinching collective action in the face of racial injustice. The Double V campaign reflected the growing militancy within black activist communities, and it expanded the realm of possibilities for future activists.

NOTES

1. Burma is now called Myanmar. For the purpose of situating John Adams and Frank Bolden in their historical moment, I use the name Burma throughout the opening passage of this chapter.
2. "Pittsburgh Boys Enjoy Happy Reunion on Stillwell Road," *Pittsburgh Courier*, June 30, 1945.
3. For James Adams, see 1920 U.S. census, Lexington, Davidson, North Carolina. For Lucy Wade, see 1900 U.S. Census, Yanceyville, Casell, North Carolina. Lucy's marriage certificate from July 14, 1917, can be found on Ancestry.com.
4. John Adams, 1930 U.S. census; John Adams, U.S. WWII draft cards, young men, 1940–47, Ancestry.com; John Adams and Pearl Parrott, Pennsylvania, marriages, 1852–1968, Ancestry.com, and Pearl Parrott, 1940 U.S. census.
5. "Cite Engineers in Burma for Construction Feats," *Pittsburgh Courier*, June 9, 1945.
6. See Frank Bolden Sr., 1920 U.S census, Washington Ward 3, Washington, PA; Frank Bolden, 1940 U.S. census, Pittsburgh, Allegheny, PA. Also see the documentary film

titled *Frank Bolden: The Man behind the Words*, produced, written, and directed by Daniel Love (Pittsburgh: Daniel Love, 2001), www.humanitydocs.com. For additional biographical information, see Cristina Rouvalis, "Reporter, Raconteur Frank Bolden Dies at 90," *Pittsburgh Post-Gazette*, August 29, 2003.

7. As one of the first black war correspondents, Bolden filed his dispatches with the National Negro Publishers Association, which distributed his stories to major black weeklies across the United States. See Cristina Rouvalis, "Reporter, Raconteur Frank Bolden Dies at 90," *Pittsburgh Post-Gazette*, August 29, 2003.

8. "Pittsburgh Boys Enjoy Happy Reunion on Stillwell Road," *Pittsburgh Courier*, June 30, 1945.

9. John Adams, interview in *Newspaper of Record: The Pittsburgh Courier, 1907–1965*, produced and directed by Kenneth Love (Pittsburgh: Kenneth A. Love International, 2009), www.humanitydocs.com.

10. Alan Dawley, *Struggles for Justice: Social Responsibility and the Liberal State* (Cambridge, MA: Belknap Press of Harvard University Press, 1991), 359–60; Dennis Dickerson, *Out of the Crucible: Black Steelworkers in Western Pennsylvania, 1875–1980* (Albany: State University of New York Press, 1986), 128.

11. E. E. Lewis, "Black Cotton Farmers and the AAA," *Opportunity*, March 1935, 72–74.

12. Harvard Sitkoff, *A New Deal for Blacks: The Emergence of Civil Rights as a National Issue*, thirtieth anniv. ed. (New York: Oxford University Press, 2009), 35–40.

13. T. Arnold Hill, "Uncle Sam's Payroll," *Opportunity*, February 1935, 54–55; "Negroes Outnumber Whites on Relief Roles in Penna.," *Philadelphia Tribune*, January 17, 1935.

14. CCC press release, October 17, 1935, box 9, folder 403, Urban League Records, University of Pittsburgh Archives Service Center. Of the 3,485 black enrollees in Pennsylvania, about 1,100 of them came from the Pittsburgh area. See Grace Lowndes, editorial, *Informer*, ca. 1936, box 6, folder 275, Urban League.

15. "CCC Non-Comms are Fired," *Pittsburgh Courier*, March 9, 1935.

16. "New Deal and Race Discussed at Conference," *Chicago Defender*, June 1, 1935.

17. For critiques of the New Deal in *Opportunity*, see Lester Granger, "Labor—That Work-Relief Bill," March 1935, 86, Robert Weaver, "The New Deal and the Negro," July 1935, 200–202, E. E. Lewis, "Black Cotton Farmers and the AAA," March 1935, 72–74, and T. Arnold Hill, "Uncle Sam's Payroll," February 1935, 54, 62. For critiques in black newspapers, see "Hope Abandoned in New Deal," *Chicago Defender*, May 11, 1935, "Negroes and the NRA," *Pittsburgh Courier*, September 9, 1933, and "New Deal Designed to Promote J.C., Says Davis," *Baltimore Afro-American*, July 6, 1935.

18. Sitkoff, *A New Deal for Blacks*, 186.

19. See Bruce M. Stave, "Pittsburgh and the New Deal," in *The New Deal*, vol. 2, *The State and Local Levels*, ed. John Braeman, Robert H. Bremner, and David Brody (Columbus: Ohio State University Press, 1975), 390–91. According to William E. Hill, who served as industrial secretary of the Urban League of Pittsburgh for several years during the Depression, African Americans represented about 17 percent of all unemployed persons in Pittsburgh—a very high figure considering they constituted only 8 percent of the city's total population ("The Negro Wage Worker," in *The WPA History of the Negro in Pittsburgh*, ed. Laurence Glasco [Pittsburgh: University of Pittsburgh Press, 2004], 223). Additionally, African Americans represented 22 percent of all

employment seekers at Allegheny County's Emergency Association. See "Two Groups of the Unemployed in Pittsburgh," *Pittsburgh Business Review*, October 29, 1931, 12–16.
20. At its peak in January 1934, the CWA provided employment for 319,000 Pennsylvanians, and later the PWA in Pennsylvania employed more people than in any other state except New York (Stave, "Pittsburgh and the New Deal," 392).
21. R. Maurice Moss, quoted in Arthur J. Edmunds, *Daybreakers: The Story of the Urban League of Pittsburgh, the First Sixty-Five Years* (Pittsburgh: Urban League of Pittsburgh, 1999), 86–87.
22. Grace Lowndes, editorial, *Informer*, ca. 1936, box 6, folder 275, Urban League Records.
23. Stave, "Pittsburgh and the New Deal," 390–391; Grace Lowndes, editorial, *Informer*, ca. February 1934, box 6, folder 275, Urban League Records.
24. Dickerson, *Out of the Crucible*, 119–23.
25. For the quote regarding Vann, see Ralph M. Bashore, Pennsylvania secretary of forests and waters, to unknown recipient, March 20, 1935, box 27, folder 14, Robert L. Vann Papers, Percival Prattis Collection, Moorland-Spingarn Research Center, Howard University. For the ULP report on African Americans in the County Emergency Relief Board, see Grace Lowndes, editorial, *Informer*, ca. February 1934, box 6, folder 275, Urban League Records.

For additional information about Vann, Pennsylvania Democrats, and patronage appointments, see Andrew Buni, *Robert L. Vann of the* Pittsburgh Courier: *Politics and Black Journalism* (Pittsburgh: University of Pittsburgh Press, 1974), 203–4, 217; Ruth Louise Simmons, "The Negro in Recent Pittsburgh Politics" (MA thesis, University of Pittsburgh, 1944), 17; Stave, "Pittsburgh and the New Deal," 380.
26. "Application for Approval of Civil Works Project," December 12, 1933, box 10, folder 449, Urban League Records.
27. R. Maurice Moss, "The Negro In Pittsburgh's Industries," *Opportunity*, February 1935, 40–42, 59. The league additionally supported graduate research on African Americans in the steel industry and race relations in Pittsburgh's South Side, proposed a survey of black religious life in the city, and sponsored a study on black employment in the food industry. See Pauline Redmond, "Race Relations on the South Side of Pittsburgh as Seen through the Brashear Settlement" (MA thesis, University of Pittsburgh, 1936), F. Alden Wilson, "Status of the Negro in the Iron and Steel Industry in Pittsburgh and Environs" (MA thesis, University of Pittsburgh, 1934), ULP, "A Survey of the Religious Life of the Negro in Pittsburgh," September 12, 1935, box 10, folder 452, Urban League Records, and ULP, "The Relation of the Negro to Unemployment in Food Products," 1933, box 10, folder 448, Urban League Records.
28. Hill, "The Negro Wage Worker," 226; "Workers on Housing Projects Earn $67,000," *Pittsburgh Courier*, November 18, 1939. M. Nelson McGeary noted that contractors complied with the requirement to furnish African Americans with 29 percent of the unskilled construction jobs, but they often fell short of the 4.5 percent skilled-position quota. PHA officials threated to withhold funds from contractors for this infraction, but contractors blamed local unions for not furnishing skilled black workers. When questioned, unions claimed there were not enough skilled black workers available, but local African Americans denied this claim and charged them with discrimination. See McGeary, *The Pittsburgh Housing Authority* (State College: Pennsylvania State College, 1943), 30–31.

29. According to *Courier* reports from February 4, 1939 ("Construction To Start on Bedford Dwellings Next Month") and November 18, 1939 ("Workers on Housing Projects Earn $67,000"), the Bedford Dwellings project included 430 housing units, the Terrace Village 1 project featured 825 units, and the Terrace Village 2 project included 1,851 units; altogether, these projects provided 3,106 units. Estimating an average of three people per unit, these projects might have accommodated about 9,318 people by early 1940.
30. Historian Bruce M. Stave notes that as late as 1937 African Americans in Pittsburgh "paid $4.40 per room per month for dwellings that were usually in much worse condition than those rented by white families for $4.23 per month" ("Pittsburgh and the New Deal," 397).
31. For reports on housing conditions in the 1910s and 1920s, see Abraham Epstein, "The Negro Migrant in Pittsburgh" (senior thesis, University of Pittsburgh, 1917), 16–17, and Hill, "The Negro Wage Worker," 225. For studies of health conditions in the black community, see Carolyn Leonard Carson, "And the Results Showed Promise . . . : Physicians, Childbirth, and Southern Black Migrant Women, 1916–1930," in *African Americans in Pennsylvania, Shifting Historical Perspectives*, ed. Joe Trotter and Eric Ledell Smith (University Park: Pennsylvania Historical and Museum Commission and Pennsylvania State University Press, 1997), 331, ULP, "Pittsburgh's Second Annual Negro Health Education Campaign," 1919, box 6, folder 242, Urban League Records, and program of health activities, 1929, box 2, folder 51, Urban League Records.
32. Soon after Bedford Dwellings opened, William E. Hill accepted a position as its director. See "W. E. Hill Named Bedford Manager," *Pittsburgh Courier*, December 9, 1939. For the *Courier's* observation that Bedford Dwellings was among the first government housing projects to feature integrated occupancy, see "Hill Joins Race Relations Group," *Pittsburgh Courier*, February 10, 1945.
33. Stave, "Pittsburgh and the New Deal," 397.
34. Thomas Sugrue, *Sweet Land of Liberty: The Forgotten Struggle for Civil Rights in the North* (New York: Random House, 2008), 52–53.
35. Buni, *Robert L. Vann of the* Pittsburgh Courier, 205–7.
36. See Percival Prattis, "Days of *Courier* Past," in *Perspectives of the Black Press: 1974*, ed. Henry G. La Brie III (Kennebunkport, ME: Mercer House Press, 1974), 70–71.
37. James H. Brewer, "Robert Lee Vann and the *Pittsburgh Courier*" (MA Thesis, University of Pittsburgh, 1941), 27–39.
38. Brewer, "Robert Lee Vann and the *Pittsburgh Courier*," 91; Buni, *Robert L. Vann of the* Pittsburgh Courier, 257, 270–71.
39. See, for example, the following articles in *Courier*: "Negro Workers Lead in Great Lakes Steel Drive," July 31, 1937; "Harlem Boasts 42,000 Negro Labor Unionists," August 21 1937; and "Union Drive Slows in Border Cities," September 11, 1937.
40. For instance, CCC workers slept in segregated barracks. Thousands of black sharecroppers faced eviction because of the Agricultural Adjustment Act, and white landowners often kept for themselves the subsidies the government paid them to reduce crop production. See Sitkoff, *A New Deal for Blacks*, 35–40.
41. Brewer, "Robert Lee Vann and the *Pittsburgh Courier*," 93–95; Buni, *Robert L. Vann of the* Pittsburgh Courier, 280–91.
42. Buni, *Robert L. Vann of the* Pittsburgh Courier, 280–91.
43. State Democrats had pledged earlier that 10 percent of the available government ap-

pointments would be set aside for loyal black Pennsylvanians. After the primary, Lawrence, Jones, Vann, and Guffey met to reconcile the party divide, but when Vann asked Jones about the patronage promise Lawrence interceded by telling Jones not to answer. Insulted, Vann walked out of the meeting. See Brewer, "Robert Lee Vann and the *Pittsburgh Courier*," 95-98.

44. Brewer, "Robert Lee Vann and the *Pittsburgh Courier*," 96-97.
45. Buni, *Robert L. Vann of the* Pittsburgh Courier, 290-98.
46. Brewer, "Robert Lee Vann and the *Pittsburgh Courier*," 70, 99-100; Buni, *Robert L. Vann of the* Pittsburgh Courier, 316-21.
47. Ira F. Lewis, speech, October 10, 1943, box 31, Robert L. Vann Papers.
48. "Leading Americans from All Walks of Life Extol Leader," *Pittsburgh Courier*, October 16, 1943.
49. Trotter and Day, *Race and Renaissance*, 42.
50. Sugrue, *Sweet Land of Liberty*, 46.
51. Beth Tompkins Bates, *Pullman Porters and the Rise of Protest Politics in Black America, 1925-1945* (Chapel Hill: University of North Carolina Press, 2001), 152.
52. Trotter and Day, *Race and Renaissance*, 41.
53. Sugrue, *Sweet Land of Liberty*, 47.
54. Sugrue, *Sweet Land of Liberty*, 47.
55. E. Pauline Myers to George De Mar, chairman of the Pittsburgh MOWM, April 17, 1943, box 6, folder 265, Urban League Records. Myers had been involved in racial advocacy since her days as a student at Howard University in the late 1920s. For additional information about Myers and MOWM, see David Lucander, *Winning the War for Democracy: The March on Washington Movement, 1941-1946* (Urbana: University of Illinois Press, 2014), 63-64.
56. Trotter and Day, *Race and Renaissance*, 41-42.
57. Percival Prattis, The Horizon (column), *Pittsburgh Courier*, March 18, 1944.
58. Percival Prattis, The Horizon (column), *Pittsburgh Courier*, March 18, 1944.
59. Quoted in Eric Ledell Smith and Kenneth C. Wolensky, "A Novel Public Policy: Pennsylvania's Fair Employment Practices Act of 1955," *Pennsylvania History* 69, no. 4 (2002): 501. Also see "Brown Bill Gets Wide Support," *Pittsburgh Courier*, March 31, 1945.
60. See the May 1945 issue of the ULP's journal, *Informer*, box 6, folder 241, Urban League Records.
61. "Local FEPC Fight On; Leaders' Views Differ," *Pittsburgh Courier*, December 8, 1945. Despite the opposition of Brown, Moss, and others, by the late 1940s city FEPCs began forming across Pennsylvania. A Philadelphia FEPC law passed in 1948, and city officials in Pittsburgh passed an FEPC law in 1953. Finally, the Pennsylvania legislature passed a statewide FEPC law in 1955. See Smith and Wolensky, "A Novel Public Policy," 506-17.
62. "Both Parties Pledge FEPC Plank," *Pittsburgh Courier*, September 14, 1946.
63. Smith and Wolensky, "A Novel Public Policy," 501-17.
64. "Should I Sacrifice to Live 'Half-American?,'" *Pittsburgh Courier*, January 31, 1942.
65. For accounts of the Double V emblem's design, see Frank Bolden, interview in *Newspaper of Record: The* Pittsburgh Courier, *1907-1965*, produced and directed by Kenneth Love (Pittsburgh: Kenneth A. Love International LLC, 2009), www.humanitydocs.com, and Patrick S. Washburn, "The *Pittsburgh Courier*'s Double V Campaign in 1942," *American Journalism* 3, no. 2 (1986): 73-75, 79.

66. "The *Courier's* Double 'V' for a Double Victory Campaign Gets Country-Wide Support," *Pittsburgh Courier*, February 14, 1942.
67. Washburn, "The *Pittsburgh Courier's* Double V Campaign in 1942," 80.
68. Frank E. Bolden, "White Supremacists Are a Nuisance to the Nation's War Effort," *Pittsburgh Courier*, February 21, 1942.
69. For information on prominent African Americans who posed for Double V photographs, see Washburn, "The *Pittsburgh Courier's* Double V Campaign in 1942," 4, and "Nationwide Support Grows for 'Double V,'" *Pittsburgh Courier*, March 14, 1942.
70. Phyl Garland, interview in *Newspaper of Record*.
71. L. C. Johnson and Andy Razaf composed "A Yankee Doodle Tan." See Washburn, "The *Pittsburgh Courier's* Double V Campaign in 1942," 75–78.
72. "Nationwide Support Grows for 'Double V,'" *Pittsburgh Courier*, March 14, 1942.
73. Quoted in Washburn, "The *Pittsburgh Courier's* Double V Campaign in 1942," 76.
74. "Nationwide Support Grows for 'Double V'," March 14, 1942, *Pittsburgh Courier*.
75. E. Pauline Myers to George De Mar, April 17, 1943, box 6, folder 265, Urban League Records.
76. Lee Finkle, "The Conservative Aims of Militant Rhetoric: Black Protest during World War II," *Journal of American History* 60, no. 3 (1973): 692–713.
77. Ethan Michaeli, *The Defender: How the Legendary Black Newspaper Changed America* (Boston: Houton Mifflin Harcourt, 2016), 243.
78. Quoted in Washburn, "The *Pittsburgh Courier's* Double V Campaign in 1942," 81.
79. Michaeli, *The Defender*, 243.
80. Quoted in Washburn, "The *Pittsburgh Courier's* Double V Campaign in 1942," 81.
81. Frank Bolden, interview in *Newspaper of Record*.
82. Moreover, Office of Facts and Figures director Archibald MacLeish urged U.S. attorney general Francis Biddle to demand the black press tone down its rhetoric. However, Biddle decided against pursuing any formal or informal action against the black press. See Patrick S. Washburn, *A Question of Sedition: The Federal Government's Investigation of the Black Press during World War II* (New York: Oxford University Press, 1986), 99–107, quote on 107. Likewise, Franklin Roosevelt rejected J. Edgar Hoover's recommendation to indict certain black editors for sedition. See Washburn, "The *Pittsburgh Courier's* Double V Campaign in 1942," 81.
83. Washburn, "The *Pittsburgh Courier's* Double V Campaign in 1942," 76.
84. James Edmund Boyack, "Dewey Endorses *Courier's* 'Double V' Campaign," *Pittsburgh Courier*, February 28, 1942; James Edmund Boyack, "Willkie Blasts 'Hate,'" *Pittsburgh Courier*, July 31, 1943; John R. Williams, "Epochal Radio Speeches Reflect *Courier's* 'Double V' Theme," *Pittsburgh Courier*, July 31, 1943. For the quote from New York governor Herbert Lehman, see Patrick S. Washburn, "The *Pittsburgh Courier's* Double V Campaign in 1942," paper presented at the annual meeting of the Association for Education in Journalism, East Lansing, Michigan, August 1981, 6–7.
85. John R. Williams, "Epochal Radio Speeches Reflect *Courier's* 'Double V' Theme," *Pittsburgh Courier*, July 31, 1943; Horace Cayton, "UAW-CIO Adopts *Courier* 'Double-V' Program," *Pittsburgh Courier*, August 15, 1942.
86. Quoted in Washburn, "The *Pittsburgh Courier's* Double V Campaign in 1942," 82.
87. Washburn, "The *Pittsburgh Courier's* Double V Campaign in 1942," 84.

CONCLUSION

The Legacy of the Black Reform Era

Evelyn Cunningham had just checked in to her room at a hotel in Montgomery on January 30, 1956, when she heard a bomb explode. Alarmed, she dropped her bags and rushed outside, where she saw smoke spewing from the home of Martin Luther King Jr. Gradually, and perhaps cautiously, Cunningham made her way to the scene, not knowing whether the immediate danger had passed. Many others did the same. By the time she reached King's house, a large crowd of African Americans had assembled, armed, angry, and ready to fight back. The unsympathetic white police officers who showed up soon afterward only added to the growing tension. King's grand strategy of nonviolence seemed poised to die in its infancy.[1]

It was an ominous beginning to Cunningham's new assignment. The seasoned reporter for the *Pittsburgh Courier* had been sent to cover the Montgomery bus boycott and write a series of articles that would appear in the paper in March and April.[2] She had come a long way to get to this point in her career. Cunningham spent her early childhood in Elizabeth City, North Carolina, before her parents decided to migrate to Harlem in the early 1920s. Her father worked as a cab driver and hotel porter, and her mother earned money as a seamstress, but they had higher aspirations for Evelyn. She earned high school and college degrees in New York, and in 1940, the year Robert L. Vann died, the *Courier* offered her a job. The paper had well over two hundred thousand subscribers by then, more than any other black weekly, and it presented Cunningham with an opportunity to establish herself as a legitimate journalist. Yet if she came to work on her first day with lofty dreams of beat reporting and writing exposés, she initially had to check them at the door. Cunningham spent her first few years performing fairly mundane tasks, mostly reviewing the *New York Times* for stories pertinent to African Americans and then rewriting those stories for the *Courier*. But gradually her role expanded. Recognizing her knack for composing serious yet engaging stories, *Courier* editors began sending her on assignments to cover lynchings, protests, and other important issues. Cunningham was the first woman to report "hard news" for the black weekly. Almost without exception, her female predecessors had been relegated to writing gossip columns or discussing fashion.[3] But covering hard news could be dangerous, especially for a black female journalist in the South.

Standing in front of King's house, Cunningham saw dozens of African American men around her armed with pipes, broken bottles, rocks, and pistols.[4] The police started shoving some people in an effort to clear the streets, but the crowd only got larger and angrier. "Now you got your .38 and I got mine," one of them said to a patrolman, "so let's battle it out." Things seemed to be getting out of hand when King stepped out on to his smoldering porch. "We are not advocating violence," he thundered to the crowd, trying as best as he could to appear calm and unshaken. Urging everyone to drop their weapons, he reminded them that "what we are doing is right. What we are doing is just. And God is with us."[5] What followed next, Cunningham would remember for the rest of her life.

> I just stood there: awed, frightened, not believing what I was seeing. ... And the dropping of the weapons, which I can hear at this moment, I will never forget the significance of hearing these things fall to the ground one by one by one, until it appeared that nobody had a weapon in his or her hand. They were just riveted then on what Dr. King had to say.[6]

King's words had their effect, as they often did. Disarmed, both figuratively and literally, the crowd dispersed and the strategy of nonviolence survived an early test. Yet for the remainder of the civil rights movement, King struggled to balance militancy and moderation. A social movement that lacked bold goals would fail to generate grassroots enthusiasm. But that enthusiasm, once created, had to be channeled in productive ways: too confrontational in its approach, and the movement might alienate its less radical members and drive off allies; too broad in its objectives, and it could lose focus and fail to produce substantive results.[7]

To an extent, interwar-era black reformers grappled with a similar challenge. The extraordinarily difficult political and social climate in which they operated inclined them to reject Marxist and separatist approaches as unrealistic and to adopt a pragmatic posture that placed attainable progress above utopian goals. Often, this meant putting idealism aside to take advantage of immediate opportunities to improve material conditions in the black community. In the 1910s and 1920s, almost all local unions in Pittsburgh excluded black workers, and white workers on the shop floor (both native and foreign born) often impeded black occupational advancement.[8] Reformers also could not count on support from local, state, or federal authorities in the years before the New Deal. Thus, with few allies available, and lacking basic government services in the black community, staff in the Urban League of Pittsburgh (ULP) rhetorically linked racial justice to the economic interests of Pittsburgh's business elite in order to gain financial support—which they used to stitch together a social safety net in the inner city.

The league's methods, though conservative by contemporary standards, yielded physical results. Its lobbying efforts prompted city officials to build a free public bathhouse in the Hill District and convinced steel executives to improve lodging for their black workers. The ULP's room registry program secured housing for hundreds of southern black women entering the city. Several thousand black infants received medical screenings through the league's health campaigns. And league staffers went to local schools and juvenile justice centers to advocate for children and young women, while supporting black adults at parole hearings.

This is not to say that reformers lacked class identities. While they harnessed middle-class values to extract concessions from white elites, they also used them to enact change from within the black community. Urban Leaguers often viewed migrant folkways as fundamentally unsuited for the urban environment. Hence, to counter crude antiblack stereotypes and pursue what they called racial uplift, they worked to inculcate migrants with middle-class notions of respectability, including thriftiness, workplace reliability, sexual monogamy, sobriety, and genteel public behavior. Leaders like R. Maurice Moss delivered speeches on "proper" public conduct, for instance, while league women engaged in campaigns to teach migrant families about good housekeeping.[9] Certainly not all migrants appreciated serving as the objects of "adjustment work," and historians such as Kevin Gaines have called attention to how this approach implicitly blamed migrants for racial inequality, since it implied that economic deprivation stemmed from bad behavior.[10]

But black reformers' conception of activism expanded well beyond the bounds of racial uplift ideology, something historians have often missed. Journalists in the *Courier* worked to build political solidarity in Pittsburgh's black community, elect African Americans to key government positions, and pressure the major parties to address racial inequality. In 1932, the *Courier* leveraged its influence over the black vote to extract concessions from the Democrats in the form of patronage appointments and proportional representation in local work-relief projects. Meanwhile, Urban Leaguers lobbied local industries to open skilled positions to African Americans and promoted the integration of the industrial labor movement through its workers' councils and labor rallies. Staff in the local NAACP successfully prosecuted police officers for assaulting unarmed black men, secured the release of African Americans arrested at the Highland Park pool, and brought public scorn on the law enforcement community in Beaver County for its mishandling of the "shanghai case." Moreover, reformers either spearheaded or provided critical support for several major human rights initiatives, including the Pennsylvania Civil Rights Act in 1935, the state investigation of the Allegheny County School Board in 1937, and the antidiscrimination clause in the Pennsylvania labor relations bill the same year.[11]

By 1945, black Pittsburghers found themselves in a considerably stronger economic and political position than at the start of the Great Migration in 1915. Mortality rates for black infants and adults, though still disproportionately high, had declined precipitously. Meanwhile, thousands of black steelworkers now stood alongside white workers in interracial unions, and while they rarely gained leadership positions in those unions, they nevertheless saw improvements in wages, working conditions, and job security. Civil rights had improved in the city as well, and African Americans could now patronize many (but not all) restaurants, stores, and hotels that they could not before.

At the close of World War II, it had never been harder for white politicians to ignore the concerns of black Pittsburghers. The city saw a new wave of black migrants come in as industrial jobs opened during the war, increasing the black population from sixty-two thousand in 1940 to eighty-six thousand by 1950.[12] And even though Vann had died, his paper continued expanding during the war, along with its ability to affect the outcome of elections. Meanwhile, increasing numbers of black Pittsburghers gained seats in the Pennsylvania legislature.

Pittsburgh's black activist community saw continuity and change in the postwar years. With the help of talented journalists such as Evelyn Cunningham, the *Courier* continued its longstanding commitment to highlight black achievement, to call attention to racial injustice, and to offer a platform from which black leaders could discuss and debate vital issues of the day. Yet the experience of World War II showed a younger generation of activists that international developments sometimes created new opportunities on the home front to use more forceful tactics. Through the March on Washington Movement and the *Courier*'s Double V campaign, they saw how dramatic displays of nonviolent protest pressured federal authorities to act.

During the 1940s, dozens of new interracial civil rights organizations, such as the Congress of Racial Equality (CORE), emerged in cities across the country. In 1947, sixteen white and black CORE activists rode a bus through the Upper South to challenge segregation in interstate travel. Harried all along the way, they drew national attention through their "journey of reconciliation" and inspired similar tactics during the classic civil rights period. One of CORE's founders, James Farmer, played a leading role in organizing the freedom rides of the early 1960s.

Interracialism flowered in Pittsburgh as well. After leaders in the *Courier* and other organizations successfully pressured the Pittsburgh Trolley Company to hire a black trolley driver in 1945, inspired local activists formed the Interracial Action Council (IAC). As its first objective, the IAC took on Pittsburgh's largest department stores—such as Frank and Seder, Gimbels, and Rosenbaum's—which had long excluded African Americans from sales positions. When the department stores refused to negotiate, IAC members launched a letter-writing campaign that flooded retailers with forty-five thousand postcards and handbills. Although many concerned customers cancelled their accounts because of the campaign, the stores still refused to compromise.[13]

In response, one IAC member, K. LeRoy Irvis, took the lead in organizing a mass-protest demonstration in front of the stores on a busy shopping day in December 1947. The twenty-six-year-old Irvis had recently joined the ULP as its public relations director, and in this role he increased its visibility across the city. His threatened picket concerned both Mayor David L. Lawrence and store managers, and they arranged a meeting with him on the day of the scheduled protest. Irvis agreed to meet them but also remained prepared to carry out his plan. When negotiations broke down, as he expected, he gave his wife a signal from the window of the city hall building, and she commenced the demonstration. For the next three days, hundreds of black and white activists, carrying banners and signs, marched through downtown Pittsburgh to protest racial injustice. Major media outlets took note of the occasion as well, and during the week correspondents from *Time*, *Business Week*, and network radio descended upon the city.[14] As Irvis recalled:

> There were both white and Negro veterans, clergymen, social workers, newspaper editors in the line, handing out throwaway [protest flyers] to the gaping crowds of Christmas shoppers who read the huge, lettered accusations: "This store is un-American. It refuses to hire Negro sales clerks."[15]

Where letters and negotiations failed, direct action worked. By December 15, 1947, four of the five major department stores began hiring black salesclerks. Yet the victory came at a cost for Irvis. During and immediately following the demonstrations, ULP executive secretary R. Maurice Moss received dozens of angry letters and telegrams from local business leaders. "Is this the reason we finance the Urban League," one of them asked, "so you can send young people downtown to embarrass us?" Under this pressure, Moss fired Irvis.[16]

The incident illustrates an important point. Reformers sometimes imprecisely gauged the possibilities available and missed opportunities. Moss started with the Urban League in the 1920s, first in Baltimore and later in Pittsburgh, when it depended on its alliance with business leaders. Ultimately, his experiences as a child in the Upper South during the rise of Jim Crow, as a student of social work in New York, and as a league officer at city branches, worked against him in the late 1940s. They limited his vision at a moment when others saw more expansive possibilities. "He was a product of his times," Irvis explained. "He was neat when the rest of us weren't so neat.... I was a young firebrand who was upsetting things around the nest."[17]

Like the Vann dedication ceremony four years earlier, the department store picket revealed a generational divide between interwar and postwar activists, and it offered one of several indications that the pace of activism had quickened. Moss's career neared its end as Irvis's had just begun. Following the department store incident, the ULP's executive board, led by Tom Barton, the league's first black president, reversed Moss's decision and reinstated Irvis to his position. Irvis, who resigned the next day, went on to have a distinguished political career, eventually becoming the first African American

A 1957 banquet honoring Daisy Lampkin, who continued fighting for equal rights until her death in 1965, with K. Leroy Irvis seated to her right.
Teenie Harris Archive, Carnegie Museum of Art, Pittsburgh.

Black and white activists protest outside Woolworth's department store in downtown Pittsburgh, 1960.
Teenie Harris Archive, Carnegie Museum of Art, Pittsburgh.

Speaker of the Pennsylvania House of Representatives. Possibly sensing he had lost the board's support, Moss left Pittsburgh in 1948, after more than eighteen years with the ULP, and went on to serve as the associate director of the National Urban League in New York.[18]

In the mid-1950s, as black men and women boycotted public busses in Montgomery, a new generation of activists in Pittsburgh—such as Byrd Brown, Marion Bond Jordon, and the Reverend Charles Foggie—helped organize protest marches at the Highland Park Pool, Woolworth's, and other public places that continued to practice racial segregation.[19] Although the careers of old guard reformers drew to a close during the 1950s, many of them enthusiastically supported the tactics and goals of the civil rights movement, including Daisy Lampkin of the NAACP and Percival Prattis of the *Courier*. Indeed, as the paper's executive editor, Prattis chose to cover the movement extensively, thereby helping to attract national support for it. For her part, Evelyn Cunningham did not just write about the protests; she actively participated in them. In 1961, she joined a group of NAACP activists at a sit-in demonstration at the Double T Diner in Rosedale, Maryland, where police arrested and fined her.[20]

Despite its successes, the civil rights era witnessed setbacks as well. Even as Pittsburgh's public pools, restaurants, and hotels opened to African Americans, many saw their houses, businesses, and history destroyed when city officials ordered the demolition the lower Hill District in 1956 as part of their "urban renewal" project. While the influx of a second wave of migrants during the 1940s enhanced black political power in the city and resulted in the elections of Robert Williams, Harry Fitzgerald, Irvis, and other African Americans, they faced entrenched problems that had no easy solutions. Even after the city passed a fair housing ordinance in 1952, black Pittsburghers continued to live apart from whites in segregated neighborhoods. And while black teachers gained entry to jobs in the city's public education system, prevailing housing patterns effectively trapped black students in severely underresourced schools.[21] Even so, activists in the fifties operated from a much stronger position than reformers did during the interwar years.

Defeats and limitations characterized the black reform era as much as victories and achievements. And in the final analysis, it may be that the act of striving—the flawed but relentless struggle for citizenship—served as an end in itself. By trying, experimenting, failing, and succeeding, black reformers built up the institutional strength of their communities, established procedures and precedents for facing new challenges, and gained the experience and confidence needed to pursue Canaan.

Through thirty years of persistence, reformers helped change the moral tone of American race relations for future generations. Dozens of campaigns, scores of mass-protest meetings, hundreds of court cases, thousands of studies, and millions of newspaper articles slowly chipped away at the edifice of white supremacy and affected the way people discussed race, rights, and human dignity. This collective effort pushed multiculturalism closer to the mainstream of American political culture outside the South and ultimately helped make possible the formation of powerful interracial coalitions committed to direct-action tactics. Liberal white college students in 1915 followed a curriculum that included craniometry, social Darwinism, and eugenics. In the 1960s, they went on freedom rides and participated in sit-in demonstrations alongside African Americans. Charles Foggie, K. LeRoy Irvis, Evelyn Cunningham, and Martin Luther King Jr. inherited this new social milieu, along with its possibilities.

NOTES

1. Evelyn Cunningham, interview in *Newspaper of Record: The Pittsburgh Courier, 1907–1965*, produced and directed by Kenneth Love (Pittsburgh: Kenneth A. Love International, 2009), www.humanitydocs.com.
2. For examples of some of the stories Cunningham wrote about the Montgomery protests, see the following articles in the *Pittsburgh Courier*: "'More Determined Than Ever': Fight for Freedom Goes On," March 3, 1956, "Pastor No. 1 Target at Montgomery Trial," March 24, 1956, "Boycott Fund: $50,000," March 31, 1956, and "Dull Moments Were Few at Pastor King's Trial," March 31, 1956. For the final installment in Cunningham's Montgomery series, see "Why and How This Young Pastor Became Leader of Bus Boycott," April 21, 1956.
3. See the biographical sketch and oral history interview available through the National Visionary Leadership Project at visionaryproject.org. Also see Daniel Lovering, "Evelyn Cunningham, Civil Rights Reporter, Dies at 94," *New York Times*, April 29, 2010. For information on Cunningham's early life, see the 1920 U.S. census, Elizabeth City, Ward 4, Pasquotank, North Carolina, and the 1925 New York State census. The 1930 and 1940 census records also locate her in New York. She is listed as Early E. Long (1920), Evelyn Long (1925), Evelyn E. Long (1930), and Evelyn Sherrer (1940). Cunningham's parents were named Clyde Long and Mary Long. Evelyn got married and divorced four times, but she kept the surname of her third husband: Cunningham.
4. Cunningham, interview in *Newspaper of Record*.
5. Martin Luther King Jr., "The Bombing," in *The Autobiography of Martin Luther King Jr.*, ed. Clayborne Carson (New York: Grand Central Publishing, 1998), 78–80.
6. Cunningham, interview in *Newspaper of Record*.

7. For King's desire to balance militancy and moderation, see *The Autobiography of Martin Luther King Jr.*, 59. Pages 316–19, which outline his concerns with the Black Power slogan, relate to this topic as well.
8. Polish workers, whose numerical dominance of certain departments in local plants enabled them to reserve positions for kin and friends, militated against outside intrusion by black migrants. See John Bodnar, Michael Weber, and Roger Simon, "Migration, Kinship, and Urban Adjustment: Blacks and Poles in Pittsburgh, 1900–1930," *Journal of American History* 66, no. 3 (1979): 548–65.
9. For an account of the "politics of respectability," see Evelyn Brooks Higginbotham, *Righteous Discontent: The Women's Movement in the Black Baptist Church, 1880–1920* (Cambridge, MA: Harvard University Press, 1993). For the Moss speech, see "Fanning the Flames," box 3, folder 124, Urban League Records, University of Pittsburgh Archives Service Center.
10. Kevin K. Gaines, *Uplifting the Race: Black Leadership, Politics, and Culture in the Twentieth Century* (Chapel Hill: University of North Carolina Press, 1996), 2. Notwithstanding noteworthy scholarship by Evelyn Brooks Higginbotham, Darlene Clark Hine, Stephanie Shaw, and others, studies in the 1990s and 2000s usually offered dismissive portrayals of black reformers and mainstream racial organizations. See the introduction of this book for a detailed bibliography.
11. For an example of the *Courier*'s effort to marshal black voting strength, see Robert L. Vann, "The Patriot and the Partisan," September 11, 1932, box 31, folder 2, Robert L. Vann Papers, Percival Prattis Collection, Moorland-Spingarn Research Center, Howard University, and "5,000 Negroes in Huge Crowd Which Greets Governor Here," *Pittsburgh Courier*, October 22, 1932. For examples of how reformers promoted black inclusion in the industrial labor movement and secured an antidiscrimination clause, see William Hill, "The Negro Wage Worker," in *The WPA History of the Negro in Pittsburgh*, ed. Laurence Glasco (Pittsburgh: University of Pittsburgh Press, 2004), 228, William Hill to Homer Brown, memo, February 23, 1937, box 1, folder 3, Homer Brown Collection, University of Pittsburgh Archives Service Center.
12. Laurence Glasco, "Double Burden: The Black Experience in Pittsburgh," in *City at the Point: Essays on the Social History of Pittsburgh*, ed. Samuel P. Hays (Pittsburgh: University of Pittsburgh Press, 1989), 88–91; Joe W. Trotter and Jared N. Day, *Race and Renaissance: African Americans in Pittsburgh since World War II* (Pittsburgh: University of Pittsburgh Press, 2010), 90–140.
13. Eric Ledell Smith and Kenneth C. Wolensky, "A Novel Public Policy: Pennsylvania's Fair Employment Practices Act of 1955," *Pennsylvania History* 69, no. 4 (2002): 502.
14. Arthur J. Edmunds, *Daybreakers: The Story of the Urban League of Pittsburgh, the First Sixty-Five Years* (Pittsburgh: Urban League of Pittsburgh, 1999), 113–14.
15. Smith and Wolensky, "A Novel Public Policy," 502.
16. Edmunds, *Daybreakers*, 114–15.
17. Edmunds, *Daybreakers*, 114–15.
18. Edmunds, *Daybreakers*, 115.
19. Glasco, "Double Burden," 88–91; Trotter and Day, *Race and Renaissance*, 90–140.
20. See Cunningham, the National Visionary Leadership Project, visionaryproject.org.
21. Glasco, "Double Burden," 69–109; Trotter and Day, *Race and Renaissance*, 90–140.

INDEX

Adjustment programs. *See* Racial uplift
Agricultural Adjustment Administration, 210; Agricultural Adjustment Act, 234n40. *Also see* New Deal
Aliquippa, Pennsylvania, 4, 22, 41–42, 49n50, 161, 189, 193
Allegheny County school board, 40, 42, 64, 66, 160–63, 240
A.M. Byers Company, 51n90, 53n117, 78n27
American Federation of Labor (AFL), 59, 171–74, 185–86, 199n9, 210, 218. *See also* Congress of Industrial Organizations; Gompers, Samuel; Steel Workers Organizing Committee
Amos 'n' Andy radio program, 119–20. *See also Pittsburgh Courier*; Racial discourse
Aurora Reading Club. *See* Black clubs
Austin, Reverend J.C., 47n13, 90, 105n30, 140n35, 140n42, 145n17, 193

Bagnall, Robert, 41, 52n99, 93, 157
Baltimore and Ohio (B&O) Railroad, 5, 23, 36, 55, 76n3, 149
Barton, Tom, 74, 76n5, 221, 242
Beaver County, 83–84, 97–103, 107n60–61, 107n63, 151, 193, 240
Bethune, Mary McLeod, 153, 188, 217

Birth of a Nation, 8, 36, 90. *See also* Ku Klux Klan
Bolden, Frank, 119, 140, 206, 207, 209, 227, 231n1, 231n6, 232n7, 235n65, 236n81
Black churches, 19–21, 31–34, 44, 47n12–13, 49n42–45, 49n47–48, 56, 94, 169, 179, 193, 204n85, 225, 246n9. *See also* Storefront churches
Black clergy, 3, 47n12–13, 49n45, 71, 170, 193; reverends, 22, 25, 36, 44, 47n13, 49n45, 90, 94, 130, 140n35, 140n42, 144n87, 157, 161, 170, 179, 193, 200n26, 225, 244
Black clubs, 11, 19, 20, 32, 132, 135, 141n45, 144n99, 146n130, 164n7, 169, 227; Aurora Reading Club, 19, 170, 198n5; Frogs, 20, 141n45; Loendi, 19, 20, 141n45
Black industrial workers, 5, 7, 10–12, 15n12, 16n16, 32–44, 51n90, 53n117, 57–63, 66, 75, 77n9, 77n20, 78n21–22, 108–35, 153, 157, 169–84, 190–98, 208, 222–25, 233n28, 239. *See also* Black migrants
Black migrants: Adams, John, 205, 207, 210, 231n1, 231n4, 232n9; "Alice," 147–150, 164n1; Dempsey, Matthew, 41; Gant, Harrison, 12, 18–19, 23, 26, 38, 45, 46n1, 48n25, 28n35, 51n83, 70, 108–9, 138n1–2, 169, 171, 189, 198n2, 203n72; Lindsey,

247

Black migrants (continued)
  Nola, 54, 76n1; Lynch, Merril, 51n88, 77n11, 130, 136, 144n86, 146n120, 195–98, 204n92–94, 204n97; McChester, LeRoy, 38–39, 51n88, 77n11, 198, 204n97; "Ruby," 108, 147–149, 164n1; Simmons, James, 22, 39, 47n17, 52n92, 125, 142n55; Tipper, Bartow, 22, 26, 48n19, 48n36, 129, 144n85; Williams, Joe, 83–84, 98, 104n2. *See also* Black industrial workers; Great Migration
Black newspapers, 18, 22, 47n16, 111, 120, 131–42, 217, 219, 232n17, 236n77; *Baltimore Afro-American*, 106n42, 133, 142n60, 145n103, 165n21, 189, 202n67, 202n68–69, 217, 232n17; *Chicago Defender*, 14n8, 126, 137, 142n66, 165n18, 211, 217, 232n16, 232n17; *New York Age*, 46n9, 141n48; *New York Amsterdam News*, 78n24, 126, 142n60, 164n6–7, 165n11
Black sporting life: Negro Leagues, 32–33, 62–63, 215, 227; Pittsburgh Crawfords, 32–33, 215; Homestead Grays, 32–33
Bond, Sadie, 54–55, 64, 76n1
Brotherhood of Sleeping Car Porters, 179–80, 184, 201n40, 222. *See also* Randolph, A. Phillip
Brown, Homer, 10, 12, 25, 44, 50n61, 75, 84, 90–107, 120–22, 140n37 140n39, 149–67, 170–71, 179, 184–86, 190, 201n48–49, 202n50–52, 202n57, 203n76, 207, 209, 220–25, 235n59, 235n61, 246n11
Bunche, Ralph, 141n43, 153, 183, 188, 192, 195

Careathers, Ben, 13n3, 42–43, 189–93, 203n70–73. *See also* Communists
Carnegie Steel, 37, 54, 62, 64, 143n84, 197, 223
Charleston, Oscar, 33
Centre Avenue, Pittsburgh, 25, 32, 35, 42, 106n34, 117, 133, 152, 207. *See also* Wylie Avenue
Civilian Conservation Corps (CCC), 153, 210–12, 232n14–15, 234n40. *See also* New Deal
Civil Works Administration (CWA), 210–12, 233n19. *See also* New Deal
Clark, John T., 11, 15n13, 18–21, 42–53, 55–81, 88, 90, 104n9, 104n11, 105n14, 105n28–29, 138n10, 177–178

Clark, John L., 115, 141n44
Communists, 3, 5, 10, 13n3, 16n16, 42–43, 74–75, 78n22, 132, 145n102, 169, 171, 186–98, 202–4, 229; American Communist Party (CPUSA), 186–90, 202n64; International Labor Defense (ILD), 186–88; Workers School, 189–90, 203n74–75. *See also* Careathers, Ben
Conference for Progressive Labor Action. *See* McKinney, Ernest Rice; Socialists
Congress of Industrial Organizations (CIO), 10–12, 17n23, 42–43, 168–69, 174, 185, 192–98, 202n56, 204n95–96, 217–18, 221, 223, 230, 236n85. *See also* American Federation of Labor; Steel Workers Organizing Committee; United Mine Workers
Coolidge, Calvin, 126, 132
Criminal justice system, 6, 14n9, 35, 67, 83, 85, 96, 103, 122; disproportionate incarceration, 35, 85, 90; police conduct, 4, 6, 23, 34, 35, 36, 41, 44, 67, 83–106, 151, 155, 188, 189, 237, 238, 240, 244; Western State Penitentiary, 35, 50, 66, 89,90, 105n26–27. *See also* Juvenile delinquency; Pittsburgh NAACP; Shanghai case
Crisis, 50n69, 52n99, 105n23–24, 187, 199n24, 202n64
Crucible Steel, 83
Cunningham, Evelyn, 237–38, 241, 244–46

Davis, John P., 169, 192, 203n83–84
De Castrique, Anthony, 98–101. *See also* Shanghai case
Democratic Party, 9, 45, 94, 109, 113, 131–38, 151, 153–54, 164n6, 169, 173, 214; Democrats, 5, 9, 21, 58, 109, 112–13, 125, 130–36, 139n15, 145n103, 145n113, 146n119, 146n126, 153–55, 173, 185, 187, 191, 202n68–69, 208–19, 224, 233n25, 234n43, 240; David L. Lawrence, 156, 185, 218, 221, 235n43, 241; Joseph Guffey, 131–32, 137, 185, 217–18, 235n43; George Earle, 151, 155, 157, 165n21, 185–86; James Farley, 131. *See also* New Deal; *Pittsburgh Courier*
Detroit, 21, 23, 58, 123, 128, 136, 194, 229
Discriminatory hiring practices, 8, 9, 11, 35–44, 53n114, 64, 75, 119, 153, 161–63, 208, 214–16, 222, 224, 242

INDEX 249

Disease, 32, 43, 45, 49n50, 55, 65, 67, 69, 87, 127, 177; infant mortality, 4, 12, 31, 69, 70, 72, 81n74, 105n14, 159, 239, 240; mortality, 6, 31, 67, 69, 70, 72, 81n74, 2; pneumonia, 4, 31, 67, 69, 80n60; tuberculosis, 4, 31, 70, 72, 190. *See also* ULP health campaigns; Washington, Jeannette; Kinner, Marie

Domestic workers, 4, 7, 15n13, 20, 39, 67, 76n1, 87, 112, 128, 161, 177, 180, 200n28

Double V campaign, 7, 11, 17n23, 110, 209, 221, 225-31, 235n65-80, 236n82-87, 241. See *Pittsburgh Courier*

Du Bois, W. E. B., 1-3, 13n1, 17n20, 42, 52n99, 74, 91, 93, 115, 123-24, 137, 139n26, 141n43, 142n53, 175, 183, 187-88, 199n24-25, 202n63

Duquesne, Pennsylvania, 36, 41, 54, 61, 62, 78n25, 109, 138n2

Earle, George. *See* Democratic Party
Eldridge, Roy. *See* Jazz in Pittsburgh
Epstein, Abraham, 23, 26, 37-38, 44, 48n23, 48n48, 49n42, 51n78-86, 58, 59, 70, 77n9-13, 79n36, 79n50, 80n60, 80n62, 105n21, 198n6, 234n31
Ethiopia, 122, 141n45, 217
Ethnicity, 3, 4, 10, 25, 57, 110, 173, 175, 189, 217; European immigrants, 25, 37, 38, 43, 55, 57, 110, 136; Jews, 25, 81n68, 89; Italians, 4, 6, 14n10, 25, 34, 39, 48n31, 49n51, 57, 93, 95, 96, 138n7, 143n81, 173, 175, 217, 229; Poles, 4, 14n10, 37-39, 48n31, 49n41, 51n81, 138n7, 143n81, 173, 175, 246n8

Fair Employment Practices Commission (FEPC), 223-25, 231, 235n61-62; FEPC Act in Pennsylvania, 153, 207, 209, 223-25, 235n59, 246n13
Farley, James. *See* Democratic Party
Federal Bureau of Investigation (FBI), 41, 229-30. *See also* Hoover, J. Edgar
Ford, James, 169. *See also* Communists; Socialists
Foster, William Z., 43, 74, 78n22. *See also* Communists; Socialists
Frazier, E. Franklin, 14n10, 16n16

Gant, Harrison. *See* Black migrants

Garvey, Marcus, 17n20, 40-41, 47n13, 52n99, 115, 139n26, 192. *See also* Universal Negro Improvement Association
Gary, Indiana, 38-39, 194, 230
Gibson, Josh, 33
Givens, Joseph, 96-98
Gompers, Samuel, 59-60, 77n19. *See also* American Federation of Labor
Granger, Lester, 188, 192, 212, 232n17
Great Depression, 10, 13n2, 15n13, 15n15, 16n16, 42, 46n4, 60, 72, 75, 82n84, 103, 108, 109, 126-30, 135, 140n35, 142n56, 142n59, 143n81, 143n84, 144n89-90, 169-78, 191-92, 202n59, 203n70, 204n89, 217, 232n19. *See also* Unemployment
Great Migration, 2-12, 13n2, 14n8, 15n10, 19-24, 33-38, 47n16, 48n22, 51n81-82, 57, 70, 74, 76n4, 83-88, 115, 129, 138n6, 143n75, 148, 169-74, 199n10, 206-15, 240, 246n8. *See also* Black migrants
Great Steel Strike of 1919, 60, 77n20-21, 174
Greenlee, Gus, 32
Greenlee Field, 215
Greensboro, North Carolina, 54
Griffith, D.W., 8, 36, 119. See also *Birth of a Nation*
Guffey, Joseph. *See* Democratic Party

Haiti, 122, 141n45
Harding, Warren G., 112, 126, 132. *See also* Republican Party
Harlem, 16n16, 17n20, 18, 40, 55, 128, 189, 194, 202n59, 204n89, 222, 234n39, 237
Harris, Abram, 20, 35, 65, 79n36, 141n43, 183
Harrisburg, Pennsylvania, 101-2, 154, 155, 157, 163, 164n6, 225
Harris, Teenie, 92, 95, 117, 191, 196, 220, 228, 243
Highland Park pool, 4, 6, 34, 93-95, 102, 106n37, 157, 175, 240, 244
Hill, William, 42, 48n23, 51n89, 75, 77n10, 198n1, 201n40-41, 201n49, 202n52, 204n84, 246n11
Hill, T. Arnold, 37, 51n80, 127, 142n74, 169, 172, 184, 186, 188, 199n9, 200n33, 202n57, 202n62, 211-12, 222, 232n13, 232n17
Holloway, Wilbert, 73, 115, 133-34, 145n110, 226

Homestead, Pennsylvania, 32, 36, 41–42, 62–63, 197
Hoover, Herbert, 108–9, 112, 126–36, 142–45, 202n68–69, 229, 230
Hoover, J. Edgar, 229–30, 236n82
Horne, Lena. *See* Jazz in Pittsburgh
Housewives Cooperative League, 180–81, 201n43–46
Howard University, 17n21, 20, 35, 65, 71, 107n65, 138n5, 190, 211, 213, 233n25, 235n55, 246n11

Illery, Alma, 181, 201n44, 225
Immigrants. *See* Ethnicity
Imperial, Pennsylvania, 4, 36
Informer, 88, 152, 165n8, 205, 232n14, 233n22–25, 235n60. *See also* Lowndes, Grace
Industry, Pennsylvania. *See* Shanghai case
Irvis, K. LeRoy, 221, 241–45

Jazz in Pittsburgh, 32
Johnson, James Weldon, 89, 123, 141n50, 160, 166n42
Johnson, Reginald, 173, 186, 199n16, 201n48, 202n57
Johnstown, Pennsylvania, 4, 36, 41, 50n69–70, 89, 105n23–25, 193
Jones, Eugene K., 18, 44, 77n19, 113, 137, 153, 212
Jones, Julia Bumbrey, 115
Jones, Reverend Augustus, 44, 49n45, 53n115, 90
Jones, Richard F., 91, 161
Jones and Laughlin Steel Company, 22, 38, 41, 59, 64, 108, 128, 130, 136, 169, 189, 193, 198, 203n73
Juvenile delinquency, 5, 12, 34–35, 55, 67, 85–86, 89, 239; morals court, 5, 12, 55, 65, 67, 79n41, 79n49, 81n84, 85–88, 105n20. *See also* Criminal justice system; Lowndes, Grace

King Jr., Martin Luther, 237, 245, 245n5, 246n7
Kinner, Marie, 71
Ku Klux Klan, 4, 8, 34, 36, 41, 51n71, 57, 89, 126, 203n75, 231

Labor Age. *See* Communists; Socialists
Lampkin, Daisy, 17n24, 20, 25, 44, 46n7, 90–94, 106n33, 106n36, 152, 157, 159, 163, 166n32, 181, 187, 201n44, 202n60, 220–21, 243–44
Lawrence, David L. *See* Democratic Party
Leonard, Buck, 33
Lett, Harold, 75, 129, 143n82–83, 176, 200n27, 200n29, 214
Lewis, Ira, 17n21, 115, 116, 124, 219, 220–21, 235n47
Lewis, John L., 174, 199n17, 203n83, 204n96, 217
Lindsey, Nola. *See* Black migrants
Lodging, 25, 47n16, 55, 65, 98, 143n84, 157, 188, 239; boardinghouses, 4, 26, 27, 31, 55; company bunkhouses, 26, 36, 62; housing, 4, 6, 9, 16n16, 20, 24–26, 35, 43–46, 47n13, 48n40, 53n116, 54–56, 61–63, 66–74, 79n36, 100, 111, 119, 124, 133, 177, 234n31–32, 239, 244; Housing Projects, 180, 215–216, 233n28, 234n29; tenements, 4, 26, 27, 55. *See also* Diseases; Pittsburgh Housing Authority
Lowndes, Grace, 12, 20–21, 25, 46n9, 57–75, 79n41, 79n49, 82n84, 86–88, 104n10, 105n19–20, 152, 159, 201n44, 205, 232n14, 233n22–23, 233n25
Lynch, Merril. *See* Black migrants

March on Washington Movement (MOWM), 11, 221–23, 226, 229, 231, 235n55, 241
May, Edwin, 70, 200n35
McChester, LeRoy. *See* Black migrants
McKinney, Ernest Rice, 10, 25, 41–42, 47n14, 49n52, 52n100–4, 115, 121, 140n41, 161, 166n45, 170, 174–75, 189–94, 199n20, 203n79–80. *See also* Socialists
Mencken, H.L. 23, 49n48
Messenger. *See* Brotherhood of Sleeping Car Porters
Meyer, John D. *See* Shanghai case
Midland, Pennsylvania, 83, 98, 103
Miller, Kelly, 190, 203n77
Montgomery, Alabama, 237, 244, 245n2
Moss, R. Maurice, 20, 25, 46n9, 52n95, 53n114, 65, 75, 76n5, 81n84, 157, 161, 163,

182, 201n40, 212–14, 225, 233n21, 233n27, 235n61, 239, 242, 244, 246n9
Moton, Robert R., 59–60, 77n17, 77n19
Murray, Phillip, 10–11, 43, 52n106, 168–179, 189, 193–194, 196, 198n1, 198n3, 204n85–87, 230. *See also* Congress of Industrial Organizations; Steel Workers Organizing Committee

National Association for the Advancement of Colored People (NAACP). *See* Pittsburgh NAACP
National Industrial Recovery Act, 170, 173–74, 212, 214
National Labor Relations Act (Wagner Act), 10, 174, 179, 180, 184, 210; lack of nondiscrimination clause, 153, 165n10, 170–71, 184–86, 201n48
National Negro Congress (NNC), 43, 75, 155, 169, 171, 192–97, 203n82, 203n84
National Urban League (NUL), 7, 13n5, 14n10, 15n14, 18, 32–44, 52n107, 59, 65, 66, 75, 77n7, 77n14, 81n78, 113, 127, 137, 153, 167n50, 169–84, 192, 211–12, 222, 244
Nearing, Scott, 31
Negro League Baseball. *See* Black sporting life
Nelson, Thelma, 161
Neighborhoods of Pittsburgh: East Liberty, 20, 24–26, 42, 71, 152, 156; fifth ward, 24, 146n19, 151; Homewood, 20, 25; North Side, 67, 71; Strip District, 24; third ward, 136, 146n24
Nelson, Grover. *See* Welfare workers
New Deal, 9–10, 16n16, 17n22, 34–35, 48n26, 50n67, 78n23, 94, 131, 138–46, 153, 165n12–20, 167n50, 170–79, 187–89, 190, 198, 199n7–19, 200n34, 201–19, 239
New York City, 15n13, 16n16, 18, 20, 65, 75, 88, 146n124, 160, 170, 177, 212
New York Times, 238, 245n3

Old Pittsburghers, 20–21, 25, 31, 190
Opportunity Magazine, 49n48, 52n108, 53n109, 79n45, 141n43, 142n74, 143n82–83, 167n50, 172, 177, 178, 199n7–16, 200n29–38, 201n48, 202n62, 211, 214, 232n11–17, 233n27

Paige, Satchel, 33
Pan-Africanism, 40. *See also* Ethiopia; Haiti; Racial discourse
Park, Robert E., 43
Parry, Florence Fisher, 120, 122, 140n36
Pearce, Georgine, 12, 148–50, 159, 161, 164n1–3
Pennsylvania Equal Rights Act (Reynolds bill), 154–55, 157, 165n16–25, 166n27, 219
Pennsylvania Labor Relations Act (McGinnis bill), 153, 165n10, 171, 184, 186, 240; nondiscrimination clause, 153, 165n10, 170–71, 184–86, 201n48
Pickens, William, 51n73, 53n115, 90–91, 106n31, 123–24, 141n51, 153
Pinchot, Gifford, 89, 98–103, 107n51–62, 126, 144n89, 151, 165n18
Pittsburgh Housing Authority, 180, 215, 233n28; Bedford Dwellings, 215–16, 234n29, 234n32; Terrace Village, 215–16, 234n29. *See also* Lodging
Pittsburgh Courier, 3, 7–17, 20, 42, 45–60, 70, 73, 78, 80–81, 91–103, 104–46, 151, 154–55, 161–246. *See also* Federal Bureau of Investigation; Double V campaign; Racial discourse
Pittsburgh NAACP (PNAACP), 3, 6, 10, 12, 17n24, 36, 42, 44, 45, 53n115, 75, 83–85, 90, 91, 94, 96–103, 106n34, 110, 111, 120, 121, 149, 150–52, 155, 156–59, 161, 163, 164, 166n39, 174, 179, 184, 187, 207, 221, 222, 240. *See also* Brown, Homer; Shanghai case
Pittsburgh Post-Gazette, 121, 140n39, 190, 232n6–7
Pittsburgh Press, 50n61, 98, 101, 106n47, 107n51, 107n60–63, 120–22, 140n36, 149, 167n52–53
Policing. *See* Criminal justice system
Prattis, Percival, 107n65, 119, 139n29, 140n32–33, 179, 209, 213, 220, 221, 224, 233n25, 234n36, 235n57–58, 244, 246n11
Progressive Era, 3, 16n18; Progressives, 3, 44, 135, 157, 219
Prostitution, 5, 12, 32, 35, 49n50, 55, 67, 79n49, 81n84, 85–89, 186; brothels, 32, 67, 86, 104n12. *See also* Lowndes, Grace
Public Health Nursing Association. *See* Washington, Jeannette

Public Works Administration, 210, 211, 233n20. *See also* New Deal

Racial discourse, 3, 8, 11, 17n20, 41, 47n13, 119, 121, 224, 229, 239; Black representation, 122, 153. *See also* Amos 'n' Andy; *Pittsburgh Courier*, Parry, Florence Fisher; Rogers, Joel

Racial uplift, 2, 7, 8, 15n14, 16n16, 31, 46n2, 69, 77n7, 113, 176, 177, 200n26, 239, 240, 246n10; adjustment programs, 2, 21, 43, 44, 51n81–n82, 56, 69, 176, 239, 246n8; moral reform, 2, 56; social reorganization theory, 43. *See also* Respectability politics

Randolph, A. Phillip, 42, 133, 169, 179, 191, 192, 195, 222, 223

Reader, Frank E., 99, 102, 103

Reid, Ira, 32, 35, 49n48, 50n65, 50n68, 65, 66, 77n11, 79n36, 79n46–48, 90, 105n26–27, 199n7–8, 212

Republican Party, 12, 109, 124–36, 138n4, 138n15, 142n56, 142n66, 144n89, 151, 218, 224, 225; GOP, 9, 11, 75, 94, 109, 111, 112, 125–37, 139n15, 142n66, 155, 219, 225, 230; Republicans, 5, 58, 94, 111–13, 127, 130–35, 144n89, 151, 153, 155, 185, 203n75, 224, 225

Respectability politics, 5, 19, 20, 31, 49n47, 221, 239, 246n9. *See also* Racial uplift

Reynolds, Hobson, 136, 155, 157, 221. *See also* Pennsylvania Equal Rights Act

Rogers, Joel, 115, 122, 217

Roosevelt, Franklin Delano, 9, 11, 75, 94, 103, 109–112, 121, 125, 126, 130–37, 139n15, 142n60, 142n66, 144n91, 144n99, 145n112–17, 151, 153, 170, 173, 178, 187, 207–12, 216–25, 229, 230, 236n82

Roosevelt, Eleanor, 153, 213, 221

Schools. *See* Teaching jobs

Schnader, William, 99, 100, 101, 102, 203n1, 203n3, 106n47, 107n55–70, 151. *See* Shanghai case

Schuyler, George, 70, 80n62, 102, 107n65, 115, 116, 119, 140n32, 141n45, 193, 194, 204n88–89, 220–22, 229

Scott, Jeanne, 158–160, 163, 166n33–40

Scottsboro case. *See* Communists; NAACP; Parry, Florence Fisher

Shanghai case, 85, 97, 98, 106n47–51, 158, 240; Industry abduction, 84, 97, 98, 102, 103, 107n51, 107n53; migrant deportation, 6, 36, 44, 93, 97–101, 103; investigation of, 84, 97, 99–101. *See also* De Castrique, Anthony; Meyer, John D.; Reader, Frank E.; Schnader, William

Simmons, James. *See* Black migrants

Smith, Alfred E., 136

Socialists, 3, 10, 42, 58, 91, 132, 161, 174, 190, 191, 203n79. *See also* McKinney, Ernest Rice

Social Darwinism, 8, 43, 245

Social researchers, 26, 43, 65, 214, 215; social science, 3, 5, 8, 121, 140n43. *See also* ULP fellows program

Social workers, 2, 5, 8, 10, 17n20, 19, 25, 42, 43, 52n100, 57, 62, 64, 65, 121, 157, 166n39, 170, 203n80, 208, 242

Spingarn, Joel, 91

Steel Workers Organizing Committee (SWOC), 10, 168, 170, 174, 179, 189, 191, 196, 204n94. *See also* Congress of Industrial Organizations

St. Louis, 7, 15n13, 20, 46n1, 74, 75, 81n78–79, 178, 194, 222, 229

Storefront churches, 31, 49n48, 132. *See also* Black churches

Strayhorn, Billy. *See* Jazz in Pittsburgh

Sweet, Ossian, 91, 123

Teaching jobs, 10, 64, 150, 151, 160–162; Black teachers, 9, 35, 40, 42, 64, 66, 160, 161, 163, 244

Thayer, Alonzo, 53n114, 75

Time Magazine, 106n32, 165n9

Tipper, Bartow. *See* Black Migrants

Tolliver, Reverend Harold, 25, 36, 47n11, 47n13, 48n30, 51n74, 130, 144n87, 157, 161, 200n26

Travelers' Aid Society, 55, 64, 76n1

Tyson, Francis, 44, 49n45, 79n36, 179, 214

Unemployment, 31, 39, 75, 81n84, 127–29, 135, 142n70, 142n72, 143n74, 143n80, 144n89, 176, 177, 192, 200n29, 200n30, 210, 212, 232n19, 233n27. *See also* Great Depression

Union Station, 12, 18, 23, 24, 54, 64, 67, 76n1, 79n37, 86
Unions. *See* American Federation of Labor; Congress of Industrial Organizations; Steel Workers Organizing Committee; United Mine Workers
United Mine Workers, 174, 196. *See also* Congress of Industrial Organizations
Universal Negro Improvement Association (UNIA), 40, 41. *See also* Garvey, Marcus
Urban League of Pittsburgh (ULP): fellows program, 17n20, 65, 79n36, 122; health campaigns, 5, 70–73, 80n67, 239; home economics program, 68–74, 80n56–59, 88, 159; workers council program, 75, 171, 178–180, 193, 200n38–39, 215. *See also* Clark, John T.; Disease; Hill, William; Kinner, Marie; Lett, Harold; Pearce, Georgine; Social researchers; Washington, Jeannette
U.S. Steel, 196, 204n94

Vann, Robert L. See *Pittsburgh Courier*
Victorian morality, 5, 31, 112. *See also* Racial uplift; Respectability politics
Virginia Union University, 90, 101, 113

Wagner Act. *See* National Labor Relations Act
Walls, Jean Hamilton, 161, 166n46
Washington, Booker T., 1, 44, 59, 74, 113, 171, 173, 199n25
Washington, Jeannette, 12, 64, 71, 73, 79n37, 159

Watt Street School, 34, 135, 163, 195
Western Pennsylvania Negro Labor Conference, 168, 171, 193
Western State Penitentiary. *See* Criminal justice system
Westinghouse Electric and Manufacturing Company, 38
Welfare workers, 5, 15n12, 32, 49n52, 62, 63, 68, 78n28, 88
White, Walter, 17n20, 53n115, 84, 97–99, 101, 104–7, 116, 120, 123, 124, 139n26, 140n37, 141n47, 157, 158, 166n33–40, 174, 186, 187, 199n17, 202n51–60, 222
Williams, Joe. *See* Black migrants
Williams, Smokey Joe, 33
Willkie, Wendell, 11, 17n23, 219, 230, 236n84
Wilson, W. Rollo, 115
World War I, 21, 38, 42, 58, 171
World War II, 9, 11, 13n2, 14n9–10, 45, 52n103, 104n5, 106n41, 138n8, 163, 166n38, 201n43, 207, 208, 219, 221–23, 236n76, 236n82, 240, 241
Wright, Richard, 175, 188, 199n21
Wylie Avenue, 25, 28, 29, 32, 34, 106n34, 108, 109, 115, 122, 141n44, 183. *See also* Centre Avenue YMCA

Yellow journalism. See *Pittsburgh Courier*
YMCA. *See* Centre Avenue YMCA
Young, W.P. *See* Welfare workers

www.ingramcontent.com/pod-product-compliance
Lightning Source LLC
Chambersburg PA
CBHW011755220426
43672CB00018B/2970